War Crimes

OTHER BOOKS OF RELATED INTEREST

OPPOSING VIEWPOINTS SERIES

The Breakup of the Soviet Union
Eastern Europe
Human Rights
The Vietnam War
War
World War II

CURRENT CONTROVERSIES SERIES

Hate Crimes
Interventionism
Nationalism and Ethnic Conflict

AT ISSUE SERIES

Anti-Semitism
Ethnic Conflict
The United Nations
U.S. Policy Toward China

DISCARD

War Crimes

Henny H. Kim, *Book Editor*

David L. Bender, *Publisher*
Bruno Leone, *Executive Editor*
Bonnie Szumski, *Editorial Director*
David M. Haugen, *Managing Editor*
Brenda Stalcup, *Series Editor*

Contemporary Issues
Companion

Greenhaven Press, Inc., San Diego, CA

Every effort has been made to trace the owners of copyrighted material. The articles in this volume may have been edited for content, length, and/or reading level. The titles have been changed to enhance the editorial purpose. Those interested in locating the original source will find the complete citation on the first page of each article.

No part of this book may be reproduced or used in any form or by any means, electrical, mechanical, or otherwise, including, but not limited to, photocopy, recording, or any information storage and retrieval system, without prior written permission from the publisher.

Library of Congress Cataloging-in-Publication Data

edited by

War crimes / Henny H. Kim, ~~book editor~~.
 p. cm. — (Contemporary issues companion) *440*
 Includes bibliographical references and index.
 ISBN 0-7377-0171-4 (lib. : alk. paper). —
ISBN 0-7377-0170-6 (pbk. : alk. paper)
 1. War crimes. I. Kim, Henny H., 1968– . II. Series.
K5301.W367 2000
341.6'9—dc21
                                                    99-16391
                                                        CIP

©2000 by Greenhaven Press, Inc.
P.O. Box 289009, San Diego, CA 92198-9009

Printed in the U.S.A.

CONTENTS

Foreword   7

Introduction   9

Chapter 1: An Examination of War Crimes

1. War Crimes Violate the Laws of War   13
   John H.E. Fried

2. The Persistence of Genocide   24
   Samantha Power

3. Recognizing Rape and Sexual Violence as War Crimes   32
   Valerie Oosterveld

4. The Clear and Present Danger of War Crimes   35
   David J. Scheffer

5. War Crimes Are Determined by Those in Power   42
   Sharon Clarke

Chapter 2: War Crimes: A Historical Overview

1. The Development of the Laws of War   47
   Telford Taylor

2. Holocaust: Hitler's Final Solution   56
   Amy Newman

3. Judgment at Nuremberg   64
   Robert Shnayerson

4. War Crimes in Vietnam   76
   Eric Norden

5. War Crimes on Trial   90
   Neil J. Kritz

Chapter 3: Personal Reflections on War Crimes

1. The Prison Camps   101
   Peter Maass

2. War Crimes Inflict Permanent Damage   112
   Lisa Chiu

3. Perpetrating the Crimes   115
   Yuasa Ken, as told to Haruko Tayo Cook and Theodore F. Cook

Chapter 4: How Should War Crimes Be Addressed?

1. War Crimes Must Be Confronted Immediately   122
   Ed Vulliamy

2. International War Crimes Trials Are Necessary   129
   Gary Jonathan Bass

3. Military Force Is a More Effective Deterrent than
    International Trials   135
    David Rieff

4. A Stronger United Nations Can Prevent War Crimes   139
    Robert C. Johansen

5. Powerful Governments Should Be Held Accountable for
    Their War Crimes   144
    Ramsey Clark

6. Difficult Questions About Appropriate Punishment   152
    David Fromkin

7. The Evil That Perpetuates War Crimes Should Be Studied   155
    Paul Shore

Appendix: The Nuremberg Principles
    and the Geneva Convention   158

Organizations to Contact   165

Bibliography   169

Index   172

FOREWORD

In the news, on the streets, and in neighborhoods, individuals are confronted with a variety of social problems. Such problems may affect people directly: A young woman may struggle with depression, suspect a friend of having bulimia, or watch a loved one battle cancer. And even the issues that do not directly affect her private life—such as religious cults, domestic violence, or legalized gambling—still impact the larger society in which she lives. Discovering and analyzing the complexities of issues that encompass communal and societal realms as well as the world of personal experience is a valuable educational goal in the modern world.

Effectively addressing social problems requires familiarity with a constantly changing stream of data. Becoming well informed about today's controversies is an intricate process that often involves reading myriad primary and secondary sources, analyzing political debates, weighing various experts' opinions—even listening to first-hand accounts of those directly affected by the issue. For students and general observers, this can be a daunting task because of the sheer volume of information available in books, periodicals, on the evening news, and on the Internet. Researching the consequences of legalized gambling, for example, might entail sifting through congressional testimony on gambling's societal effects, examining private studies on Indian gaming, perusing numerous websites devoted to Internet betting, and reading essays written by lottery winners as well as interviews with recovering compulsive gamblers. Obtaining valuable information can be time-consuming—since it often requires researchers to pore over numerous documents and commentaries before discovering a source relevant to their particular investigation.

Greenhaven's Contemporary Issues Companion series seeks to assist this process of research by providing readers with useful and pertinent information about today's complex issues. Each volume in this anthology series focuses on a topic of current interest, presenting informative and thought-provoking selections written from a wide variety of viewpoints. The readings selected by the editors include such diverse sources as personal accounts and case studies, pertinent factual and statistical articles, and relevant commentaries and overviews. This diversity of sources and views, found in every Contemporary Issues Companion, offers readers a broad perspective in one convenient volume.

In addition, each title in the Contemporary Issues Companion series is designed especially for young adults. The selections included in every volume are chosen for their accessibility and are expertly edited in consideration of both the reading and comprehension levels of the audience. The structure of the anthologies also enhances accessibility. An introductory essay places each issue in context and provides helpful facts such as historical background or current statistics and legislation that pertain to the topic. The chapters that follow organize the material and focus on specific aspects of the book's topic. Every essay is introduced by a brief summary of its main points and biographical information about the author. These summaries aid in comprehension and can also serve to direct readers to material of immediate interest and need. Finally, a comprehensive index allows readers to efficiently scan and locate content.

The Contemporary Issues Companion series is an ideal launching point for research on a particular topic. Each anthology in the series is composed of readings taken from an extensive gamut of resources, including periodicals, newspapers, books, government documents, the publications of private and public organizations, and Internet websites. In these volumes, readers will find factual support suitable for use in reports, debates, speeches, and research papers. The anthologies also facilitate further research, featuring a book and periodical bibliography and a list of organizations to contact for additional information.

A perfect resource for both students and the general reader, Greenhaven's Contemporary Issues Companion series is sure to be a valued source of current, readable information on social problems that interest young adults. It is the editors' hope that readers will find the Contemporary Issues Companion series useful as a starting point to formulate their own opinions about and answers to the complex issues of the present day.

Introduction

Defining the term "war crime" is a complex task. On the simplest level, a war crime is a violation of the laws of war. Beyond that, however, an understanding of war crimes requires an examination of some of the historical circumstances surrounding the establishment of standards of warfare. In his book *Nuremberg and Vietnam: An American Tragedy*, Telford Taylor traces the origins of the laws of war to "medieval notions of knightly chivalry" and to an even older fundamental principle that "the ravages of war should be mitigated as far as possible by prohibiting needless cruelties." This principle was informally and sporadically followed in many nations until the "formalization of military organization in the eighteenth century brought the establishment of military courts," according to Taylor.

These laws of war continued to be modified and expanded. In 1863, Francis Lieber, a German immigrant and law professor, prepared a code of military conduct for the U.S. Army during the Civil War. The code's 157 articles included provisions forbidding "unnecessary cruelty" and mistreatment of enemy soldiers. At the turn of the nineteenth century, representatives from European nations met at The Hague, Netherlands, to establish the Hague Conventions. The conventions, which sought to protect civilians as well as prisoners of war, are considered the first comprehensive international agreements on the rules of war. This international effort made possible some of the legal and political strategies that were used to address the atrocities committed during World War II.

The central issue emerging from the Second World War was Germany's slaughter of six million Jews in the Holocaust. The United States led the international community in holding Nazi leaders legally responsible for the Holocaust and other war crimes. While some of the primary Nazi leaders, including Adolf Hitler, committed suicide at the end of World War II, others were captured and brought to trial. In the Nuremberg Trials, which began in 1945 in Nuremberg, Germany, twenty-four defendants were tried for conducting a war of aggression and exterminating millions of Jews and other minority populations. Although not all of the guilty parties were charged or even tried because of legal complications, a number of Nazi leaders were convicted, the term "genocide" was recognized as a violation of international law, and a precedent was set for addressing war crimes.

These trials were especially significant because it was the first time in history that an international court successfully tried and convicted war criminals. In the October 1946 edition of the *New Republic*, Thomas Karsten and James Mathias, two members of the Nuremberg prosecution team, asserted that "a great moral principle has been judiciously established—the principle that the planning and waging of aggressive war is the greatest crime known to mankind and that those guilty of perpetrating it shall be punished." Karsten and Mathias also cautioned that the principle alone could not be effective without implementation by a strong, internationally formed organization.

"Never again" became the rallying cry of those who felt that the world community should prevent the atrocities of World War II from happening again. Time has shown, however, that the vow of "never again" did little to prevent further war crimes from occurring. In the late 1970s in Cambodia, for example, the communist Khmer Rouge government directed the killing of nearly a million civilians. The United States itself drew accusations of war crimes during the Vietnam War when news emerged that some American soldiers had tortured and massacred innocent Vietnamese civilians. During the 1980s, the Kurds, a separatist ethnic group located in northern Iraq, were the victims of chemical warfare—a war crime believed to have been sanctioned by Iraq's leader, Saddam Hussein. These and other accounts of war crimes surfaced from around the world, yet the international community made no move to bring the suspected war criminals to trial, indicating to some that the vow of "never again" referred to never holding another war crime tribunal.

During the 1990s, however, two events led to heightened public opinion in favor of reestablishing war crimes tribunals. In Rwanda, a civil war broke out between two ethnic groups—the majority Hutus and the minority Tutsis—which resulted in the mass killing of the Tutsis. Around the same time, as the former communist country of Yugoslavia broke into independent nations, the Serbs began a bloody campaign of "ethnic cleansing" against all non-Serbs, including Croats, Muslims, and Kosovar Albanians. As news of the horrendous atrocities in these war zones spread across the world, more and more people began to call for justice against the criminals who perpetrated such inhumane acts.

In 1995, fifty years after the first international war crimes trials, the international community again took legal action with the trial of Dusan Tadic, the first suspected war criminal to be tried since the end of World War II. Tadic, a former civilian guard in the Serbian death camp of Omarska, was accused of committing murder, rape, and torture against Muslim prisoners. The hearing at The Hague took a few years because of legal technicalities and tactics to extend the trial by Tadic's lawyer, who argued that the United Nations Security Council had no authority to create an international tribunal. Nevertheless, on July 14, 1997, Tadic was found guilty on eleven counts and sentenced to twenty years in prison.

Although Tadic's trial represented a significant step in prosecuting war criminals, it seemed somewhat overshadowed by the abundance of difficulties faced by the international court. One serious complication is that not every nation will agree to the orders of an international court. In the international Yugoslavian tribunals, for example, more than seventy-five indictments had been issued against suspected war criminals, but most of these suspects were not brought to trial because they were hidden under the protection of their local authorities.

Other difficulties lie in addressing the overwhelmingly high number of atrocities committed throughout the world. The mass killings in Rwanda, Cambodia, and Iraq attest to the disturbing reality of wartime actions in modern times. David Scheffer, head of the U.S. Office of War Crimes Issues, gives his perspective: "I sometimes liken war crimes to a growth industry, sadly enough. Every day we awaken to another report of mass killing or a mass grave or an emerging conflict that holds the potential of another atrocity." The sheer extent of the problem makes it extremely difficult to surmount.

However, Scheffer asserts that despite the discouraging situation, his organization and others in the international community continue to work toward attaining justice for the victims of war crimes and preventing further atrocities. Indeed, many experts share the belief that it is essential to hold war criminals accountable for their actions despite the difficulties faced by the international court. Some suggest that stronger military backing of the United Nations and giving representative countries greater vested interest in U.N. activities through equal political weight would help to surmount these difficulties. Others have championed the creation of a permanent international criminal court to deal with war crimes as they occur. At present, the way that war crimes are addressed often seems to depend on which nation or ethnic group is directly or indirectly affected, which raises important questions as to the relative nature of justice and the practical relevance of an international war crimes court. However, as accounts of worldwide atrocities increase, discussions and debate over how to best deal with the problem of war crimes become more relevant than ever.

War Crimes: Contemporary Issues Companion examines the issues surrounding international war crimes tribunals, as well as a wide range of other topics concerning war crimes. The following chapters focus on the definition of war crimes, the historical and legal development of the term, personal reflections of people who have been affected by war crimes, and how war crimes should be addressed. The selections included in this anthology provide a comprehensive overview of the historical and political aspects of war crimes and offer some suggestions for solving this age-old problem.

CHAPTER 1

AN EXAMINATION OF WAR CRIMES

WAR CRIMES VIOLATE THE LAWS OF WAR

John H.E. Fried

In the following selection, John H.E. Fried defines "war crimes" as acts that violate an internationally developed body of laws that regulate acceptable behavior in the context of war. Fried delineates the historical development of the laws of war, showing their emergence from unwritten rules of conduct to documented military standards. Although these rules are not always honored, he writes, they still have improved the treatment of civilians and prisoners during times of war and have allowed for appropriate punishment of those who commit war crimes. Fried is a professor of political economy at New York University. He formerly served as special legal consultant to the U.S. War Crimes Tribunals during the Nuremberg Trials.

War crimes are violations of the rules of war. These rules, which limit the type and extent of violence permissible in war, are partly laid down in written treaties (laws) and partly consist of unwritten customs.

There are at least four compelling reasons for the existence of rules of war. First, every belligerent has a selfish interest not to provoke reprisals from the enemy, and not to provoke neutrals to join the enemy. Second, wars, however bitter, are to usher in a new era of peace. Hence, reconciliation should not be made too difficult: yesterday's enemy may be needed as a friend tomorrow. Third, nations do not wish their armed forces to "get out of hand" for, as history has also shown, they may otherwise easily turn against their own government and conationals. Last, but not least, war has always been decried, for humanitarian and many other reasons; if wars cannot be prevented their cruelty and destructiveness must at least be limited, for the purpose of sheer self-preservation. For all of these reasons, the law of war is the oldest and one of the most important parts of international law. Especially since the Middle Ages, the rules of war—as well as the conditions under which it is lawful to start a war—have greatly occupied the attention of governments, jurists, and, indeed, military men.

Rules of War

The rules of war fall into several categories:

1. Rules concerning the status of combatants. These determine whether or not a person has the right to engage in combat and other military activities. For example, professional and conscripted soldiers may kill enemy soldiers in battle, but neither an individual civilian nor a soldier disguised as a civilian may do so.

2. Rules concerning the conduct of hostilities. These circumscribe the type and extent of damage and suffering that may be inflicted upon the people and territory of the enemy, the treatment of prisoners of war, and the like.

3. Rules dealing with the behavior of the occupying power in occupied enemy territory. The longer a wartime occupation lasts (for example, in the war which ended in 1945, Japan occupied large parts of China for over a decade), the more important are these rules.

4. Rules pertaining to such important matters as the rights and duties of the belligerents and their citizens toward neutral nations and their citizens, and to the behavior of the parties under a truce and during an armistice.

Offenses against any of these rules, whether established by treaties or by international custom, constitute war crimes.

Historical Developments

At different periods of history, the laws and customs of war varied greatly; and for long stretches of time, and in many regions of the world, practices were considered acceptable which at other times were regarded as utterly repugnant and not permissible. Nor did this evolution constitute a continuous process of amelioration. For some periods of time, or in some parts of the world, usages would improve, only to relapse again into barbarity. For example, the periods of the Crusades and, again, of the Thirty Years' War (1618–1648) were marked by a cruelty of military customs which had been overcome in previous periods and elsewhere.

Surveying the history of warfare, we find that often it was considered permissible to plunder or even physically to destroy a conquered city, and to slay the inhabitants, irrespective of sex and age. At other times, at least certain places—such as places of worship—had to be spared, and/or persons who had found rescue there, and/or women and children. For example, the Old Testament (Deuteronomy 20:19, 20) forbids the destruction of fruit-bearing trees in enemy territory. The Greeks of the heroic age had very cruel usages of war; thus, indignities were inflicted even on the corpse of a fallen enemy leader—as shown in the description, by Homer, of the treatment of Hector's body by Achilles. On the other hand, quarter was given during the Trojan wars even during battle, if ransom was offered. And the ancient code of Manu, the legendary legislator of India, ordered long before the Trojan wars that an enemy must not be harmed if he is asleep, or naked, or turning to flight, or defenseless, or folding his hands to ask for mercy. But at diverse periods of history, captured enemy soldiers were slain, or at least it was permitted to slay them.

Slavery as a Tactic

A relative improvement in the law of war was the gradually developed custom not to slay prisoners but to make them into slaves (agricultural workers, household servants, and the like) or to exchange them for one's own soldiers who had fallen into captivity of the other side. Yet, for example, Hemocratus, a general in the service of Syracuse (on the island of Sicily), was condemned to exile by his government for having ordered his troops to treat the invading Athenian armies with moderation, while Julius Caesar was not reprimanded for having sold, rather than killed, 33,000 Belgian prisoners during his second campaign in Gaul.

Under the law permitting the enslavement of conquered people, the Hebrews were taken in servitude to Egypt. The custom of selling enemy prisoners at slave auction developed into the custom of allowing the payment of ransom for their liberty. There are examples of freeing captives without ransom, while on the other hand, in the 16th and 17th centuries it was again considered permissible to make slaves of prisoners.

Religious views greatly influenced the rules of war. When the outcome of war was regarded to be the judgment of heaven, or the vanquished were regarded as being abandoned by the gods, such doctrines were used as justification for the cruel treatment of the defeated. On the other hand, the Stoics (for example, Marcus Tullius Cicero, 106–43 BC) taught that the vanquished must be spared; and according to the law as it existed at certain times in antiquity, generals who had received the surrender of towns or even nations actually became their patrons.

At some periods, more lenient rules applied in wars between "equals" (for example, conflicts between Christian princes or between Muslims) than in wars against "outsiders" or "infidels" (for example, between Christians and Muslims). Thus, in 1179, Pope Alexander III requested that enslaving be limited to non-Christians.

Early Transgressions

Very important to the development of international law was the fact that, however brutal the rules of war may have been, the violations of such limitations as did exist were considered as grievous wrongs; and in times of deep religious convictions punishments of a religious nature were threatened as the most powerful deterrent available. Thus, during the 11th century, church councils proclaimed the so-called "Truce of God," forbidding warfare on certain days and the harming during hostilities of certain categories of persons, especially priests, women, pilgrims, and merchants (and also sometimes of beasts of burden), under penalty of excommunication. Similarly, in wars between peoples of different religions, "treachery"—the violation of a treaty-created or customarily sacrosanct rule, such as the molestation of heralds of truce, or the breach of a promise of free conduct—would be "punished" by severest reprisals.

The first war crimes trial in history in the technical sense of the term (that is, punishment of transgression of the law of war through judicial procedure) appears to have been the trial by an English court in 1305 of the celebrated Sir William Wallace, for waging a war of extermination against the English population, "sparing neither age nor sex, monk nor nun." Since the latter part of the Middle Ages, customs and practices have evolved which eventually led to the modern law of war; and, in the words of a leading British jurist, Lord Wright of Durley (Robert Alderson Wright), chairman of the United Nations War Crimes Commission, "there have been hundreds of cases in which national military tribunals have tried and convicted enemy nationals of breaches of the laws of war." To illustrate, during the Franco-Prussian War of 1870–1871, the Germans executed numerous French *francs-tireurs* (irregular combatants) for violations of the laws of war.

The teachings of jurists and philosophers of the 17th and 18th centuries did much to humanize the conduct of belligerents. For example, Montesquieu (1689–1755) held that to murder prisoners of war is contrary to all law, and Jean Jacques Rousseau (1712–1778) added that they must not be held in dungeons or prisons, or put in iron, but should be placed in healthy conditions and liberated after the end of the war. Rules to such effect were agreed upon in the Treaty of Commerce and Friendship between the United States and Prussia, signed by Benjamin Franklin and King Frederick the Great.

Geneva and The Hague

Decisive progress in the evolution of the laws of war was made after the 1860's partly under the impact of the horrors of the Crimean War and the American Civil War, through international treaties concluded between states. The Geneva Conventions of 1864 and 1906, for example, were to ameliorate the conditions of wounded soldiers in the field. The most important among the treaties adopted prior to World War I were the various conventions and regulations approved at international conferences held at The Hague in 1899 and 1907, and especially the Convention respecting the Laws and Customs of War on Land and the Regulations of the same name, annexed to the convention of 1907. The rules and principles laid down therein constitute the most ambitious effort so far to "define with greater precision" the rules and customs of war on land.

Although subsequently further refined by various international conventions—for example, the Geneva Prisoner of War Convention of 1929 and the Geneva conventions of 1949—the Hague Regulations of 1907 (as they are called for short) have continued to form the core of the law of war of the 20th century. They have been so generally accepted by the community of nations that, as numerous tribunals have stated, they are binding upon all states and all individuals, which means that their violation constitutes war crimes.

Some of the provisions of the 1907 regulations, cited here at random, may indicate their range and significance: "Volunteer corps" (now often known as organized partisans or guerrillas), if fulfilling specific conditions laid down in the regulations, have the same rights and duties as have armies. Prisoners of war must be humanely treated. For example, their board, lodging, and clothing must be "on the same footing as furnished to the troops who captured them." "It is especially forbidden to employ poison or poisoned weapons" or "to kill or wound an enemy who has surrendered" or "to declare that no quarter will be given." "The attack or bombardment, by whatever means, of towns, villages, dwellings, or buildings which are undefended is prohibited." "Escaped prisoners who are retaken before being able to rejoin their own army are liable only to disciplinary punishment. Prisoners who, after succeeding in escaping, are again taken prisoner, are not liable to any punishment on account of the previous flight." In belligerently occupied territory, "family honor and rights, the lives of persons, and private property, as well as religious convictions and practices, must be respected. Private property cannot be confiscated. Pillage is formally forbidden. No general penalty, pecuniary or otherwise, shall be inflicted upon the population on account of the acts of individuals for which they cannot be regarded as jointly and severally responsible." "The property of municipalities, that of institutions dedicated to religion, charity and education, the arts and sciences, even when State property, shall be treated as private property"—that is, must be "respected" and cannot be confiscated by the occupant.

Basic Principles Regarding War Crimes

Since the rules of war are part of international law, no nation can one-sidedly change them. No legislature or government or general can decree that something which is a war crime is permitted to their own forces. In 1842, Daniel Webster, United States secretary of state, declared: "The law of war forbids the wounding, killing, impressing into the troops of the country, or enslaving or otherwise maltreating the prisoners of war unless they have been guilty of some grave crime, and from the obligations of this law no civilized state can discharge itself." War crimes can be punished, not only by the organs of the country of which the offender is a citizen—for example, a guard who tortures, or a camp commander who orders the torturing of, prisoners of war will in a civilized country be court-martialed by his own authorities—but also by the enemy. The right of the enemy to try a war crime suspect has been uncontested throughout the centuries. In fact, since the rules of war are *international* law, such enemy suspects may be tried, and, if found guilty, punished even by a nation which has *not* passed any legislation for such procedures. Hence, Gen. George Washington acted correctly when in 1780, during the American Revolutionary War, he had Maj. John André tried by a Board of General Officers, and André was correctly convicted by them as a spy "under the laws of war" (that is, under the then existing *international* rules of war) even though no *American* legislature had by 1780 stipulated the criminality of André's behavior. The matter was lucidly stated by United States Attorney General James Speed in 1865 in connection with the trial of President Abraham Lincoln's assassins: "The laws of war exist and are of binding force upon the departments and citizens of the government though not defined by any law of Congress. When war comes, the laws and customs of war come also, and during the war are part of the law of the land." Similarly, the United States Supreme Court stated shortly after the Civil War (in *Dew v. Johnson*): "What is the law which governs an army invading an enemy's country? It is not the civil law of the invaded country; it is not the civil law of the conquering country; it is the law of war." War crimes are very serious offenses. In the words of the United States basic field manual: "All war crimes are subject to the death penalty, although a lesser penalty may be imposed." Not only military personnel are bound by the law of war. Hence, any civilian may become guilty of a war crime—for example, a physician who subjects an enemy citizen to inhuman "medical experiments," or a businessman participating in the plunder of enemy property. Even in the heat of war, persons suspected of war crimes may not be punished without their guilt being properly established. To shoot them out of hand constitutes itself a war crime. International law does not lay down the procedure to be followed. Summary procedure may suffice, if it affords the accused the minimum guarantees of a fair trial according to the general principles of law as recognized by civilized nations. In a wider sense, the term "war crimes" covers two other types of behavior violating international law, namely "crimes against peace" and "crimes against humanity."

Crimes Against Peace

These consist in planning, preparing, initiating, or waging of war of aggression. After World War II, the International Military Tribunal at Nuremberg (composed of one each American, British, French, and Russian judge) tried top leaders of Adolf Hitler's Germany, and the International Military Tribunal for the Far East, at Tokyo (composed of one judge each from Australia, Canada, pre-Communist China, France, Great Britain, India, the Netherlands, New Zealand, the

Philippines, the USSR, and the United States), tried top leaders of Japan. Both tribunals stated in their judgments that to unleash a war of aggression "is not only an international crime; it is the supreme international crime." But both tribunals emphasized that only persons actually formulating or influencing governmental policy can be charged with "crimes against peace." For example, the Tokyo judgment declared that "the duty of an army is to be loyal." Hence, neither privates nor generals of an aggressor nation can be blamed if they "merely performed their military duty of fighting a war waged by their government," as long as they did not personally participate in the making of the policy of aggression.

The concept that aggression is a crime is intimately connected with the distinction between "just" and "unjust" war. "Unjust" war means, in essence, aggressive war, and includes especially aggression made in violation of a solemn pledge (treaty) *not* to attack. The distinction between just and unjust war goes back for more than 2,000 years. It has been insisted upon, for example, by Roman statesmen and jurists in antiquity; by the two most influential "doctors" of the Catholic Church, St. Augustine in the 5th century and St. Thomas Aquinas in the 13th century; by the father of the modern law of nations, Hugo Grotius (1583–1645), and other famous Dutch jurists; and by Spanish scholastics and French and German thinkers of the age of enlightenment. Approximate precedents for the proposition that "crimes against peace" are punishable also exist. Thus, the Senate of Rome requested the extradition for trial of Hannibal for inciting nations to make war upon Rome, and of Brutulus Papius of Samnium for attacking Rome in breach of treaty. (Both committed suicide.) In 1474, Sir Peter of Hagenbach, governor of Breisach, was tried by a court composed of Austrian and Swiss judges and executed for having waged a terroristic war.

During the period of absolutism in Europe, the distinction between just and unjust war fell into oblivion. But when in 1815, Napoleon Bonaparte, violating his pledge, escaped from Elba to France and rekindled the war, the Great Powers of Europe declared him an outlaw "as an enemy and disturber of the tranquility of the world who has incurred public vengeance." Thereafter, Britain, with the consent of the other Great Powers, punished him by banishing him to the grim island of St. Helena.

Trials for Peace

Under the Versailles Treaty (1919), the German emperor William II was to be tried by an international tribunal "for a supreme offence against international morality and the sanctity of treaties" (especially including the violation of the German-guaranteed neutrality of Belgium and Luxembourg). But the Netherlands, where William had fled, refused to extradite him, and the trial never took place.

During the interwar period, several international pronouncements condemned wars of aggression as illegal and criminal. Thus, in February 1928, the sixth Pan American Conference of 21 American republics resolved that "war of aggression constitutes an international crime against the human species," all aggression is illicit. The Nuremberg and Tokyo international tribunals attached special importance to the General Treaty for the Renunciation of War (Kellogg-Briand Pact) of Aug. 27, 1928, because it was ratified before World War II by virtually all countries of the world. The pact does not specify that aggression is criminal, but the Nuremberg international tribunal declared: "The solemn renunciation of war as an instrument of national policy pledged in the Kellogg-Briand Pact involves the proposition that such a war is illegal in international law; and that those who plan and wage such a war, with its inevitable and terrible consequences, are committing a crime in so doing." This, as well as all other principles enunciated by the Nuremberg international tribunal, received added weight by the fact that the General Assembly of the United Nations, by a unanimous resolution of Dec. 11, 1946, identified itself with these principles, as did subsequently the 11-nation Tokyo tribunal.

It should be noted, however, that after World War II only 36 leaders (12 German and 24 Japanese), out of the many thousands of war crime suspects tried, were convicted for "crimes against peace."

Crimes Against Humanity

These are outrages (murder, extermination, deportation, torture, and other mass atrocities) and persecutions of entire racial, religious, and political groups. If the victims are enemy citizens, such deeds constitute "war crimes" in the narrow sense of the term. But if the victims were, for example, German nationals, such deeds were considered punishable under international law (that is, also by non-German courts), *provided* they were committed in connection with "crimes against peace," or "war crimes." The Nuremberg international tribunal interpreted these crimes cautiously. Its judgment states that "revolting and horrible" as was "the policy of persecution, repression and murder of civilians in Germany before the war of 1939," the tribunal was not competent to deal with them. It did, however, find certain defendants guilty of atrocities, irrespective of the nationality of the victims, because they were committed "in execution of or in connection with the aggressive war." In other words, when, for example, mentally or physically deficient persons were systematically exterminated as "useless eaters" in occupied territories as well as in Germany, or when German Jews and gypsies were transported to concentration and extermination camps just as were foreign Jews and gypsies pursuant to the Nazi master race theory, all this was part and parcel of a criminal war policy. Other war crimes tribunals which had to deal with indictments for "crimes against humanity" followed the interpretation of the Nuremberg international tribunal.

It will be noted, therefore, that the post–World War II war crimes trials left open the question as to whether mass atrocities committed by or with the complicity of a government *in peacetime* against entire groups of its *own* population constitute international crimes; that is, whether the culprits can be brought to justice before an outside court.

War Crimes Trials After World War I

The practices of "terror, in violation of the laws of war," which Germany used in World War I led to an insistent demand to punish the individuals responsible for them. The Versailles Treaty provided that Germany should hand over to the Allies the persons wanted for trial. But when in February 1920 the first such list of some 900 names—including the former imperial crown prince, Field Marshal Paul von Hindenburg, and Gen. Erich F.W. Ludendorff—was presented, German indignation was so strong that the Allies agreed to a compromise, namely, that investigations and trials would be handled by the German Supreme Court. The outcome was a farce. Of the 901 persons grievously incriminated by evidence furnished by the Allies (mainly Great Britain, France, and Belgium), 888 were either acquitted or not indicted. The whole procedure gave rise to fanatical chauvinistic demonstrations, and greatly helped the early spread of nazism. The 13 who were found guilty received insignificant prison sentences but were celebrated inside and outside the court as national heroes.

World War II Trials

The most famous trial held during World War II was that staged by the Germans at Riom (France) of French statesmen for "crimes against peace." The intention was to prove that the accused, and especially Leon Blum, the former French prime minister who was of Jewish ancestry, had been involved in a Jewish plot to start a world war against Germany. But the evidence immediately pointed in the opposite direction. The trial was quickly abandoned, and the defendants put in concentration camps. The first trial of an officer of the notorious Nazi Elite Guard extermination troops was held in Kharkov, USSR, in 1943.

In view of the unparalleled mass atrocities systematically carried out by Germany from the inception of the war, numerous formal warnings were issued by the Allies during World War II that the culprits would be brought to justice. Resolve was also strong to punish Japanese atrocities committed in the far-flung Asian and Pacific theaters of war. In 1943, a United Nations Commission for the Investigation of War Crimes, composed of representatives of 17 nations, was established with its seat in London as a clearinghouse of information and evidence. In May 1944, at the request of China, the commission established a Far Eastern subcommission.

The trial before the International Military Tribunal (Nov. 20, 1945, to Oct. 1, 1946) of Hermann Goering and 20-odd other leading personalities of the Third Reich was held at Nuremberg for symbolic reasons, Nuremberg having been the citadel of national socialism where Hitler had held his huge annual rallies. The trial was presided over by the British member of the tribunal, Lord Justice Geoffrey Lawrence. The tribunal was established and functioned pursuant to an agreement signed in London in August 1945 by representatives of the United States, Britain, France, and the USSR, and formally adhered to also by 19 other nations.

Of the 24 former leading Nazis indicted, 22 were tried, including Martin Bormann in absentia [although not present]; one of the defendants committed suicide before judgment and the other was not tried for medical reasons. Death sentences were imposed on 12 defendants, 3 were given life imprisonment and 4 lesser prison sentences, and 3 were acquitted.

Thereafter, 185 other leading German personalities—cabinet ministers, field marshals and admirals, industrialists, ambassadors, jurists, physicians, and so on—were indicted before 12 tribunals, composed exclusively of United States judges, at Nuremberg between December 1946 and March 1949 under a law issued by the Allied Control Council for Germany. Four defendants committed suicide; four were severed from the proceedings for health reasons. Of the remaining 177, these United States tribunals sentenced 25 to death, 20 to life imprisonment, 97 to lesser prison terms, and acquitted 35.

The Tokyo international tribunal was established on Jan. 19, 1946, by General of the Army Douglas MacArthur, as Supreme Commander of the Allied Powers (SCAP). The substantive and procedural law applied by it was very similar to that applied by the Nuremberg international tribunal. However, there were four chief prosecutors (one each from the four powers represented on the bench) at Nuremberg, and only one chief prosecutor (an American, Joseph B. Keenan, former assistant to the United States attorney general) at Tokyo. The trial lasted (including a seven-month recess to prepare the 1,200-page judgment) from May 3, 1946, to Nov. 4, 1948. The Australian member, Chief Justice of the Supreme Court of Queensland William Flood Webb, presided. Probably the best known of the defendants was Gen. Hideki Tojo, Japan's prime minister in 1941–1944, who was hanged as a war criminal in 1948. Of the 25 defendants brought to trial, 7 were given the death sentence, 16 were sentenced to life imprisonment, and 2 to other prison terms.

Furthermore, many trials were conducted from 1945 by American, British, French, Australian, Belgian, Dutch, Polish, Norwegian, Soviet, Czechoslovak, and other courts in many parts of Europe and the Far East. The defendants were mainly citizens of former enemy countries, but numerous nationals of the respective countries also were tried as collaborators in the war crimes of the enemy. The most famous of the latter trials were probably those of Marshal Henri Philippe Petain and Pierre Laval—respectively head of state and prime minister of France's wartime Vichy regime—and the Norwegian Vidkun Quisling, whose name had become synonymous for fifth columnist during World War II. One reason why many trials could be held was the unique fact that huge masses of official, top-secret documents of the former Axis powers had become available.

As the decade of the 1960s opened, the war crimes trials connected with World War II were not entirely over. This was particularly true of the Federal Republic of Germany, where since the 1950s many gravely incriminated persons who had lived under assumed names were brought to trial. German authorities estimated that these trials—long since held exclusively by German courts under German law—involving several additional thousands of suspects, were to come to an end by 1963. As far as these late trials were concerned, world attention focused on the trial in 1961, before the High Court of Israel, of Adolf Eichmann (who had lived incognito in Latin America, whence he was abducted to Israel in 1960), for having been a top figure in, and largely mastermind of, the extermination of millions of Jews and others considered "inferior" by the Hitler regime.

THE PERSISTENCE OF GENOCIDE

Samantha Power

According to Samantha Power, although human rights violations have decreased overall since World War II, genocide—the systematic killing of a whole national or ethnic group—still continues. The Jewish Holocaust provoked many nations to vow that such a tragedy would never be allowed to occur again, says Power, but the truth is that atrocities on a grand scale are still being committed by military states. Nonetheless, the United States and other nations choose to overlook some of these tragedies because of political reasons. Power is the director of the Human Rights Initiative at the Kennedy School of Government at Harvard University. Her upcoming book, entitled *Again and Again*, examines American responses to genocide since the Holocaust.

Fifty years ago a state-centric universe allowed governments to treat their own citizens virtually as they chose within national borders. Today the concept of human rights is flourishing, and the rights of individuals are prized (if not always protected). Across the contemporary legal, political and social landscape, we see abundant evidence of the legitimation of the movement: we see global conventions that outlaw discrimination on the basis of gender and race and outline the rights of refugees and children; a planet-wide ban on land-mines that was sparked by the outrage of a Vermonter; a pair of ad hoc international war crimes tribunals that take certain mass murderers to task; and an abundance of human rights lawyers who have acquired a respected presence at the policy-making table. In short, when it comes to human rights as a whole, states and citizens have traveled vast distances.

But one ugly, deadly and recurrent reality check persists: genocide. Genocide has occurred so often and so uncontested in the last fifty years that an epithet more apt in describing recent events than the oft-chanted "Never Again" is in fact "Again and Again." The gap between the promise and the practice of the last fifty years is dispiriting indeed. How can this be?

Reprinted, with permission, from "Never Again: The World's Most Unfulfilled Promise," by Samantha Power. This article was originally published by *Frontline* on its website "The World's Most Wanted Man," at www.pbs.org/frontline/shows/karadzic/genocide/neveragain.html.

In 1948 the member states of the United Nations General Assembly—repulsed and emboldened by the sinister scale and intent of the crimes they had just witnessed—unanimously passed the Genocide Convention. Signatories agreed to suppress and punish perpetrators who slaughtered victims simply because they belonged to an "undesirable" national, ethnic, or religious group.

The wrongfulness of such mindful killings was manifest. Though genocide has been practiced by colonizers, crusaders and ideologues from time immemorial, the word "genocide," which means the "killing" (Greek, cide) of a "people" (Latin, genos), had only been added to the English language in 1944 so as to capture this special kind of evil. In the words of Champetier de Ribes, the French Prosecutor at the Nuremberg trials, "This [was] a crime so monstrous, so undreamt of in history throughout the Christian era up to the birth of Hitlerism, that the term 'genocide' has had to be coined to define it." Genocide differed from ordinary conflict because, while surrender in war normally stopped the killing, surrender in the face of genocide only expedited it. It was—and remains—agreed that the systematic, large-scale massacre of innocents stands atop any "hierarchy of horribles."

American Support

The United States led the movement to build on the precedents of the Nuremberg war crimes trials, enshrine the "lessons" of the Holocaust, and ban genocide. Though slow to enter the Second World War, this country emerged from the armistice as a global spokesperson against crimes against humanity, taking charge of the Nuremberg proceedings and helping draft the 1948 Genocide Convention, which embodied the moral and popular consensus in the United States and the rest of the world that genocide should "never again" be perpetrated while outsiders stand idly by. President Harry Truman called on U.S. Senators to endorse the Convention on the grounds that America had "long been a symbol of freedom and democratic progress to peoples less favored," and because it was time to outlaw the "world-shocking crime of genocide."

The American people appeared to embrace these abstract principles. And though one wing of the American establishment still downplayed the importance of human rights and resisted "meddling" in the internal affairs of fellow nations, even its spokesmen appeared to make an exception for human rights abuses that rose to the level of genocide. Though Americans disagreed fervently over whether their foreign policy should be driven by realism or idealism, interests or values, pragmatism or principle, they united over the cause of combating genocide. A whole range of improbable bedfellows placed genocide, perhaps the lone universal, in a category unto itself.

In recent years this consensus has gained indirect support from the popular growth of a veritable cult of "Never Again" in the United States. The creation of a Holocaust industry of sorts has seen the establishment of a slew of Holocaust memorials and museums—the Holocaust Museum in Washington, D.C. is the most heavily frequented museum on the Mall—and an unprecedented burst of Holocaust-related news stories (be they about Schindler's List, Daniel Goldhagen's account of the role of ordinary Germans, the contemporary war crimes trials against aging Nazis like Maurice Papon, or Switzerland's fall from grace). There have in fact been more stories on Holocaust-related themes in the major American newspapers in the 1990s than in the preceding forty-five years combined. Though interest in the Holocaust does not translate into a popular outrage over the commission of contemporary genocides, it has caused many of us to question the wartime passivity of great powers and individual citizens. And American presidents have responded to these lamentations: ever since the Holocaust first entered mainstream discourse two decades ago, U.S. leaders have gone out of their way to pledge never again to let genocide happen. Jimmy Carter said it, Ronald Reagan said it, George Bush said it, and Bill Clinton said it.

Questioning Inconsistencies

But in the half century since, something has gone badly wrong. In Bosnia the men, women and children of Stupni Do, Srebrenica, Ahmici, Zvornik, Prijedor, etc., all learned in recent years that the promise of "never again" counted for little. And they were not alone. Notwithstanding a promising beginning, and a half-century of rhetorical ballast, the American consensus that genocide is wrong has not been accompanied by a willingness to stop or even condemn the crime itself.

Since the Holocaust, the United States has intervened militarily for a panoply of purposes—securing foreign ports, removing unpalatable dictators, combating evil ideology, protecting American oil interests, etc.—all of which provoke extreme moral and legal controversy. Yet, despite an impressive postwar surge in moral resolve, the United States has never intervened to stop the one overseas occurrence that all agree is wrong, and that most agree demands forceful measures. Irrespective of the political affiliation of the President at the time, the major genocides of the postwar era—Cambodia (Carter), northern Iraq (Reagan, Bush), Bosnia (Bush, Clinton) and Rwanda (Clinton)—have yielded virtually no American action and few stern words. American leaders have not merely refrained from sending GIs to combat genocide; when it came to atrocities in Cambodia, Iraq and Rwanda, the United States also refrained from condemning the crimes or imposing economic sanctions; and, again in Rwanda, the United States refused to authorize the deployment of a multinational U.N. force, and also squabbled over who would foot the bill for American transport vehicles.

Political Concerns Come First

What are the causes of this gap between American principle and American practice?

During the Cold War, one might be tempted to chalk up America's tepid responses to real-world geopolitical circumstance. With the nuclear shadow looming, and the world an ideological playground, every American intervention in the internal affairs of another country carried with it the risk of counter-intervention by its rival, and the commensurate danger of escalation. In the same vein, while the United States was embroiled in its war with the Soviet Union, it was said, humanitarian concerns could not be permitted to distract American leaders, soldiers and resources from the life-or-death struggle that mattered most. Henry Kissinger was one of many who believed it was best not to ask questions about the domestic behavior of states but to focus on how they behave outside their borders. Countries that didn't satisfy vital security needs, or serve some economic or ideological end, were of little concern. And since staging a multilateral intervention would have required Security Council clearance, the superpower veto effectively ruled out such operations.

But the end of communism eliminated many of the Cold War concerns regarding intervention. The superpower rivalry withered, leaving the United States free to engage abroad with few fears of nuclear escalation and often with the backing (and even troops) of its former nemesis. Free of the shadow of the veto, the U.N. Security Council claimed some of its intended function—as a dispatcher of troops and a proliferator of resolutions. The war against Saddam Hussein—himself a packageable panacea for the American Vietnam syndrome—seemed to usher in an era in which American-led U.N. coalitions would tackle intolerable acts of aggression and patrol the "new world order."

Yet, despite the propitiousness of circumstance, mass atrocity was rarely met with reprisal. The reasons for this are numerous—some familiar but many surprising. The most common justification for non-intervention is that, while leaving genocide alone threatens no vital American interests, suppressing it can threaten the lives of American soldiers.

What Leaders Claim

But this does not explain the American failure to condemn genocide or employ non-military sanction. Moreover, if it was so very obvious that the story ended there and that, by definition, "mere genocide" could not pass a Pentagon cost-benefit analysis, it is unlikely that Americans would be so vocal and persistent in their legal and moral commitments to prevent "another genocide."

American leaders say they are simply respecting the wishes of the American people, who have elected them, first and foremost, to fulfill the American dream of equality and freedom for all at home. Though this claim conforms with our intuitions and with the mounting data that the American public is becoming ever more isolationist, it may be misleading. Polls taken during the Bosnian war indicated that, while most Americans opposed unilateral American intervention or the deployment of U.S. ground troops, two-thirds supported American participation in multilateral efforts—flying in humanitarian air-drops or bombing Bosnian Serb positions. In the Iraqi case, likewise, a Gallup poll reported that 59 percent of Americans thought the coalition should have continued fighting until Hussein was overthrown and 57 percent supported shooting down Iraqi gun ships targeting the Kurds.

Saying the Word

If American leaders ever used the word "genocide" to describe atrocities, it is likely that this public support would have grown. A July 1994 Program on International Policy Attitudes (PIPA) poll found that when citizens were asked, "If genocidal situations occur, do you think that the U.N., including the U.S., should intervene with whatever force is necessary to stop the acts of genocide," 65 percent said "always" or "in most cases," while 23 percent said "only when American interests are also involved" and just 6 percent said "never." When asked how they would react if a U.N. commission decided that events in Bosnia and Rwanda constituted genocide, 80 percent said they would favor intervention in both places.

It is possible that such support is superficial and would fade once U.S. forces incurred casualties, but it also arose without prompting from American leaders. In no postwar case of genocide has an American president attempted to argue that mass atrocity makes military or political intervention morally necessary. Yet it is notable that when the United States has intervened for other reasons, its leaders have garnered popular support by appealing to American sensibilities regarding mass killing. In the lead-up to the Gulf War, for example, Saddam Hussein was transformed into American "Enemy #1" not so much because he seized Kuwaiti oil fields but because he was "another Hitler" who "killed Kuwaiti babies." The advancement of humanitarian values in fact appears to "sell" in a way that "protecting American oil interests" in Kuwait or "saving the NATO alliance" in Bosnia do not. When it came time to deploy American soldiers as part of a postwar NATO peacekeeping mission in Bosnia, for instance, two-thirds of Americans polled found "stopping the killing" a persuasive reason for deploying troops (64 percent, CBS/New York Times 12/9/95), while only 29 percent agreed with Clinton that deployment was necessary so as to maintain a stable Europe and preserve American leadership.

Some Help from the Media

Contrary to conventional wisdom, the modern media is probably not making intervention more likely. For starters, unlike in cases of famine or natural disaster, genocide can be exceedingly difficult to cover. Despite all the "globaloney" about reporters being "everywhere," stories about the early stages of genocide are often unattainable because the price of accessing such terrain may be the life of the reporter. And even if technological advances—such as Internet television images or flying, unmanned rescue cameras—succeed in bringing viewers live genocide, the "CNN effect" will not necessarily translate into louder or wider calls for humanitarian intervention, as television images have both attract and repel concern.

On the one hand, as we saw in Bosnia and Rwanda, the publicity given to mass atrocity can attract public interest and pull foreign governments toward intervention. On the other hand, the seeming intractability of the hatreds, the sight of the carnage, the visible danger to anyone who sets foot in the region, and the apparent remoteness of events from American homes can repel American voters and leaders and keep American troops out. In effect, this very tension may explain the United States' tendency to deliver a hearty humanitarian response but nonexistent military response to genocide.

American Hesitancy

Part of the problem in galvanizing a firm response lies in the instruments that were intended to serve as the solution. The Genocide Convention, which will celebrate its fifty-year anniversary in December 1998, never received either the commitment of the United States or the teeth for enforcement that it needed to become "law" in any meaningful sense.

Despite the indispensability of the United States in drafting the 1948 Convention—and some 3,000 speeches by Senator William Proxmire on the Senate floor on behalf of it—the Senate did not pass the Act until 1988—a full forty years after President Truman signed it. American law-makers were petrified that African- or Native Americans would haul the United States before the International Court of Justice (ICJ) on genocide charges, or that other states would infringe upon American national sovereignty. By the time the Convention had finally become U.S. law, the Congress had attached so many reservations that ratification was rendered largely meaningless. For instance, by requiring that the United States would never be brought before the ICJ on a genocide count, the Congress barred the United States (under the legal rule of reciprocity) from filing charges against other nations—such as Hussein's Iraq or Pol Pot's Cambodia. The United States has tended to further international law only so long as it does not find its sovereignty impinged or its practices or officials called before international judiciary bodies.

When it came to enforcing the convention's provisions, the drafters envisioned that a standing International Criminal Court would come into existence almost immediately. Ironically, that court was established in 1998—the very same year that the Convention celebrates its fifty-year-anniversary. And, already Washington's insistence that the United States (via the UN Security Council) retain prosecutorial authority, indicates that, as with the Convention itself, Washington's reluctance to have its own citizens and soldiers held accountable under international law may well impair the legitimacy and effectiveness of the new body.

Misusing the Term "Genocide"

The Convention's half century of impotence highlights the importance of retaining an independent arbiter of which cases should appear before the International Criminal Court. Thanks to international and national politics, and the demands of individual member states over the last fifty years, the word "genocide" itself lost salience— misused, overused and generally abused. To begin with, the Convention, which defined the crime as "a systematic attempt to destroy, in whole or in part, a national, ethnic, or religious group as such," was both under-inclusive (excluding Pol Pot's attempted extermination of a political class) and over-inclusive (potentially capturing a white racist's attempt to cause bodily injury to a carload of African-Americans). But, because it was drafted in order to satisfy all the major powers, it also ended up with wording so imprecise that the genocide label quickly became a political tool. For instance, President Truman labeled the North Koreans as genocidal perpetrators; France was charged with genocide in 1956 for its bloody involvement in Algeria; and the potent Asia-Africa block within the UN frequently charged Israel with orchestrating genocidal killing. American leaders in the fifties and sixties both levied the charge (usually against the Soviets), and found itself accused of such acts. In 1951 the Civil Rights Congress, an activist organization, published a book called "We Charge Genocide," which asserted that "the oppressed Negro citizens of the United States, segregated, discriminated against, and long the target of violence, suffer from genocide. . . ." And, two decades later, philosophers Bertrand Russell and Jean Paul Sartre established their own war crimes tribunal to try the United States for committing genocide against Vietnam. Tribunal President Sartre compared American intervention in Southeast Asia with Hitler's chosen means of conquest of Europe. In Hitler's Europe, "A Jew had to be put to death, whoever he was, not for having been caught carrying a weapon or for having joined a resistance movement, but simply because he was a Jew;" likewise, in his day, Americans were "killing Vietnamese in Vietnam for the simple reason that they are Vietnamese." Far from representing the ultimate "stain" on a nation, galvanizing swift and stern retribution, the genocide label has been applied to everything from desegregation in the United States to birth control and abortions in the developing world. And no impartial body exists to restore the word's intended meaning and use.

In the last fifty years, nothing has gone quite as planned. The Universal Declaration of Human Rights, which also celebrated its fiftieth birthday in December 1998, has become a bedrock document in international law, outlining the basic rights that individuals all over the world are entitled to claim. The Genocide Convention initially succeeded in articulating a postwar international consensus that genocide was a monstrous evil. But, as Pol Pot, Hussein, Radovan Karadzic and the Rwandan Interahamwe [Hutu militia] discovered, neither it nor the rhetorical commitments of the American leaders have translated into a willingness to halt the masterminds of genocide.

Recognizing Rape and Sexual Violence as War Crimes

Valerie Oosterveld

According to Valerie Oosterveld, although sexual violence against women during wars has occurred frequently throughout history, it has rarely been considered a war crime. However, as wartime rape has become even more widespread during the twentieth century, there has been increasing pressure to classify it as a war crime, Oosterveld reports. Accounts of mass rape in the former Yugoslavia during the 1990s spurred women's and human rights groups to political action, she writes, resulting in the recognition of rape as a war crime. So far, few war criminals have been prosecuted for rape, but as more victims testify and human rights organizations push for accountability, international tribunals may feel compelled to punish rapists harshly, Oosterveld concludes. Oosterveld practices law in Toronto, Canada. She is a contributor to *UNESCO Courier*, a publication of the United Nations Educational, Scientific, and Cultural Organization.

Violence against women during armed conflict is nothing new. With other innocent victims—children and the elderly—they have always been on the front lines of wars of all kinds—religious wars, civil wars or world wars. Historians have described how soldiers have raped women to intimidate civilian populations. But during the twentieth century the character of war has changed and this practice has become even more widespread. Where soldiers used to target other soldiers, the goal now is often to kill or terrorize civilians. Various forms of sexual assault may occur during fighting or in conjunction with looting and other crimes by armed forces overrunning an area. Soldiers may publicly rape women and detain them in special camps or brothels, where they can be tortured, raped and made pregnant.

Overwhelming Evidence

There have been many examples of this kind of violence in the 1990s. After Iraq invaded Kuwait in 1990, it was estimated that at least 5,000

Reprinted, with permission, from "When Women Are the Spoils of War," by Valerie Oosterveld, *UNESCO Courier*, August 1998.

Kuwaiti women were raped by Iraqi soldiers during the occupation. Two years later, shocking reports were published around the world about the use of rape and forced pregnancy as tools of "ethnic cleansing" in Bosnia. In 1994 and 1995, stories of sexual violence in war again appeared in the world media, this time from Rwanda. One United Nations report estimated that as many as 500,000 women and girls suffered brutal forms of sexual violence, including gang-rape and sexual mutilation, after which many of them were killed. In Algeria, the women of entire villages have been raped and killed. The government estimates that about 1,600 girls and young women have been kidnapped to become sexual slaves by roving bands from armed Islamic groups.

While men may also be victims of rape and sexual mutilation during armed conflict, it is widely recognized that sexual violence is usually targeted specifically at women. But women are often reluctant to report rape, either because they fear the social stigma or because they feel that it is useless to report the crime in conditions of chaos and societal breakdown. The extent of sexual violence often becomes evident long after the world knows the extent of other crimes. Stories of sexual violence in Rwanda emerged approximately nine months after the genocide had ended, as women began bearing babies conceived as a result of rape. According to estimates of the Rwandan National Population Office, women who survived the genocide gave birth to between 2,000 and 5,000 children, who are often known as "enfants des mauvais souvenirs"(children of bad memories). The same pattern is true of the former Yugoslavia, where women were raped until they were pregnant and then held until they were close to term. In 1993, it was estimated that between 1,000 and 2,000 women became pregnant as a result of rape.

Prosecuting Sexual Violence

Reports of mass rape in the former Yugoslavia led women's and human rights groups and then governments around the world to condemn these acts and call for an international tribunal to hold the perpetrators accountable. Following several Security Council resolutions condemning the massive, organized and systematic detention and rape of women, the International Criminal Tribunal for the Former Yugoslavia was founded in 1993. From the beginning, one of the purposes of setting up this court was to prosecute crimes of sexual violence. The tribunal was the first to recognize crimes of sexual violence as war crimes and as "grave breaches" imposing on states the duty to search for the allegedly guilty persons and bring them to court or extradite them for prosecution elsewhere. This is something new. Sexual violence is not explicitly called a grave breach in the main law of war documents—the 1949 Geneva Conventions and their 1977 Additional Protocols. However, it is generally accepted that these crimes meet the criteria of "willfully causing great suffering or serious injury to body or health" and "torture or inhuman treatment".

Sexual violence can also be regarded as a crime against humanity, like murder, extermination, enslavement, deportation, imprisonment, torture or persecution, depending on the surrounding circumstances. Historically however, crimes of sexual violence have rarely been prosecuted under any of these headings. One exception was the Tokyo World War II trial, where several Japanese officers were charged and held liable for the rape of 20,000 women during the occupation of Nanking (China) in 1937. During the prosecutions of top-ranking World War II criminals at Nuremberg, rape was not listed as a crime against humanity. However, it was prosecuted in the national trials that followed Nuremberg, and it is now accepted as belonging on the list. Both the Yugoslav and Rwandan Tribunals explicitly include it in the definition of crimes against humanity.

The experience of these two tribunals has demonstrated both the progress that has been made and the difficulties that have arisen in prosecuting crimes of sexual violence. As of August 1998, twenty-six people have been charged with committing sexual atrocities; however, many of them are still at large. In June 1996, the first indictment dealing solely with sexual violence and enslavement crimes was issued. It alleges that, in 1992 when the city of Foca (southeast of Sarajevo) was overrun by Serb forces, Muslim and Croat women were detained and repeatedly beaten and raped. Only one of the eight men accused in this indictment turned himself in to the tribunal.

Few Prosecutions

Unfortunately, the Rwanda Tribunal has publicly charged only two people with crimes of sexual violence, both in 1997—three years after it was founded. The first was Jean-Paul Akayesu, the mayor of Taba commune. Even though there had been reports of widespread sexual abuse in Taba, he was not initially charged with these crimes, and it was not until witnesses testified about rape, and a coalition of human rights and women's organizations submitted a brief, that the prosecutor amended the indictment to add sexual violence to charges of genocide, crimes against humanity and war crimes. This is the first case before the Rwandan Tribunal in which someone is specifically charged with crimes of sexual violence, and the first to address the issue of a leader's responsibility for encouraging or allowing others to commit rape.

Governments are in the process of finalizing the statute of a permanent International Criminal Court. This court will be able to build on the advances of the Yugoslav and Rwandan Tribunals and will hopefully reverse the historical trend.

THE CLEAR AND PRESENT DANGER OF WAR CRIMES

David J. Scheffer

David J. Scheffer is the U.S. Ambassador at Large for War Crimes. The following selection is taken from a speech he gave at the University of Oklahoma College of Law in Norman, Oklahoma, on February 24, 1998. Scheffer discusses the very real danger that contemporary war crimes present to victimized people and to the wider international community. According to Scheffer, the crimes against humanity committed in Iraq by Saddam Hussein stand as a potent example of the unchecked dangers that threaten the safety and freedom of people throughout the world. While there exists a strong international effort to maintain the laws of war and establish war crimes tribunals, he states, additional measures are needed to end these atrocities. One crucial objective, says Scheffer, is the creation of a structured and permanent international court to uphold the laws of war, support national and international interests, and bring war criminals to justice.

We live in a world today where threats to our security and to the security of other countries are growing in their number, their complexity, and their elusiveness. The threats include international terrorism and drug trafficking, the development and deployment of weapons of mass destruction, man-made ecological transformations, and global economic gyrations which are placing whole societies at risk. Our foreign diplomatic, military, and economic policies must confront these threats, and this is a challenge that the Clinton Administration is determined to meet.

But I have come to Norman today to speak about another clear and present danger to civilized people around the world. It is a danger that would be ignored at our peril. Crimes against humanity and war crimes are all too frequent in modern conflict and internal power struggles. Genocide has occurred in Cambodia, Rwanda, and the former Yugoslavia, and perhaps other places as well. The absence of justice is too often the norm rather than the exception in lands where armed con-

Excerpted from "The Clear and Present Danger of War Crimes," by David J. Scheffer, *Department of State Dispatch*, March 1998.

flicts and atrocities proliferate. Combatants are as likely to know as much about the laws of war as they do about quantum mechanics.

Typical among the victims are women and children—often in the thousands—raped and macheted for their mere existence. The severity of mass killings in our own time, on the eve of the millennium, reflects how little we know of ourselves, of our neighbors, and of our future. Neither our faith in the impressive march of technology nor our other aspirations of the twenty-first century can overshadow the grotesque reality of the massacres that characterize civilization, or the lack thereof, in today's troubled world.

But America has tried to lead the way since the Civil War to codify international rules to govern armed conflict and to outlaw the slaughter of civilians. Our soldiers fought to defend those principles in two world wars and throughout the Cold War, and they stand prepared to sustain those principles today.

The Iraq Example

Our principles are at stake today when we look at the track record of the present Iraqi dictatorship. U.S. military forces are deployed in the Persian Gulf because the record of Saddam Hussein and of his regime leaves us with no choice but to do whatever is required to ensure that Iraq complies fully with the UN Security Council resolutions whose fulfillment is essential to restoring peace and security to that important part of the world. The recent crisis has centered on Iraq's continued resistance to eliminating all of its weapons of mass destruction and the means to produce them.

The United States and our many allies in this effort have stood firm in backing up our diplomacy with the threat of force to persuade Saddam Hussein that the international community will not permit him to use such weapons again, as he has in the past against his neighbors and even against his own people. . . .

What must never be forgotten is the legacy of what Saddam Hussein has done against his neighbors and against his own people. What must we remember of the life and times of Saddam Hussein and of his military regime? Saddam Hussein seized power in 1979. In the 1980s he used poison gas against Iran during the Iran-Iraq war. In 1988, his forces committed crimes against humanity and perhaps even genocide during the "Anfal" campaign against the Iraqi Kurds, including the use of poison gas, which killed thousands of innocent civilians in the town of Halabja alone. During the Gulf war, Saddam's regime committed crimes against humanity and war crimes against the people of Kuwait, taking many civilians as prisoners and torturing many to death. Iraq has never answered Kuwait's anguished demands for a full accounting of Kuwaiti prisoners of war and missing civilians, which is yet another breach of Iraq's obligations under Security Council Resolution 687—yet another confirmation of the reality of Saddam's regime.

The Iraqi regime committed war crimes against coalition forces during the Gulf war, including violations of the Geneva Convention on Prisoners of War. During the Gulf war, Saddam deployed "human shields" to military targets, blatantly violating the Geneva Convention on Protection of Civilians. He used human shields in November 1997 and has threatened to commit the same war crime once again in the event our forces have to bomb military targets. Saddam has waged crimes against humanity against Marsh Arabs of southern Iraq and against Iraqi Kurds in northern Iraq since 1991. Tens of thousands of civilians have perished. And this is not an exhaustive list. Saddam Hussein is, as Secretary of State Madeleine Albright reminded us, a "repeat offender." He is the nightmare the Iraqi people have suffered since 1979. Anyone who believes otherwise or blames the international community for conditions within Iraq suffers from acute amnesia. Saddam must not be appeased, and his crimes must never be forgotten. U.S. policy reflects, and will continue to reflect, these realities.

Continuing to Bring Criminals to Trial

Though our attention is focused on Iraq at the moment, the clear and present danger of war crimes reaches beyond the regime in Baghdad. The atrocities wrought by war criminals undermine the rule of law, create chaos within societies, generate massive refugee flows, fuel wars, cost governments billions of dollars to overcome, and challenge the moral underpinnings of civilization itself. You may witness the danger only on television, but the United States is on the front line every day confronting these assaults on humanity.

In the Balkans and in Rwanda, the perpetrators of genocide, crimes against humanity, and war crimes are the targets of an international prosecutor, Justice Louise Arbour, who is succeeding, one indictee at a time, to resurrect the legacy of Nuremberg in our time. The number of indictees of the International Criminal Tribunal for the Former Yugoslavia in custody has more than tripled in 1997. Twenty-two of the 76 indicted who remain living are now in custody. Many have surrendered voluntarily; others have been arrested with the active support of the NATO [North Atlantic Treaty Organization] Stabilization Force (SFOR), acting within its mandate.

The United States has led the effort to bring indictees to The Hague, and will continue to do so. The fact that certain major indictees remain at large should lead no one to assume that we are satisfied. Those indictees who are still at large, including Radovan Karadzic and Ratko Mladic, must realize that their day before the Yugoslav Tribunal will come; that there are no deals to cut; that there is no way they can avoid a fair trial. It is important to note that the Prime Minister of Republika Srpska, Milorad Dodik, who took office in January 1998, has said that all war criminals should go to The Hague voluntarily or otherwise. Prime Minister Dodik promised to work intensively to facilitate voluntary surrenders, but he acknowledged that, under any circumstances, all those indicted must face justice. Karadzic and Mladic should take the hint and surrender now.

Support for Justice

At the International Criminal Tribunal for Rwanda in Arusha, Tanzania, 23 of 32 indictees are now in custody. Some of the major leaders of the 1994 genocide are among those in custody. More of the ringleaders will be indicted in the future, and we will provide every possible support in their apprehension and prosecution.

The Clinton Administration is determined that the international tribunals will be fully supported until their jobs are done. In December 1997 the UN General Assembly approved, for the first time, full budget requests for the tribunals, each reflecting more than a 30% increase over their 1997 budgets. That is an extraordinary development given the budgetary situation at the United Nations—and one that we are pleased to see.

This leads me to a related point. At the very moment in world history when the United States can make the critical difference in waging peace—by joining with others to enforce international law, advancing vital national security interests, and bringing war criminals to justice—our credibility and our influence with other governments is needlessly and foolishly at risk.

The failure of the United States to pay its UN debts for years has had severe repercussions in the exercise of American foreign policy. As Secretary Albright has said, we are the indispensable nation, but we cannot go it alone. We were pleased in 1997 to receive bipartisan support for legislation that would put us well on the way to satisfying our obligations at the United Nations. Unfortunately, final passage of this bill was blocked by a small group of House members who wanted to hold the legislation hostage over an unrelated issue. The American people must not let this happen again. The United States has a responsibility to pay our debts at the same time as we insist that reform at the United Nations goes forward. The pursuit of war criminals is only one reason to pay our fair share, but even standing alone it is a darn good reason. Historians will judge us not only for the good we have done, but for the good we have failed to do. We must not fail to bring to justice the genocidaires and war criminals of our era.

Attempts to Establish Strict Laws

There is at this moment a yawning gap between the judicial chambers of the Yugoslav and Rwanda Tribunals and those areas of the world where justice remains denied. There are no international mechanisms for holding individuals criminally accountable for the violations of international humanitarian law that have occurred in Burundi, in Cambodia, in Iraq, and elsewhere. I know the challenge this presents and how difficult it will be to advance the rule of law. But we have a responsibility to try in the years ahead.

One area of obvious interest in this regard is Iraq. Finding a way to hold Saddam Hussein and his regime accountable for their crimes is an issue that the Clinton Administration has long had in mind. We will remain vigilant in that objective and continue to examine with other key governments the best way forward. We have not lost sight of the possibility of supporting another government's action against the Government of Iraq on charges of genocide in the International Court of Justice. We have acknowledged the important goals of the INDICT campaign [an international campaign to indict Iraqi war criminals] that non-governmental organizations and the Iraqi opposition have launched. We were heartened by House Concurrent Resolution 137 on November 17, 1997, which called, by a vote of 396–2, for an international war crimes tribunal to prosecute Saddam Hussein.

Looking beyond Iraq, President Clinton is determined to see established, by the end of the twentieth century, a permanent international criminal court that will bring to justice future perpetrators of genocide, crimes against humanity, and war crimes. Since 1995, the United States has joined with other governments at the United Nations in talks on how to structure and establish such a permanent court. . . .

Objectives to Achieve

As head of the U.S. delegation negotiating the establishment of a permanent court, I am keenly aware of the objectives we must achieve and the national interests we must protect in creating such a court.

The rule of law, which the United States has always championed, is at risk again of being trampled by war criminals whose only allegiance is to their own pursuit of power. We believe that a core purpose of an international criminal court must be to impose a discipline of law enforcement upon national governments themselves to investigate and prosecute genocide, crimes against humanity, and war crimes, failing which the permanent court will stand prepared to undertake that responsibility. Just as the rule of extradition treaties is "prosecute or extradite," the rule governing the international criminal court must be "prosecute nationally or risk international prosecution." That discipline on national systems to fulfill their obligations under international humanitarian law has been and will continue to be central to the U.S. position in the negotiations. Our long-term vision is the prevention of these crimes through effective national law enforcement joined with the deterrence of an international criminal court.

Second, the authority of the UN Security Council under the UN Charter to restore and maintain international peace and security and to repel aggression must be fully preserved. The Security Council should play a significant role in certain procedures of the permanent court so that the dual objectives of peace and justice can be pursued most effectively. The court will need to look to the Security Council for referrals of armed conflicts or atrocities where the mandatory cooperation of states is required to hold perpetrators of crimes accountable. The court also will need to rely upon the Security Council for certain enforcement actions to ensure compliance with the orders of the court.

Third, the U.S. criminal and military justice systems are the most sophisticated and highly developed in the world. Our courts must have the primary duty of investigation and prosecution of U.S. citizens, who must not be subjected to any unwarranted, unjustified, or frivolous exposure to the jurisdiction of the permanent court.

For Duty, Not Politics

Fourth, no other country shoulders the burden of international security as does the United States. In the post–Cold War world, the U.S. military is called upon to defend our national security from a wide range of threats; to carry out mandates from the Security Council; to fulfill our commitments to NATO; to help defend our allies and friends; to achieve humanitarian objectives, including the protection of human rights; to combat international terrorism; to rescue Americans and others in danger; and to prevent the proliferation or use of weapons of mass destruction. Many other governments participate in our military alliances, and a larger number of governments participate in UN and other multinational peacekeeping operations, such as SFOR in Bosnia. It is in our collective interests that the personnel of our militaries and civilian commands be able to fulfill their many legitimate responsibilities without unjustified exposure to criminal legal proceedings. The permanent court must not be manipulated for political purposes to handcuff governments taking risks to promote international peace and security and to save human lives. Otherwise, the permanent court would undermine the effort to confront genocide, crimes against humanity, and war crimes.

We believe such a court can be structured, but much hard work lies ahead. The world desperately needs a permanent international criminal court that is fair, effective, and efficiently administered. And it will need the United States as its strongest pillar of support. We look forward to working closely with other governments and with nongovernmental organizations to forge a permanent court.

In December 1997, Secretary Albright directed me to investigate the site of a massacre of Tutsis in northwest Rwanda shortly after an attack by Hutu insurgents which left hundreds dead and hundreds more wounded. After touring the devastation of the Mudende refugee camp where the slaughter took place and seeing the mass graves, I visited Gisenyi Hospital where I saw the living horror of resurgent genocide in the anguished faces of 267 victims. The wounded were overwhelmingly women and children. Many had multiple wounds caused by gunshot, machete, and burns. The lone exhausted surgeon in the hospital told me how he literally stuffed the brains of children back into their skulls and stitched up the consequences of malicious machete attacks. I saw bloated heads that bore out the surgeon's efforts at triage. Women and babies with untreated compound fractures moaned in agony. One young beautiful girl lay paralyzed by a gunshot wound to her lower spine. There was a critical shortage of medical supplies and medical personnel.

We all have a duty to respond to this barbarity; indeed, to this clear and present danger.

WAR CRIMES ARE DETERMINED BY THOSE IN POWER

Sharon Clarke

*In the following essay, Sharon Clarke explores what she consid-
ers the hypocrisy surrounding the punishment of war crimes.
Clarke argues that there are significant inconsistencies surrounding which war criminals are actually ever brought to trial. She
asserts that American and Western European leaders hold the
power to decide who will be tried for war crimes, as well as what
acts should be considered crimes punishable by an international
court of law. The major world powers have been instrumental in
the establishing of war crimes tribunals, Clarke maintains, yet
these same nations have always found ways to avoid punishment for their own atrocities committed during wartime. At the
same time, leaders from non-Western nations have been charac-
terized as brutal murderers in order to augment the image of so-
called civilized nations such as the United States, she writes.
Clarke is the author of* Sumner Locke Elliott: Writing Life.

What better than a war crimes tribunal to demonstrate the West's
right to sit in judgement on the rest of the world?

The United Nations Security Council has decided to set up an
international tribunal to try those accused of war crimes in Yugoslavia. It is the first attempt to prosecute alleged war criminals since
the Nazis were put in the dock at Nuremberg.

Those who complain that nothing will come of it, because there
are too many legal and political complications, miss the point. It
doesn't matter if the eleven Western-appointed judges never convict
anybody. That the court exists, and is internationally recognised as
legitimate, will be sufficient for the purposes of the Western powers. It
will confirm their moral authority around the globe.

When it came into operation in September 1993, the war crimes tribunal was due to concentrate on the civil war in Yugoslavia. But there
is already talk of widening its remit to cover crimes committed by
African warlords, Iraqi generals and others. Soon Western-appointed

Reprinted, with permission, from "Why They Love a Good War Crime," by Sharon
Clarke, *Living Marxism*, July 1993.

judges could be prying into the affairs of every third world state and passing judgement on their peoples.

The assumption behind the West's war crimes initiative is that the source of violence and barbarism is to be found over there—in the East and the third world. By comparison, the great and the good over here are assumed to have clean hands, and be qualified to decide the fate of the guilty.

What the war crimes discussion means is that some of the poorest and most powerless peoples on Earth are being blamed for causing war and oppression around the world, while the wealthy and powerful in the West are absolved of all guilt. 'They' are held responsible for the crimes; 'we' are responsible for meting out the punishment.

When Is a Massacre a War Crime?

What is a war crime anyway? The term has now been accepted into the everyday language of international politics. Yet closer inspection suggests that there is really no such thing as a war crime. The notion of war crimes and war criminals is an ideological construction, used to brand those of whom the Western powers disapprove—and, by implication, to boost the moral credentials of the West itself.

The discussion of war criminals assumes that atrocities are committed by a few particularly evil men with a propensity to behave like barbarians. The implication of singling out war criminals in this way is that other combatants act like gentlemen during a war, and are guilty of nothing. In reality, war creates an environment in which all are brutalised. Atrocities are committed on all sides of every conflict. In war, anybody can become capable of doing things which were unthinkable beforehand; but some have a lot more power than others with which to do it.

The strange thing is, however, that massacres are not called war crimes when they are carried out by those with the most power to commit atrocities—the forces of the USA, Britain or their allies. Since the Nazi trials at the end of the Second World War, there has been no mention of war crimes: not when the Americans slaughtered an estimated four million people during the war in Vietnam and Cambodia; nor when the British conducted massacres while putting down anti-colonial rebellions in Kenya, Aden and Malaya; nor when British paratroopers shot dead 14 Irish civilians on Bloody Sunday; nor when the French tortured and killed Algerians who resisted their rule; nor, most recently, when the US-led alliance killed perhaps 200,000 Iraqis in the Gulf War, using everything from napalm to fuel-air explosives which suck the oxygen out of the lungs.

Few Exceptions

Of course, there have been occasions in the past when US or British forces were accused of going too far. But the inquiries and commissions reluctantly set up in response have not been declared as grandiose international tribunals, and have never suggested that the accused be considered war criminals. Indeed the common concern has been to play down the importance of these incidents, and to let those responsible off as lightly as possible.

The classic colonial example came in April 1919, when British Brigadier-General R.E.H. Dyer sought to teach rebellious natives a lesson by ordering his troops to fire unprovoked on a crowd of thousands in the Indian city of Amritsar. A fusillade of 1650 rounds left, according to official figures, 379 dead and hundreds more maimed. The Amritsar massacre created unrest across India. The British imperial authorities responded by imposing martial law, and setting up an inquiry into the killings. A year later the Hunter Committee reported; it whitewashed the massacre, suggesting only that Dyer be 'severely censured'. The House of Lords then condoned Dyer's actions, and a group of Empire loyalists presented him with a sword and a purse of £20,000.

Arbitrary Determinations

The modern American equivalent of Amritsar was probably the My Lai massacre of 1968, when US troops wiped out an entire Vietnamese village in four hours. The details of the massacre remained a US army secret for 18 months, until they were revealed by Pulitzer Prize-winning journalist Seymour Hersh in the New York Times in November 1969. Lieutenant William Calley was then tried—by the army's internal court martial—on charges of killing at least 109 'Oriental human beings', one of them two years old. In 1971 Calley was sentenced to life with hard labour. He appealed, and the sentence was reduced to 20 years. He appealed again, and it became 10 years. He appealed once more, and was released in 1975. On the personal orders of President Richard Nixon, Calley served his sentence under 'house arrest', in his army apartment. He did not spend one day in prison.

Dyer, Calley and many other Western commanders whose massacres are well documented have never been considered war criminals or paraded in chains before the world. Yet unknown Serbian, Croatian and third world soldiers, with only a fraction of the destructive firepower at the disposal of the West, have already been found guilty of war crimes by the Western media before the tribunal is even set up. Clearly the category 'war crime' has nothing to do with the numbers killed or the circumstances in which they died. It is a political label, invented by the Western allies to be stuck on to foreigners as they see fit.

The capitalist powers love a good war crime story from Yugoslavia or Somalia because it makes the West look morally superior, and lends legitimacy to its self-image as the force for civilisation on Earth. That is a particularly valuable political asset for them today, when the governing parties and institutions of the West are all facing crises of legitimacy.

In 1993, no political party can excite public support, and no established institution commands much respect. The British monarchy is up to its neck in scandal, leading Italian politicians are all accused of belonging to the mafia, President Bill Clinton's honeymoon period proved shorter than [rock musician] Bill Wyman's . . . in different ways, the pattern is repeated across the West. The combination of economic slump and political exhaustion has thrown the governmental systems of Europe and the USA into disarray.

Against that background, it is not hard to see why the Western elites are so keen to criminalise and condemn people in other parts of the world, to find an external focus through which to demonstrate their authority. Branding the East or the third world as a threat to civilised values is a backhanded way of advertising the comparative virtues of Western capitalism.

The Crimes Are Relative

This is the significance of the UN decision to set up a war crimes tribunal. It institutionalises the distinction between a morally superior West and the inferior peoples of the rest of the world. By condemning selected foreigners as war criminals in this way, the Western authorities seek to get themselves off the hook at home. In effect they are saying, 'Look, whatever you might think of our system, just thank God that you don't have to contend with these barbarians'. The global scourge of war, for which the Western powers are primarily responsible, is twisted into an argument for the defence of their authority.

In 1982, when British troops recaptured the Falkland Islands from Argentina, they were hailed as old-fashioned heroes who had gallantly 'yomped' their way to victory. A decade later, evidence has finally surfaced that British paratroopers bayoneted and shot Argentine prisoners of war. Scotland Yard has reluctantly been prodded into investigating. But even if any Paras were to be charged, we can be sure that they will not end up in the UN tribunal dock with the Serbs and the rest.

Sir Nicholas Bonsor, Tory chairman of the commons defence committee, made clear that, regardless of the facts about the bloodshed in the South Atlantic, British squaddies never, never, never shall be war criminals. 'I think it is an insult to them', he declared, 'to suggest that we committed war crimes'. In other words, it is not necessarily a war crime to bayonet an unarmed prisoner. It all depends who is on either end of the bayonet.

CHAPTER 2

WAR CRIMES: A HISTORICAL OVERVIEW

THE DEVELOPMENT OF THE LAWS OF WAR

Telford Taylor

In the public consciousness, the concept of "war crimes" brings to mind the historic Nuremberg Trials, says Telford Taylor in the following excerpt from *The Anatomy of the Nuremberg Trials: A Personal Memoir*, his account of serving as the chief prosecutor at the Nuremberg Trials. However, according to Taylor, the laws of war were in formation long before the atrocities of the Second World War made re-examination of the laws necessary. He describes the historical lineage of the laws of war, dating back to feudal times and leading up to World War II. The late Telford Taylor, who filled federal legal posts under Presidents Franklin D. Roosevelt and Harry Truman, published a number of books, including *Munich: The Price of Peace*.

Ask the passerby what the words "war crimes" bring to his mind, and the chances are that the reply will be "Nuremberg." This may be a deserved acknowledgment of the seat of the most famous war crimes trials, but it also fosters the wholly mistaken notion that the Nuremberg trials were the original source of the "laws of war." And in order to understand the anatomy of the Nuremberg trials, it is necessary to know something of the nature and scope of the laws of war before and during World War II. . . .

The root circumstances which gave rise to the laws of war as we know them today are part of the great waves of change that swept Western civilization in the eighteenth and nineteenth centuries, including the decline of the Church and the Holy Roman Empire and the rise of nation-states as the main repositories of temporal power, the Industrial Revolution, and the Age of Enlightenment. Humanitarianism played a part in the development of these laws, but the prime motivations were commercial and military. They were, in fact, very largely the product of what Dwight Eisenhower, when retiring from the presidency, called the "military-industrial complex."

Changes in the "art" of war were the most immediate cause for the customs and practices, limiting the means and manners of warfare,

Excerpted from *The Anatomy of the Nuremberg Trials*, by Telford Taylor. Copyright ©1992 by Telford Taylor. Reprinted by permission of Alfred A. Knopf Inc.

which later turned into rules and then laws. From feudal times until well into the seventeenth century, "armies" were composed largely of mercenaries, whose pay was intermittent and who, for lack of a regular supply service, had to "live off the country." This was devastating both to the effectiveness of the armies and to the economy of nearby farms and towns. Soldiers were brutalized and undisciplined. The Thirty Years War (1618–1648) left much of Europe a shambles; it is estimated that over half the German-speaking population was wiped out, and famine and pestilence were widespread.

In the Interest of Soldiers

From these disastrous years, military lessons were learned. Soldiers who were regularly fed and paid, and who did not have to forage for food and shelter, could be disciplined and trained to a pitch of efficiency that greatly raised the tactical level of operations. Troops were organized under a regular chain of command, in battalions, regiments, and other standard units. Administrative staffs handled supplies, pay, and other logistical necessities. Military police helped enforce discipline, and procedures something like courts-martial were established to punish offenders.

Thus soldiering became a profession, and the distinction between soldier and civilian was stabilized. And so were born the customs and rules governing the conduct of occupying troops, requiring respect for the lives and livelihoods of the civilian inhabitants, as long as they remained noncombatants. . . .

During these same years, customs and rules for the taking and protection of prisoners of war were also developing. The wasteful stupidity of mass killings led increasingly to exchanges of prisoners. Often such exchanges were provided for in advance of hostilities; our own 1785 treaty with Prussia provided, in the event of war, for the humane care of prisoners taken on either side.

Still it remained doubtful whether surrender into captivity was a matter of right or of grace, and whether "no quarter" could not be declared, at least in some circumstances. Napoleon Bonaparte, for one, took a very "practical" view of the matter in 1799, at the unsuccessful end of his campaign in Egypt and Palestine. In March 1799 he captured the fortress of Jaffa, where the Mameluke garrison surrendered on the promise that their lives would he spared. But the promise was not kept, and as Napoleon sailed away, Mamelukes to the number of 1,200 (as he reported) or 3,500 (as eyewitnesses testified) were slaughtered on the beaches of the Mediterranean.

A few old rules of exception to the obligation to take prisoners lingered on, one of which is still alive today: capital punishment for spies. Well settled as it is on the basis that spies do not wear uniforms, this is an odd doctrine, as no moral obloquy now attaches to espionage. Witness the case of Nathan Hale, honored by a statue on the old campus at Yale and a plaque on the wall of the Yale Club in New York City, near his place of execution. The sporting aspect of espionage is underlined by the rule that if a spy succeeds in returning from behind the enemy lines to his own army, his responsibility for espionage is erased and if subsequently captured he must be treated as a prisoner of war—just as the base runner, surprised by an improbable catch, will be safe if he can beat the ball back to base.

Today the value of prisoner interrogation for intelligence purposes and the fear of reprisals have ensured among the major powers (though by no means universally) observance of the obligation to accept surrender and grant humane treatment to prisoners of war.

A System of Laws

Although the foregoing core elements of the laws of war were in place by the middle of the nineteenth century, they remained uncodified. Largely unwritten in any official sense, they were known as "customary law." It was the United States, during the War Between the States, that took the lead in having them systematized and embodied in an officially adopted code.

The principal draftsman of this first codification of the law of war was Francis Lieber, a German who, as a young man, had fought under Field Marshal von Blücher against Napoleon. A well-educated political dissident, he emigrated to the United States and took citizenship in 1832. His talents won him a professorship at South Carolina College, but he detested slavery and in 1857 he moved to New York and became a professor at Columbia College and subsequently at the newly established Columbia Law School.

The War Between the States, in Lieber's words, "knocked rudely at my door," for his eldest son was mortally wounded fighting for the Confederacy, whose cause Lieber abominated, while his two younger sons were in the Union Army. When one of them lost an arm in Tennessee at Fort Donelson, Lieber went west to visit him, and while there met General Henry W. Halleck, at that time commander of the Union forces in the West. In July 1862, Halleck was appointed military adviser to President Lincoln with the title General in Chief.

Halleck, himself the author of a treatise on international law, had been impressed by Lieber's combination of military, legal, and political pursuits, and in December 1862 he appointed Lieber to propose "a code of regulations for the government of Armies in the field of battle authorized by the laws and usages of war." Early in 1863 Lieber submitted a draft which was promulgated in May 1863 as General Orders No. 100, entitled "Instructions for the Government of Armies of the United States in the Field." It remained for over half a century the official army pronouncement on the laws of land warfare. . . .

In its specific content, the Lieber Code did not constitute a great leap forward in a reformist sense. Its great importance was recognition of the necessity of systematizing and articulating the accumulated experience and practices of the previous century. It thus laid the basis for instruction and training of the officers and men of large wartime armies, composed chiefly of drafted civilians unfamiliar with military affairs, and established standards for compliance with the rules and for their enforcement by courts-martial and other disciplinary measures.

International Conventions

The provisions of General Orders No. 100 were derived from international usage, but the Orders did not purport to be international law; it was a domestic regulation of the United States Army. However, it was promulgated at a time when events in Europe, especially the Crimean (1853–1856) and Franco-Austrian (1859) wars, had raised problems which were moving the major powers toward international agreement as a means of mitigating war's ravages.

Despite the progress of medical science, the warring powers in Europe had failed to make adequate provision for hospitals, doctors, and medical equipment at the scene of hostilities. In the Crimea, Florence Nightingale's administrative reforms and personal dedication to care for the wounded aroused popular feelings which were intensified in 1862 by the Swiss philanthropist Henri Dunant's widely read writings which gave a shocking account of the neglect suffered by the wounded at the Franco-Austrian battle at Solferino in Italy in 1859. At Geneva in 1864, twelve European nations signed a "Convention for the Amelioration of the Condition of the Wounded in Armies in the Field," the first of a series of international Red Cross conventions for this purpose.

In the field of war crimes, however, the international breakthrough occurred at The Hague in 1899, when a "Convention with Respect to the Laws and Customs of War on Land" was signed by the United States, Mexico, Japan, Persia, Siam, and nineteen European nations, including all the major European powers. In both organization and content, the Convention leaned heavily on the Lieber Code and accordingly dealt chiefly with prisoners of war and the relations between occupation troops and noncombatant civilian inhabitants. Unlike the Lieber Code, however, the Convention included an unqualified prohibition of declaring "no quarter" or attacking enemy soldiers who have surrendered. . . .

In all of these treaties, the laws of war are stated as general principles of conduct, and neither the means of enforcement nor the penalties for violation are specified. However, the substance of many of their provisions was soon incorporated into the military law of the major powers and many other nations.

In the United States, General Orders No. 100 was replaced in 1914 by an army field manual entitled "The Law of Land Warfare" which, updated, is still in force. It sets forth that the laws of war are part of the law of the United States and that they may be enforced against both soldiers and civilians, including enemy personnel, by military or international tribunals.

Such was the state of the laws of war in 1914, when World War I began. Up to this time the laws of war contained virtually nothing dealing with aerial warfare. The Hague Convention in 1899 antedated the Wright brothers' famous flight at Kitty Hawk in 1903, and the 1907 Convention came only a few years later. Military aviation was still in its infancy in 1914 when major-power warfare was renewed.

Naval Guidelines

The naval situation was wholly different. Over the past centuries of maritime warfare, many customs and rules, sometimes embodied in treaties, had been adopted dealing with such matters as false flags and other ruses, blockade, privateers, and the treatment of neutral shipping.

The Hague meetings produced a number of agreements to internationalize both preexistent and some new naval rules. In 1907, no less than eight naval conventions were adopted, covering such matters as the status of enemy ships at the outbreak of hostilities, the converting of merchant ships into warships, minelaying, and coastal bombardment.

Most of these rules were of such a nature that their violation would lead to reprisals, or claims for compensation, rather than criminal prosecutions. Navies do not ordinarily occupy enemy territory nor take large quantities of prisoners. These factual differences no doubt explain why there was no general naval code comparable to the Hague Conventions on land warfare.

None of the Hague Conventions, nor the predecessor concepts on which they were based, imposed any limitation on the sovereign right to make war. Wars had played a large part in the rise and proliferation of nation-states, whose leaders generally scorned as sentimental rubbish the "just and unjust war" concept of earlier centuries. To be sure, governments might still give reasons for resorting to war that stressed the righteousness of their cause, but none of this was of any legal significance. . . .

In 1914, there was nothing in the acknowledged content of international law that made any state or individual liable to criminal charges for declaring and engaging in war. But the Hague Conventions, and other treaties and conclaves in the preceding half century, had internationalized the whole subject of limits on warfare and laid the basis for an extraordinary expansion of public and political concern with "war crimes" throughout the course and aftermath of World War I. . . .

The First World War

Historians still debate the apportionment of responsibility for the onset of World War I, but no one contends that Belgium started it by attacking Germany. The German High Command conceived that their forces needed the deployment space of Belgium for a speedy victory over France, and as soon as there was a state of war between Germany and France, the German government sent Belgium a demand to allow the transit of German troops. When the Belgians declined, the German Army attacked across the Belgian frontier, in violation of the multinational Belgian neutrality treaty of 1839, which the German Chancellor Theobald von Bethmann-Hollweg publicly scorned as a "scrap of paper." A few hours later Britain, invoking the 1839 treaty, declared war on Germany.

The Germans' ruthless attack on a small neutral country not only ensured British hostility but also scandalized world opinion. With the invasion came reports of wanton destruction and brutalities by the Germans: the ancient city of Louvain was sacked and its world-famous library destroyed by fire; innocent civilians were taken hostage and often shot; in some places the invading soldiers were said to have raped women and killed adults and children alike. Soon there were comparable reports from German-occupied areas in France, where the troops of a brigade commanded by General Karl Stenger had denied quarter to French soldiers, including the wounded.

During 1915 the pitch of public indignation climbed even higher. In January the huge German lighter-than-air ships known (after their designer) as zeppelins started bombing raids over England; their military value was slight, but by the end of the year over 200 civilians had been killed and many were terrorized. The following month the German government proclaimed a "war zone" around the British Isles, in which their submarines would sink enemy merchant ships without warning. In April the huge Cunard liner *Lusitania* was sunk by a U-boat off the Irish coast with the loss of some 1,200 lives. That same month the Germans first employed poison gas as a weapon during the battle of Ypres. At about the same time the "Young Turk" government of the Ottoman Empire (which had entered the war as an ally of Germany in November 1914) began the deportation of Armenians to the Syrian desert, where they were massacred by the thousands. In October the British public was enraged by the Germans' execution of Edith Cavell, the director of a nurses' training school in Brussels. The following night a zeppelin raid over London killed 127 inhabitants. . . .

Deciding Whether to Punish

Pressure for punitive action against Kaiser Wilhelm II and other German war criminals was strongest in Britain, which was bearing the brunt of the U-boat and zeppelin operations. In 1916, Prime Minister Herbert Asquith told the House of Commons that his government was "determined to bring to justice the criminals, whoever they may be and whatever their station."

In February 1917 the German government declared a new zone

around the British Isles in which U-boats would sink enemy *and neutral* shipping alike, without warning or regard for the safety of crews or passengers. This was so contrary to maritime practice, and so hazardous to American lives and property, that two months later the United States declared war against Germany. A year later over a million American soldiers had joined the Allied forces in France.

Since American sympathies had lain with the Allies from the beginning of the war, it is not surprising that in the United States there had been almost as much discussion of war crimes trials as in Britain. In both countries the general public's wrath was directed at the Kaiser, but in legal and academic circles there was a strong current of opinion that judicial trials would promote the development of international law as an instrument of peace. This fitted well with Wilsonian internationalism and President Woodrow Wilson's insistence that the war was a crusade: a war "to end war" and "to make the world safe for democracy."

When victory came via the Armistice in November 1918, it was accompanied by the Kaiser's flight to Holland, a country with a long tradition as a haven for political refugees. This was a complicating factor, but did nothing to quell the public demand for his punishment. In Britain, Prime Minister David Lloyd George and his Cabinet pledged support for a trial of the Kaiser as part of their successful parliamentary election campaign in December 1918.

In France, the public appetite for war crimes trials had increased, partly because the Germans had carried out what amounted to a "scorched earth" policy in their final retreat through northern France. The practical French were, however, much more concerned about reparations and future national security than international justice. . . .

The Peace Conference

There was no unity of viewpoint about war crimes among the three major powers when the delegates assembled, on January 18, 1919, at the opening session of the Paris Peace Conference—a conclave dominated by British Prime Minister Lloyd George, French Premier Georges Clemenceau, and Woodrow Wilson. For the first-named, the establishment of an international tribunal to try the Kaiser, and provisions for the trial and punishment of other war criminals, was both a political necessity and a program which reflected his own and a majority of his countrymen's strong desires. But for both Clemenceau and Wilson, war crimes were collateral to their larger aims: for Clemenceau, reparations and security; for Wilson, a moderate peace, a viable democratic government for Germany, and, most of all, a League of Nations to secure future peace.

The war crimes issue was the first item on the conference's agenda, and a Commission on the Responsibility of the Authors of the War and the Enforcement of Penalties was established to study and report back on the matter. The chairman and dominant figure was the American Secretary of State, Robert Lansing, whose views on war crimes issues were fiercely conservative; he did not really believe in any supranational law and opposed any international punitive action against the Kaiser or the establishment of international courts for war crimes trials.

The commission's report, submitted in March 1919, charged Germany and her allies (the Central Powers) with extensive violations of the laws of war. Some offenders could be tried before national tribunals, but those in high authority and responsible for crimes on a large scale would be brought before a twenty-two-member international High Tribunal. The commission also found that the Central Powers had, with premeditation, launched a "war of aggression" in violation of treaties, but that this conduct did not provide the basis for a criminal charge under existing international law; it should, however, be strongly condemned and made a penal offense for the future. As for the Kaiser, the commission recommended his trial before an international tribunal on the charge that he was responsible for German violations of the laws of war.

Hindering Reservations

The report was nominally unanimous, but the American "reservations" were so fundamental that they amounted to a dissent. President Wilson was not as rigid as Lansing on these issues, but he was worried about "victors' justice" and had told Lansing that he wanted "a minority report rejecting High Tribunal and opposing trial of the Kaiser." Lloyd George, however, made it clear that he could not sign a treaty that failed to provide for the Kaiser's punishment. Confrontation then gave way to compromise, embodied in Articles 227 and 230 of the Treaty of Versailles, signed in June 1919.

Under Article 227 the Kaiser was to be tried before a "special tribunal" of five judges, one each from the United States, Great Britain, France, Italy, and Japan. He was not to be charged with responsibility for war crimes, but with "a supreme offence against international morality and the sanctity of treaties." The three ensuing articles called for trials of "persons accused of having committed acts in violation of the laws and customs of war" before "military tribunals" of the aggrieved nations, and required the German government to "hand over" the individuals so accused to any of the "Allied and Associated Powers" so requesting. Provisions comparable to Articles 228–230 were included in the later peace treaties with Austria, Hungary, and Bulgaria.

Thus the hopes of Lloyd George and other European statesmen to use the victorious peace as an occasion for confirming and expanding the international law of war foundered on the rocks of American opposition. Wilson and Lansing had won. There would be no international war crimes courts. There would be no trial to determine the Kaiser's criminal guilt. . . .

One International Treaty

Of general importance was the 1928 Treaty of Paris, which sought to outlaw war itself. The late 1920s was a period of international amity, which had begun in 1925 with the Locarno security pact among Britain, France, Germany, Belgium, and Italy guaranteeing the German-French and German-Belgian frontiers. The foreign ministers of France and Germany, Aristide Briand and Gustav Stresemann, were seeking to allay old animosities; the French ended their occupation of the Ruhr; Germany resumed reparations payments and in 1926 was admitted to the League of Nations. That year the two men shared the Nobel Peace Prize.

The tenth anniversary of the United States' entry into World War I fell on April 6, 1927, and Briand proposed to celebrate the occasion by a mutual undertaking by the two countries to renounce war. The American Secretary of State, Frank B. Kellogg, proposed making such a treaty multilateral, and on August 27, 1928, the representatives of fifteen nations met at Paris and signed the International Treaty for the Renunciation of War as an Instrument of National Policy, better known today as the Kellogg-Briand Pact and providing as follows:

> Art. I. The High Contracting Parties solemnly declare in the names of their respective peoples that they condemn recourse to war for the solution of international controversies, and renounce it as an instrument of national policy in their relations with one another.
>
> Art. II. The High Contracting Parties agree that the settlement or solution of all disputes or conflicts of whatever nature or of whatever origin they may be, which may arise among them, shall never be sought except by pacific means.

The treaty was subsequently accepted by forty-four nations, including all the Great Powers except the Soviet Union. It certainly was an impressive antiwar commitment, but did it make engaging in war a crime? Of course it was not intended to condemn resorting to war in self-defense, but what about launching an aggressive war? Opinions differed sharply at the time, and still did when World War II brought the question to a head.

Holocaust: Hitler's Final Solution

Amy Newman

In the following excerpt, author Amy Newman examines the most infamous act of genocide, the Jewish Holocaust of World War II. Newman writes of the Nuremberg Laws of 1935, the Nazi code of anti-Semitism, as being a springboard for Adolf Hitler's ultimate plans of eliminating European Jewry. With such sinister legislation on their side, the Nazis under Hitler's direction moved quickly to isolate and eventually destroy Jewish communities through escalating acts of violence. The terror culminated in the deportation of millions of Jews to concentration camps, where they were starved, overworked, and systematically killed in the gas chambers that have now come to symbolize the true atrocity of the Nazi dream. Amy Newman is the author of a book on the Nuremberg Laws, from which this selection is taken.

The Nazis promised to bring law and order to Germany, but they only half-succeeded. They brought law, but not order. In fact, some Nazi laws, especially the Nuremberg Laws, brought about disorder—riots, beatings, and eventually mass death.

Few Germans could foresee where the Nuremberg Laws would lead their nation. From a historical perspective, however, the Nuremberg Laws can clearly be seen as a bridge spanning the chasm between relegating a group of people to a second-class status and packing them in freight trains like cattle and sending them off to be murdered in one of the *Vernichtungslagern,* extermination camps.

There are three basic ways in which the Nuremberg Laws made it possible for Germany to murder millions of Jews. They removed any hope of protection from the state or any recourse to authority. They forbade Jews from forming bonds that might tie them to German citizens who would have the ability to protest and perhaps protect them. Finally, and most ominously, they defined who—when the cattle cars were loaded—would stay and who would go. . . .

Excerpted from Amy Newman, *The Nuremberg Laws*. San Diego: Lucent Books, 1999.

People of No Land

Of the three Nuremberg Laws, the Reich Citizenship Law had the most direct and immediate consequences. From the time they gained power in 1933 until the end of World War II, the Nazis constructed a grillwork of laws and decrees that herded the once-successful and assimilated German-Jewish community into an economic, social, and ultimately physical ghetto. The Nazis set up prohibitions that dictated what work Jews could do, what foods they could buy, what modes of transportation they could use, what they could do in their leisure time, what kind of education they could get, and even what names they could have. (All German Jews had to take the name Israel or Sara beginning in 1938.) The Reich Citizenship Law helped make these actions possible.

The Reich Citizenship Law stripped millions of people of even the most meager rights. As the Nazi agenda turned from humiliation and oppression to genocide, the Reich Citizenship Law determined who would die and who would not.

Unlike the other two parts of the Nuremberg Laws, the Reich Citizenship Law was applied to all Jews, regardless of whether they were religious Jews with few ties to the German community or ultra-assimilated Jews who had all but left their Jewishness behind. [Holocaust survivor] Ezra Ben Gershom describes his brother Leon's girlfriend Lore, who scarcely knew she was Jewish until the Nazis reminded her and her family of their roots:

> Lore belonged to a family that had become completely estranged from the Jewish tradition. She had been unaware of her Jewishness until the Race Laws were introduced. There was something touching in the way she asked about the details of our religious customs and tried to understand the links between the Jewish faith and the persecutions, ancient and modern, suffered by Jewry.

Not all Jews reacted favorably to being reminded of their Jewish status. In the WW II Warsaw ghetto in Poland, the Jewish police force (a group of Jews who worked for the Nazis) was headed by a Jew by the name of Sherinsky, a man who had renounced his faith and converted to Christianity. He was well known for his hatred of Jews and used his position to harass and attack the Jews of the ghetto. Ultimately, he was murdered by the ghetto underground.

The danger of being labeled a Jew was real and immediate after the passage of the Reich Citizenship Law. Daniel Lang, author of *A Backward Look*, describes a lunch with acquaintances in Germany in 1970. His hostess commented on the danger that befell her husband during the course of the war when he was almost classified as a non-Aryan. "Karl had a terrible time in the war," she said. "He was mistaken for a Jew." She went on to explain that because their last name was sometimes considered a Jewish name, a Nazi official suspected he was a Jew passing as an Aryan. For four months, while the Nazis investigated his background, there was constant danger that he would be sent off to a concentration camp.

Oil and Water

Because it sought to regulate intimate personal relationships, the Law for the Protection of German Blood and German Honor was more difficult to enforce. Enforcing the ban on marriages between Aryans and non-Aryans was simple enough, but dealing with couples who had married prior to the law was trickier, especially when many Germans refused to divorce their Jewish spouses.

Leaving aside the theories of race defilement put forth by the Nazis, in a very real sense the prohibition of mixed marriages was crucial to the success of the Nazis' genocidal plans. In addition to the protection such a marriage afforded an individual Jew, it often gave him or her an opportunity to save Jewish relatives. For example, in his book *The Last Jews in Berlin,* author Leonard Gross tells of a Jewish woman named Anna who was hidden by her brother Max Rosenthal, who was protected from deportation by his marriage to a Christian woman.

The aftermath of the Law for the Protection of German Blood and German Honor created very hard choices for people in mixed marriages. Ruth Thomas, a Jewish woman who survived the war in hiding and whose story is told in *The Last Jews in Berlin,* describes a close friend who was told by the Nazis that if she did not divorce her Jewish husband, she would lose all her property. The friend, like many other Germans in mixed marriages, was torn by her desire to stay with her husband and her fear for his safety.

During World War II, the Nazi leadership in different countries under German control took different approaches to these mixed marriages. For example, in Holland, Jews in mixed marriages were subjected to forced sterilization. The Dutch Nazis were determined to prevent the mixing of blood from one generation to the next.

The seriousness with which Nazis took the matter of "blood" can look ridiculous in hindsight. For example, Leonard Gross tells of a young Jewish boy named Gert Rosenthal who had contracted polio at the age of two (before a vaccine for polio was available). Unlike millions of other victims of this crippling disease, Gert made a complete recovery. Doctors decided to give his blood serum to other polio patients in an effort to help cure them. The Nuremberg Laws brought an end to this experimentation. The Nazis believed that Jewish blood posed a greater threat to Germans than polio did.

Not just Jewish blood but any contact with Jews was suspect. In April 1943 an official at the Ministry of Justice wrote a letter to Hitler informing him of a case that had come to the ministry's attention:

> A full Jewess, after the birth of her child, sold her mother's milk to a woman doctor and concealed the fact that she was a Jewess. With this milk, infants of German blood were fed in a clinic. The accused is charged with fraud. The purchasers of the milk have suffered damage, because the milk of a Jewess cannot be considered food for German children.

During *Kristallnacht,* the Night of Broken Glass, November 9, 1938, mobs roamed Germany's streets, destroying synagogues and Jewish businesses and assaulting Jews. Germans who murdered Jews in the course of the night were not punished in any way, but those who raped Jewish women were. This peculiar sense of justice did not reflect a Nazi concern with the well-being of Jewish women. Rather, it revealed the seriousness with which the Nazis guarded the purity of Aryan blood. To the Nazis, the rapists had committed a crime the Nazis believed worse than killing a human being: They had violated the Law for the Protection of German Blood and German Honor. The rapists were immediately expelled from the Nazi Party and turned over to the courts for prosecution.

Mischlinge

Even more than marriages between Germans and Jews, the children of those marriages presented a dilemma to the Nazis throughout the war. The Nazis used all the power of the industrialized, bureaucratic state to build a universe of death, a world in which people—or "units," as the Nazi architects of genocide referred to them—died (at least on paper) at one-minute intervals, in alphabetical order, and of the same cause. This world was the logical result of laws that divided everyone into categories of black and white, us and them, predator and prey. It was also a world singularly ill-prepared to handle the many shades of gray of the *Mischlinge.* In fact, representatives of . . . [the] Ministry of the Interior argued against declaring any *Mischlinge* to be Jews on the grounds that it would alienate the German parts of mixed families and cause them to resist the Nazis.

Although being qualified as part-Jewish protected a person in theory, it did not always work out that way. Historian Leonard Gross tells the story of a German woman who lost her half-Jewish sons to the Nazis. One son, Ernst, was deported to Buchenwald despite his status as a *Mischling* and the fact that he was married to a Christian woman. He was singled out for punishment because he refused to wear the Star of David badge that was mandated for Jews and part-Jews. Three weeks after he was sent away, his mother received notification that he had died of illness. A second son, Heinz, began a forbidden relationship with a German woman after the Nuremberg Laws were passed. He was picked up by the Gestapo and tortured for two weeks, and died soon after he was released. . . .

A Sort of Civil War

The Nuremberg Laws perverted normal relations between people. It gave an individual with a grudge against another person the power to send that person to his or her death. Ruth Thomas, who hid in Berlin during the war, lost her cousin Werner because of his variety of female companionship. One of his girlfriends, upset after the end of their relationship, denounced him for violating the Law for the Protection of German Blood and German Honor when she found out he was having an affair with another Christian woman. Werner spent several years in prison. When the Germans began deporting Jews to the death camps of Poland, he was sent there and perished in a *Vernichtungslager*.

Germans were free to invoke the Nuremberg Laws for the most petty reasons. For example, Otto Stahmer, who served as [Nazi official Hermann] Göring's lawyer at the International Military Tribunal after the war, arranged the deportation of a Jewish woman named Frau Noak, who had up to that point been protected by her marriage to a Gentile, to the Theresienstadt concentration camp simply because he did not like her living in his building.

Holocaust

Nine days after the passage of the Nuremberg Laws, Hitler called a meeting of his top officials to discuss the issue of the *Mischlinge*. One of the attendees was Bernhard Lösener, the racial theorist who consulted on the laws, who remarked later that he thought the führer spoke very knowledgeably on the subject. During the discussion, Hitler suddenly switched topics from the *Mischlinge* to war plans. Historian Lucy Dawidowicz notes that Lösener thought Hitler was rambling, but there can be no doubt that the two ideas were clearly linked in Hitler's mind. When the war began, the attack on the Jews would begin in earnest.

The years between the passage of the Nuremberg Laws and the horror of genocide were difficult ones for the Jews. The Nazis continued their legislative assault of the Jews, forcing the Jews to sell their businesses to Aryans at extremely low prices, denying Jews the right to own or use telephones, eventually forcing Jews to live in overcrowded ghettos. Jews were forced to wear the identifying Star of David badge at all times, and their ration cards were marked with a letter J. Jews received less food and could only shop at inconvenient hours when the stocks in stores were mostly depleted. Despair overtook the community. By 1938 approximately one hundred German Jews were committing suicide each month.

World War and War on the Jews

As Hitler undoubtedly understood, the outbreak of war would provide the perfect cover for his plans for the Jews. On July 30, 1941, Göring ordered Reinhard Heydrich, the head of the *Sicherheitsdienst* (or SD, the SS Security Service), to "take all preparatory measures . . . required for the final solution of the Jewish question in the European territories under German influence." The preparation yielded three main results: death from starvation and disease, death from overwork (what the Nazis called *Vernichtung durch Arbeit*—elimination through work), and death from gassing or shooting.

The Nazis concentrated Jews in large cities, herding Jews back into the ghettos they had been emancipated from hundreds of years before. The ghettos made physical the spiritual, social, and economic separation Hitler had worked so hard to build between the Jews and their neighbors and which was clearly outlined in the Nuremberg Laws. In the ghettos, the Jews were easy targets for the Nazi genocidal impulse. The ghettos housed far more people than the area could safely hold. The clearly foreseen and immediate outcome was a high death rate due to infectious diseases such as typhus. Jews were allowed only 800 calories of food per day, far below what an adult needs to stay healthy. Being sent to the ghetto was being sentenced to a death by slow starvation.

German industry benefited tremendously from the Holocaust. The concentration camps served as huge pools of slave labor. Jews were not protected by labor laws, and so they were literally worked until they died. When a Jew died while working in a German factory, no explanation was needed. Factory managers simply ordered a replacement. The work was backbreaking, and no matter how dangerous the conditions, safety equipment was never provided. The prisoners worked in the thinnest of rags no matter how severe the weather. At the Mauthausen camp in Austria, prisoners worked in a quarry, breaking stone with picks and axes. According to Paul Johnson, they then carried the granite blocks up 186 very steep steps. The average life expectancy of a quarry worker upon entering the camp was between six weeks and three months.

Einsatzgruppen

The link between the war and the Holocaust grew stronger as German troops spread throughout Europe. For example, when the German army invaded Russia in the spring of 1941, four mobile killing units followed in its wake. These units, known as *Einsatzgruppen,* were responsible for the deaths of more than eight hundred thousand Jews in occupied Russia. They had a simple but effective mode of operation. They moved into a town, rounded up all the Jews, put them on whatever mode of transportation was available, and moved them to remote areas where mass graves had been dug. The Jews were sent into the pits or forced to stand along their edges and shot down with machine guns. The deadliest "action," as the murders were called, took place near Kiev, at the Babi Yar ravine. In two days—September 29 and 30, 1941—thirty-three thousand Jews were murdered.

The Germans who made up the *Einsatzgruppen* shared Hitler's racial beliefs. One SS officer wrote a letter to a Wehrmacht general about the defenseless men, women, and children he was murdering:

> I thank my lucky stars for having been allowed to see this bastard race close up. . . . Syphilitics, cripples and idiots were typical of the lot. . . . They weren't men, but monkeys in human form. Oh, well, there is only a small percentage left of the 24,000 Jews of Kamentez-Podolsk.

Gas Chambers

The actions of the killing squads were bloody, and traumatizing, and the Nazis took pains to find faster, cleaner, and more efficient ways of murdering Jews, experimenting with carbon monoxide and various toxic gases until German doctors and technicians settled on a chemical called Zyklon-B. In the spring of 1942, a group of extermination camps—Auschwitz, Majdanek, Treblinka, Belzec, Chelmno, and Sobibor—were built in Poland. Auschwitz was capable of killing sixty thousand people in a single day.

In the camps, the process of depersonalization that had begun in 1933 and been codified into the Nuremberg Laws reached its apex. A guard in a concentration camp is reported to have called his dog *Mensch* (human being or person). He would encourage the animal to attack prisoners by shouting, "Mensch, go after the dogs."

The "Jewish Question"

The Nuremberg Laws demonstrate the fear the Nazis had of "blood poisoning," and the Holocaust was designed to ensure that there would be no Jewish blood left to mingle with that of Aryans. It is nearly impossible to accurately ascertain exactly how many people the Nazis murdered. Estimates of the Jewish dead range from 4.2 to 6 million. Historian Paul Johnson states that of the 8,861,000 Jews in the parts of Europe that fell under Nazi control, 67 percent, or 5,933,900, died.

In addition to the 6 million Jews who perished, it is estimated that the Nazis killed 15 million Russians, 2 million Poles, another 2 million Greeks and Yugoslavs, and 200,000 Gypsies. Countless more civilians died of the hunger and disease that World War II brought with it.

Conceiving of the Inconceivable

Although there is no doubt that most people were aware that Jews were being murdered, the Germans did their best not to speak of it. Written orders were kept to a minimum, and euphemisms were used to maintain an intellectual distance from the reality of the Holocaust. A letter from an employee of industrial conglomerate IG Farben, who visited Auschwitz and described the effects of starvation and the result of escape attempts, provides a perfect example:

> That the Jewish race is playing a special part here you can well imagine. The diet and treatment of this sort of people is in accordance with our aim. Evidently an increase of weight is hardly ever recorded for them. That bullets start whizzing at the slightest attempt of a "change of air" is also certain, as well as the fact that many have already disappeared as a result of a sunstroke.

Deportation to the death camps of Poland was called "resettlement in the east," mass shootings in ditches were called "special treatment." Rare indeed in its candor is a speech [Nazi leader] Heinrich Himmler made to leaders of the SS:

> Among ourselves, this once, it shall be uttered quite frankly, but in public we will never speak of it. . . . I am referring to the evacuation of the Jews, the annihilation of the Jewish people. This is one of those things that are easily said. "The Jewish people is going to be annihilated," says every party member. "Sure, it's in our program, elimination of the Jews, annihilation—we'll take care of it." And then they all come trudging, eighty million worthy Germans, and each one has his one decent Jew. Sure, the others are swine, but this one is an A-1 Jew. Of all those who talk this way, not one has seen it happen, not one has been through it. Most of you must know what it means to see a hundred corpses lie side by side, or five hundred, or a thousand. To have stuck this out and—excepting cases of human weakness—to have kept our integrity, this is what has made us hard. In our history, this is an unwritten and never-to-be-written page of glory.

It is a straightforward matter to record the facts of the Holocaust. Perhaps no other event in modern history has been more thoroughly documented. No matter how many explanations and theories are laid forward, there is no satisfactory answer to the question of how it happened. That human beings pass laws to discriminate against other humans can be proven by a look at the shelves of any law library. That people conspire to kill other people is part of the human condition. But how can a man look at the systematic murder of 6 million people—the young and the old, the sick and the well, men, women, and children—and label it glory? There is no answer.

JUDGMENT AT NUREMBERG

Robert Shnayerson

In November 1945, the international trial of Nazi war criminals began at Nuremberg, Germany. Robert Shnayerson describes the events leading up to the trial, as well as the trial proceedings and outcome. He posits that although the circumstances leading up to the trial were marked with difficulties and struggles over legality, the gravity of the situation proved enough to move prosecutors and judges toward action. As Shnayerson reveals, the trial did not necessarily result in fair sentences, nor were all of the potentially guilty parties subjected to trial. But as a means for setting a precedent in dealing with war crimes, he concludes, the judgment at Nuremberg proved significant. Shnayerson, formerly the editor of *Harper's* magazine, has written extensively on the U.S. Supreme Court and on legal matters.

In the war-shattered city of Nuremberg, 51 years ago, an eloquent American prosecutor named Robert H. Jackson opened what he called "the first trial in history for crimes against the peace of the world." The setting was the once lovely Bavarian city's hastily refurbished Palace of Justice, an SS prison only eight months before. In the dock were 21 captured Nazi leaders, notably the fat, cunning drug addict Hermann Göring.

Their alleged crimes, the ultimate in 20th-century depravity, included the mass murders of some six million Jews and millions of other human beings deemed "undesirable" by Adolf Hitler. "The wrongs which we seek to condemn and punish," said Robert Jackson, "have been so calculated, so malignant and so devastating, that civilization cannot tolerate their being ignored because it cannot survive their being repeated."

Here were satanic men like Ernst Kaltenbrunner, the scar-faced functionary second only to Heinrich Himmler in overseeing the death camps and the Nazi police apparatus; Alfred Rosenberg, cofounder of the Nazi Party and chief theorist of anti-Semitism; and Hans Frank, the vicious and venal Nazi proconsul in Poland. At the time, many asked why such messengers of evil were to be allowed even one day in

Reprinted, with permission, from "Judgment at Nuremberg," by Robert Shnayerson, *Smithsonian*, October 1996.

court, much less the 403 sessions they were about to undergo. It was a question that Jackson, on leave from his job as a Justice of the U.S. Supreme Court to prosecute this case, quickly addressed in his opening statement.

Justice Without Vengeance

With the kind of moral clarity that marked American idealism at the time, Jackson declared, "That four great nations, flushed with victory and stung with injury stay the hand of vengeance and voluntarily submit their captive enemies to the judgment of the law is one of the most significant tributes that Power ever has paid to Reason. . . . The real complaining party at your bar is Civilization. . . . [It] asks whether law is so laggard as to be utterly helpless to deal with crimes of this magnitude."

So began, in November 1945, the century's most heroic attempt to achieve justice without vengeance—heroic because the victors of World War II had every reason to destroy the vanquished without pity. Heroic because they ultimately resisted the temptation to impose on the Germans what the Nazis had imposed on their victims—collective guilt. Instead, they granted their captives a presumption of innocence and conducted a ten-month trial to determine their personal responsibility.

Locked up in solitary cells each night, constantly guarded by American M.P.'s mindful of recent suicides among high-ranking Nazis, the defendants spent their days in a giant courtroom built for 400 spectators, listening to evidence drawn from 300,000 affidavits and meticulous German documents so voluminous they filled six freight cars. Nearly all were ready to acknowledge the horrific facts while cravenly assigning blame to others. (Göring, who died unrepentant, was the exception.) When it was all over in October 1946, and ten defendants had been hanged messily in the Palace of Justice's gymnasium, this first Nuremberg trial stood as the judicial Everest of those who hoped, as Jackson did, that the rule of law could punish, if not prevent, the atrocities of war. . . .

Controversy over the Extent of Punishment

How this trial, and the 12 that followed, came to be held is a story in itself. In April 1944, two Jews who escaped the Auschwitz death camp described its horrors to the world. They detailed Germany's technology of genocide, such as the camp's four new gas-and-burn machines, each designed to kill 2,000 prisoners at a time. They pinpointed a huge slave-labor operation at nearby Birkenau, run by Germany's fine old industrial names (I.G. Farben and Siemens among others), where Allied prisoners and kidnapped foreign laborers were fed so little and worked so hard that as many as one-third died every week. Their testimony paved the way to Nuremberg.

The Allied leaders had little trouble agreeing that German war crimes must be punished. But punished how? Treasury Secretary Henry Morgenthau jr. urged that all captured Nazi leaders be shot immediately, without trial, and that Germany be reduced to the status of an agricultural backwater. Secretary of War Henry Stimson thought dooming all Germans to a kind of national execution would not do. It violated the Allied (if not Soviet) belief in the rule of law. It would deny postwar Germany a working economy and perhaps, ultimately, breed another war.

President Franklin D. Roosevelt, who wanted to bring G.I.'s (and their votes) home promptly, sought a compromise between Morgenthau and Stimson. The man asked to find it was Murray Bernays, a 51-year-old lawyer turned wartime Army colonel in the Pentagon.

Defining Boundaries

Immediately, a basic but legally complex question rose to the fore—what is a war crime, anyway? At the end of the 19th century, the increased killing power of modern weapons led to the various Hague and Geneva conventions, binding most great powers to treat civilians humanely, shun the killing of unarmed prisoners and avoid ultimate weapons, such as germ warfare, "calculated to cause unnecessary suffering." Such "laws of war" are quite frequently applied. They have saved thousands of lives. In combat the basic distinction between legitimate warfare and atrocities occurs when acts of violence exceed "military necessity."

Before Nuremberg, jurisdiction over war crimes was limited to each country's military courts. After World War I, when the victors accused 896 Germans of serious war crimes, demanding their surrender to Allied military courts, the Germans insisted on trying them and accepted a mere 12 cases. Three defendants never showed up; charges against three others were dropped; the remaining six got trivial sentences.

Bernays envisioned a different scenario: an international court that held individuals liable for crimes the world deemed crimes, even if their nation had approved or required those actions. The accused could not plead obedience to superiors. They would be held personally responsible.

Other big questions remained. One was how an international court trying war crimes could legally deal with crimes committed by the Nazis before the war. Another involved the sheer volume of guilt. The dreaded Schutzstaffel, or SS (in charge of intelligence, security and the extermination of undesirables), and other large Nazi organizations included hundreds of thousands of alleged war criminals. How could they possibly be tried individually? Bernays suggested putting Nazism and the entire Hitler era on trial as a giant criminal conspiracy. In a single stroke, this would create a kind of unified field theory of Nazi depravity, eliminating time constraints, allowing prosecution of war crimes and prewar crimes as well. He also suggested picking a handful of top Nazi defendants as representatives of key Nazi organizations like the SS. If the leaders were convicted, members of their organizations would automatically be deemed guilty. Result: few trials, many convictions and a devastating exposé of Nazi crimes.

Roosevelt promptly endorsed the plan, with one addition. The Nazis would be charged with the crime of waging "aggressive" war, or what the eventual indictments called "crimes against peace"—the first such charge in legal history.

Preparing for the Trial

Nobody was more enthusiastic about the strategy than Robert Jackson. Then 53, Jackson was a small-town lawyer from western New York with a gift for language. He had served in various posts in New Deal Washington before Roosevelt elevated him to the Supreme Court in 1941. By July 21, 1945, barely two months after Germany surrendered, Jackson had won President Harry Truman's approval for a four-power International Military Tribunal and had persuaded the Allies to conduct it in Nuremberg.

A master list of 122 war criminals was put together, headed by Hermann Göring, the ranking Nazi survivor. (Adolf Hitler, Heinrich Himmler and Joseph Goebbels were dead by their own hand. Martin Bormann, Hitler's secretary, had vanished, never to be found.) Reichsmarschall Göring, a daring World War I ace, had not allowed defeat to tarnish his reputation for candor, cunning and gluttony. He had turned himself in at a weight of 264 pounds (he was 5 feet 6 inches tall). His entourage included a nurse, four aides, two chauffeurs and five cooks. His fingernails and toenails were painted bright red. His 16 monogrammed suitcases contained rare jewels, a red hatbox, frilly nightclothes and 20,000 paracodeine pills, a painkiller he had taken at the rate of about 40 pills a day. He managed to charm some of his captors to the point of almost forgetting his diabolism.

On August 8, 1945, the Charter of the International Military Tribunal (IMT), unveiled by the victorious Allies in London, declared aggressive war an international crime. The IMT charter was grounded in the idea that Nazism was a 26-year-long criminal conspiracy. Its aim: to build a war machine, satisfy Hitler's psychopathic hatred of Jews and turn Europe into a German empire. Judges representing the four powers (the United States, Great Britain, France and the Soviet Union), plus four alternates, were named. They were to take jurisdiction over high-ranking Nazis deemed personally guilty of war crimes, conspiracy to commit war crimes, crimes against peace and crimes against humanity.

The 24 men named in the original indictment represented a wide spectrum of Germany's political-military-industrial complex. With Martin Bormann (tried in absentia), the list of those actually presented for trial was further reduced by two surprise events. Robert Ley, the alcoholic, Jew-baiting boss of the German Labor Front, which had governed the lives of 30 million German workers, hanged himself in his cell on the night of October 25. And, at the last moment, the prosecutors realized their key industrial defendant, the weapons maker Alfried Krupp, had not personally run his family's slave-labor factories until after the war began, giving him an easy defense against the prewar conspiracy charge. (Krupp was later sentenced to 12 years for war crimes, but he was released from prison in 1951.)

The Trial Begins

The trial of the remaining defendants began on the morning of November 20, 1945. In the refurbished courtroom, floodlights warmed the new green curtains and crimson chairs, illuminating the two rows of once fearsome Nazis sitting in the dock guarded by young American soldiers. Göring had shed 60 pounds during his six months of confinement, acquiring what novelist John Dos Passos, reporting for *Life*, called "that wizened look of a leaky balloon of a fat man who has lost a great deal of weight." Next to him in the front row were the ghostly Rudolf Hess, feigning amnesia; Joachim von Ribbentrop, Hitler's foreign minister; and Field Marshal Wilhelm Keitel, the Führer's Wehrmacht chief. Next in order of indictment came Ernst Kaltenbrunner (ill and absent for the first three weeks), Alfred Rosenberg and Hans Frank, who somehow thought his captors would spare his life when he handed over one of the trial's most damning documents—his 38-volume journal. (He would be sentenced to hang.)

Throughout that first day, as black-robed American, British and French judges and their two uniformed Soviet colleagues peered somberly from the bench, listening via earphones to translations in four languages, the prosecutors droned an almost boring litany of sickening crimes—shooting, torture, starvation, hanging—to which, in descending tones of indignation, from Göring downward, the accused each pleaded not guilty.

Opening Statements

The next morning, Robert Jackson opened the prosecution case on Count One, conspiracy to commit war crimes. "This war did not just happen," Jackson told the judges. The defendants' seizure of the German state, he continued, "their subjugation of the German people, their terrorism and extermination of dissident elements, their planning and waging of war . . . , their deliberate and planned criminality toward conquered peoples—all these are ends for which they acted in concert."

"We will not ask you to convict these men on the testimony of their foes," Jackson told the court. There was no need. Allied agents had found 47 crates of Alfred Rosenberg's files hidden in a 16th-century castle, 485 tons of diplomatic papers secreted in the Harz Mountains, and Göring's art loot and Luftwaffe records stashed in a salt mine in Obersalzberg.

One especially incriminating find—indispensable to the conspiracy theory—was the notes of Hitler aide Col. Friedrich Hossbach from a meeting between Hitler, Göring and other Nazis in Berlin on November 5, 1937. Hossbach quoted Hitler insisting that, as Europe's racially "purest" stock, the Germans were entitled to "more living space" in neighboring countries, which he planned to seize, he said, "no later than 1943–45."

Documented Horror

During the opening weeks, the pace of the trial was slow. Most of the American prosecution team neither read nor understood German. What with translation gaffes, repetitions and monotone readings, the documentary evidence—reams of it—at times had judges yawning and the defendants themselves dozing off.

Of course, the banality of overdocumented evil did not soften the prosecution's gruesome narrative. And a month into the recitation of Hitler's prewar aggressions from the Rhineland to Austria to Czechoslovakia, the Americans suddenly animated the documents by showing films of Nazi horrors. One German soldier's home movie depicted his comrades in Warsaw, clubbing and kicking naked Jews. In one scene, an officer helped a battered young woman to her feet so that she could be knocked down again.

An American movie documented the liberation of concentration camps at Bergen-Belsen, Dachau and Buchenwald, filling the darkened courtroom with ghastly images of skeletal survivors, stacked cadavers and bulldozers shoveling victims into mass graves. In his cell that night, Hans Frank burst out: "To think we lived like kings and believed in that beast!" Göring was merely rueful. "It was such a good afternoon, too—" he said, "and then they showed that awful film, and it just spoiled everything."

An Extremist History

Even when badly translated, Jackson's documents made a mesmerizing record of Hitler's appalling acts on the road to Armageddon. They revisited his rise to power as the people's choice in the depression year 1932. Billing himself as Germany's economic savior, the Führer immediately began spending so much on weapons that in six years, the treasury was almost empty. A diversion was called for.

Thrilling his admirers—millions of still worshipful Germans—Hitler bullied British and French leaders into selling out Czechoslovakia at the pusillanimous Munich conference in 1938. Next, Nazi thugs were unleashed on *Kristallnacht*, the "Night of Broken Glass" (November 9)—a nationwide campaign of anti-Semitic violence. Huge chunks of Jewish wealth wound up in Nazi pockets. Göring, the biggest thief, further demeaned his victims by ordering German Jews to pay the regime a "fine" of one billion marks ($400 million). As he explained it, "The Jew being ejected from the economy transfers his property to the state."

Hjalmar Schacht, then head of the Reichsbank, warned Hitler in January 1939 that his arms race was fueling runaway inflation. Hitler immediately fired Schacht and ordered new currency, largely backed by stolen Jewish property. Schacht, long a Hitler apologist, then began working secretly for U.S. intelligence and wound up at Dachau. Now, to his disgust, he sat in the Nuremberg dock.

According to trial documents, Hitler's profligacy helped propel his aggressions. By 1941, Hitler had made his suicidal decision to renege on the nonaggression pact signed with Stalin in 1939 and invade the Soviet Union. "What one does not have, but needs," he said, "one must conquer."

It began well, on June 22, 1941, and ended badly. By late 1942, with German casualties soaring at Stalingrad, Hitler had lost so many soldiers in Russia that he had to keep drafting German workers into the army, replacing them with foreign laborers, mainly French and Russian prisoners. In early 1943, with more than five million industrial slaves already toiling in Germany, the surrender at Stalingrad forced Hitler's manpower boss, Nuremberg defendant Fritz Sauckel, to kidnap 10,000 Russian civilians per day for work in Germany. Few survived longer than 18 months—a powerful incentive for Russians still at home to flee the kidnappers and join Soviet guerrillas in killing German troops.

Aryan Atrocities

Hitler's campaign to "Aryanize" Germany began before the war with the deliberate poisoning of incurably sick people and retarded children—labeled "garbage children." The regime's contempt for non-Aryan life conditioned millions of Germans to turn a blind eye to more and more epidemic evils—the death camps, the ghastly medical experiments, the relentless massacres of those Hitler called "Jews, Poles, and similar trash."

Listening to the facts, the almost incomprehensible facts, even the defendants longed for some answer to the overpowering question— why? Why did one of the world's most advanced nations descend to such acts so easily? So swiftly? The trial provided few answers. Hitler's truly diabolic achievement, French prosecutor François de Menthon observed, was to revive "all the instincts of barbarism, repressed by centuries of civilization, but always present in men's innermost nature."

For weeks, the prosecution cited such acts as the use of Jewish prisoners as guinea pigs in military medical experiments to determine the limits of high-altitude flying by locking them in pressure chambers, slowly rupturing their lungs and skulls. How long downed German pilots could last in the ocean was determined by submerging prisoners in icy water until they died. To develop a blood-clotting chemical, the doctors shot and dismembered live prisoners to simulate battlefield injuries. Death did not end this abuse. A Czech doctor who spent four years imprisoned at Dachau, where he performed some 12,000 autopsies, told investigators that he was ordered to strip the skin off bodies. "It was cut into various sizes for use as saddles, riding breeches, gloves, house slippers, and ladies handbags. Tattooed skin was especially valued by SS men."

The Reign of Fanatics

The scale of Hitler's madness was almost beyond imagination. The documents showed that after conquering Poland in 1939, he ordered the expulsion of nearly nine million Poles and Jews from Polish areas he annexed for his promised Nordic empire. The incoming colonists were "racially pure" ethnic Germans imported from places like the Italian Tirol. The SS duly began herding the exiles from their homes toward ethnic quarantine in a 39,000-square-mile cul-de-sac near Warsaw. Opposition grew; progress slowed. In righteous rage, the SS unleashed hundreds of *Einsatzgruppen*—killer packs assigned to spread terror by looting, shooting and slaughtering without restraint. Thereafter, the SS action groups murdered and plundered behind the German Army as it advanced eastward.

By January 1946, prosecutor Jackson was at last animating his documents with live witnesses. The first was a stunner. Otto Ohlendorf, blond and short, looked like the choirboy next door. In fact he was 38, a fanatic anti-Semite and the former commander of Einsatzgruppe D, the scourge of southern Russia. He testified with icy candor and not an iota of remorse.

How many persons were killed under your direction? asked Jackson. From June 1941 to June 1942, Ohlendorf flatly replied, "90,000 people."

Q. "Did that include men, women, and children?" A. "Yes."

Rather proudly, Ohlendorf asserted that his 500-man unit killed civilians "in a military manner by firing squads under command." Asked if he had "scruples" about these murders, he said, "Yes, of course."

Q. "And how is it they were carried out regardless of these scruples?"

A. "Because to me it is inconceivable that a subordinate leader should not carry out orders given by the leaders of the state."

The prosecution rested after three months, capped off by another movie distilling still more Nazi horror, and displays of macabre human-skin lampshades and shrunken Jewish heads submitted as evidence.

A Weak Defense

German defense lawyers then spent five months trying to cope with major handicaps. Most had grown to abhor their clients. All were unfamiliar with adversarial cross-examinations used in the United States and Britain, to say nothing of key documents that the Americans tended to withhold before springing them in court.

They managed to outflank the court's ban on tu quoque evidence (meaning, "If I am guilty, you are, too")—a stricture aimed at keeping Allied excesses, notably the mass bombing of German cities, out of the trial. In the dock was Adm. Karl Dönitz, accused of ordering U-boats to sink merchantmen without warning and let the crews drown whenever a rescue attempt might jeopardize the Germans. Dönitz never denied the charge. Instead, his lawyer produced an affidavit from Adm. Chester Nimitz, commander of the wartime U.S. Pacific fleet, stating that American submariners had followed the same policy against Japanese ships. (In the end, he was sentenced to ten years; upon release in 1956, he lived 24 more years, to age 88.)

The prosecution had depicted a vast conspiracy to wage war and commit atrocities. But in choosing representative Nazis as defendants, it wound up with 21 men who, though all pleaded ignorance or powerlessness, were otherwise so different that many hated one another. Each tried to save himself by accusing others. As a result, the defense naturally failed to muster a united front, and the prosecution's conspiracy theory steadily unraveled.

The trial's highlight was the star turn of its one wholly unabashed defendant, Hermann Göring. In three days of direct examination, Göring sailed through an insider's history of Nazism, defending Germany's right to rearm and reoccupy territory lost by the Versailles treaty. He laughed off the notion that his fellow defendants were ever close enough to Hitler to be called conspirators. "At best," he said, "only the Führer and I could have conspired."

Jackson's cross-examination was a disaster. Göring understood English well; while questions were translated into German, he had time to improvise his answers. At one point, Jackson prodded Göring to admit that the Nazis' plan to occupy the Rhineland, enacted without warning in 1936, was a Nazi secret, hidden from other countries. Göring smoothly answered, "I do not believe I can recall reading beforehand the publication of the mobilization preparations of the United States."

A Key Witness?

Jackson conducted a bizarre cross-examination of Albert Speer, Hitler's personal architect of gigantic edifices and stage manager of the Nuremberg rallies. Smart, suave, handsome, not yet 40, the wellborn Speer ranked high among Hitler's few confidants and was chief of all Nazi war production for the regime's last three years. He oversaw 14 million workers; he could hardly claim ignorance of their condition or how they were recruited. In the spring of 1944, for example, he ordered 100,000 Jewish slave workers from Hungary as casually as if they were bags of cement.

On the witness stand, Speer said he had become totally disillusioned with Hitler when the Führer responded to Germany's inevitable defeat by ordering a nationwide scorched-earth policy: the total destruction of everything in the path of the Allied armies. Rejecting Hitler's monomania, which he called a betrayal of ordinary Germans, Speer told the court, "It is my unquestionable duty to assume my share of responsibility for the disaster of the German people." And he revealed—offering no proof—that in February 1945 he had set out to assassinate Hitler by dropping poison gas through an air shaft in the Führer's bunker, only to find the shaft sealed off.

Speer, the most attractive defendant at Nuremberg, had been debriefed by interrogators avid for his special knowledge of how German war factories managed to keep humming despite immense Allied bombing. Some saw him as just the kind of man needed to rehabilitate postwar Germany. Under cross-examination, he got mostly easy questions, typically prefaced by Jackson's disclaimer, "I am not attempting to say that you were personally responsible for these conditions."

That Speer actually received a 20-year sentence seems remarkable, given his adroit performance. That his equally (or perhaps less) culpable colleague, Fritz Sauckel—brutal, low-born, ill spoken—was sentenced to death, seems as legally unfair as it was morally deserved.

Considering the Accused

After Robert Jackson's powerful summation of the trial's "mad and melancholy record," the case went to the trial judges, from whom no appeal was permitted. The great unspoken issue at Nuremberg was the question of collective guilt, and hindsight clarifies the extraordinary dilemma those eight judges faced in 1946. Collective guilt had tainted the Versailles treaty and helped ignite the Holocaust. It is the fuel of human barbarism, currently on display from Rwanda to Serbia. And though the Nuremberg judges were given every reason to savage the Nazi tyranny, they came to believe that justice could be served only by asserting the principle of individual responsibility. Justice required, in fact, a virtual rejection of the United States' whole grand conspiracy concept.

The Nazi Party founders had been charged with conspiring for 26 years (1919–45) to launch World War II and related atrocities. All 22 defendants (including Bormann) stood accused of planning aggressive war; 18 were charged with wartime crimes and crimes against humanity, such as genocide. If the court approved, seven Nazi organizations would also be convicted, rendering all their thousands of members guilty without trial.

Conspiracy Charges

The problem was that conspiracy is a crime of joint participation. Conviction required proof that two or more people knowingly agreed at a specific time and place to use criminal means to achieve criminal ends. But the distinguished French judge, Donnedieu de Vabres, urged his colleagues to observe that the defendants had seemed to act less in cahoots with, than in bondage to, a megalomaniac. Jackson's documents showed the "Führer Principle" in practice—the madness of Hitler's erratic orders, executed by lackeys too blind, venal or terrified to disobey. The evidence seemingly proved chaos, not organized conspiracy.

The judges, risking a backlash from Europe's Nazi victims by sharply limiting their verdicts to the hard evidence, ruled that the war conspiracy began not in 1919 but on November 5, 1937, at the "Hossbach conference" in which Hitler's aides heard his schemes for conquering Germany's neighbors.

The conspiracy charge (Count One) was restricted to eight defendants (led by Göring) who knowingly carried out Hitler's war plans from 1938 onward. In effect, the defendants were liable only for actual wartime crimes beginning September 1, 1939—a dizzying number of crimes but one that eliminated perhaps a third of the prosecution's evidence and produced three acquittals, including that of Schacht.

Under such an approach, guilt for simply belonging to the Nazi organizations was impossible. The court held that only the SS, the Gestapo-SD and the top Nazi leadership had been proved "criminal," meaning that their members had voluntarily joined in committing war crimes after 1939. That left several million potential defendants for lower courts to handle. But since the Nuremberg judges ruled them all innocent until proven guilty, relatively few were ever tried—the prosecutorial job was too formidable.

The trial removed 11 of the most despicable Nazis from life itself. In the early morning hours of Wednesday, October 16, 1946, ten men died in the courthouse gymnasium in a botched hanging that left several strangling to death for as long as 25 minutes. Ribbentrop departed with dignity, saying, "God protect Germany." Göring had cheated the hangman 2½ hours earlier. He killed himself in his cell, using a cyanide capsule he had managed to hide until then. In one of four suicide notes, he wrote, "I would have consented anytime to be shot. But the Reichsmarschall of Germany cannot be hanged."

One Step Toward Peace

The Nuremberg trial never remotely enabled the world to outlaw war. By 1991, the wars of the 20th century had killed more than 107 million people. And given Nuremberg's uniqueness—winners in total control of losers—the court of 1945 may seem irrelevant to the wars of the 1990s, in which ethnic killers, such as Gen. Ratko Mladic, the

Bosnian Serb implicated in the mass murder of unarmed prisoners, manage to avoid justice.

Yet the United Nations' seven "Nuremberg Principles" hold that no accused war criminal in any place or position is above the law. What the Nuremberg judges really achieved, in fact, has never been more relevant. By rejecting group guilt and mass purges, the 1945 judges defied hatred and struck a blow for peace that may yet, half a century later, help temper the madness of war.

WAR CRIMES IN VIETNAM

Eric Norden

Although the war in Southeast Asia lasted from 1954 to 1975, American involvement became pronounced in the mid-1960s when President Lyndon Johnson increased U.S. military support against communist North Vietnam. In this 1966 article, Eric Norden provides accounts of atrocities committed in Vietnam, blaming the U.S. military for what he sees as government-sanctioned war crimes. Norden uses reports from major news publications and government disclosures to substantiate his claim that American soldiers indiscriminately tortured and killed Vietnamese men, women, and children. He also charges U.S. military advisors with condoning war crimes committed by South Vietnamese soldiers. Norden contends that these actions clearly constitute war crimes under the Geneva Convention and the Nuremberg Principles. Norden is an investigative journalist who has frequently written about political controversies.

In the bitter controversy over our Vietnamese policies which has raged across the nation since President Lyndon Johnson's decision in February 1965 to bomb North Viet-Nam, there is only one point which supporters of U.S. policy will concede to the opposition: the sheer, mindnumbing horror of the war. Despite the barrage of official propaganda, reports in the American and European press reveal that the United States is fighting the dirtiest war of its history in Viet-Nam. The weapons in the American arsenal include torture, systematic bombing of civilian targets, the first use of poison gas since World War One, the shooting of prisoners and the general devastation of the Vietnamese countryside by napalm and white phosphorus. Not since the days of the American Indian wars has the United States waged such unrelenting warfare against an entire people.

Torture of prisoners and "suspects" by Vietnamese troops and their U.S. advisers is a matter of public record. "Anyone who has spent much time with Government units in the field," writes William Tuohy, *Newsweek*'s Saigon correspondent, "has seen the heads of prisoners held under water and bayonet blades pressed against their throats. . . .

Reprinted from "American Atrocities in Vietnam," by Eric Norden, *Liberation*, February 1966.

In more extreme cases, victims have had bamboo slivers run under their fingernails or wires from a field telephone connected to arms, nipples or testicles." (*New York Times* Magazine, November 28, 1965.)

Donald Wise, chief foreign correspondent for the London *Sunday Mirror*, reports that such torture is condoned and even supervised by U.S. officers. "No American is in a position to tell his 'pupils' to stop torturing," Wise writes from Saigon. "They are in no mood either. . . ." Some of the standard tortures described by Wise include "dunking men head first into water tanks or slicing them up with knives. . . . Silk stockings full of sand are swung against temples and men are hooked up to the electric generators of military HQ's." (London *Sunday Mirror*, April 4, 1965.)

Distinctions Are Not Made

The "Viet-Cong" use terror also, of course, but theirs is of a more selective nature, if only to avoid estranging the peasants and villagers on whom they depend for food and shelter. They will kill and mutilate the body of a Government official, but they generally pick an unpopular and corrupt victim whose death is welcomed by the peasants. U.S. and Government troops in the countryside, on the other hand, feel themselves lost in an enemy sea and tend to strike out indiscriminately at real or imagined guerrillas. Thus, no Vietnamese is exempt from mistreatment and torture. As Wise reports, "Inevitably, innocent peasants are kneed in the groin, drowned in vats of water or die of loss of blood after interrogation. But you cannot identify VC from peasants. . . ." In fact, it is assumed that every peasant is a real or potential Viet-Cong rebel. . . .

Many U.S. reporters have witnessed torture first-hand. Beverly Deepe, the New York *Herald Tribune's* correspondent in Saigon, writes:

> One of the most infamous methods of torture used by the government forces is partial electrocution—or "frying," as one U.S. adviser called it. This correspondent was present on one occasion when the torture was employed. Two wires were attached to the thumbs of a Viet-Cong prisoner. At the other end of the strings was a field generator, cranked by a Vietnamese private. The mechanism produced an electrical current that burned and shocked the prisoner. (New York *Herald Tribune*, April 25, 1965.)

Electrical torture is employed all over Viet-Nam, even on the battle-front. A small U.S. field generator used to power pack radios is often "modified" for torture purposes and is prized for its high mobility. The device generates sufficient voltage to provide strong and sometimes deadly shocks. . . .

Less sophisticated methods than electrical torture are also used. According to Beverly Deepe:

Other techniques, usually designed to force onlooking prisoners to talk, involve cutting off the fingers, ears, fingernails or
sexual organs of another prisoner. Sometimes a string of ears
decorates the wall of a government military installation. One
American installation has a Viet-Cong ear preserved in alco-
hol. (*Op. cit.*)

There is apparently no attempt to disguise such atrocities, even for
public relations reasons. Writes A.P. correspondent Malcolm Browne:

Many a news correspondent has seen the hands whacked off
prisoners with machetes. Prisoners are sometimes castrated or
blinded. In more than one case a Viet-Cong suspect has been
towed after interrogation behind an armored personnel carrier across the rice fields. This always results in death in one of
its most painful forms. Vietnamese troops also take their
share of enemy heads. . . . (*Op. cit.*)

Technology and Torture

. . . Although torture of Viet-Cong suspects antedated the arrival in
strength of U.S. forces, American technology has given it some inter-
esting twists. The helicopter, introduced by the United States as a vital
element in the air war, is now playing a role in the "interrogation" of
prisoners. *Houston Chronicle* reporter Jonathan Kapstein reported the
innovation, termed "the long step," on his return from an assignment
in Viet-Nam.

A helicopter pilot looked up from his Jack Daniels-and-Coke
to relate what had happened to a captive he had been flying
back from a battle area. A Vietnamese army officer yelled in
the ear of the suspected guerrilla who was tied hand and foot.
The man did not respond, so the officer and a Vietnamese soldier heaved him, struggling against his ropes, out of the UH-
1B helicopter from 2,900 feet. Then over the roar of the
engine, the officer began to interrogate another prisoner who
had watched wide-eyed. The answers must have been satisfactory, the flier said, because, though kicked and roughly handled, the guerrilla was alive to be marched off when the helicopter landed. . . . (*Nation*, Dec. 21, 1964.)

A prisoner who "cooperates" after watching the exit of his comrade
is not always rewarded. *Herald Tribune* Saigon correspondent Beverly
Deepe reports an instance when "Two Viet-Cong prisoners were interrogated on an airplane flying toward Saigon. The first refused to
answer questions and was thrown out of the airplane at 3,000 feet
The second immediately answered all the questions. But he, too, was
thrown out." (New York *Herald Tribune*, April 25, 1965.) Sometimes

there is not even the pretense of "questioning." Jack Langguth, Saigon correspondent for the *New York Times,* reports a case where "One American helicopter crewman returned to his base in the central highlands last week without a fierce young prisoner entrusted to him. He told friends that he had become infuriated by the youth and had pushed him out of the helicopter at about 1,000 feet." *(New York Times,* July 7, 1965.) . . .

As U.S. casualties have mounted even the pretense of preliminary interrogation has been dropped. Captured and wounded Viet-Cong are now executed summarily. Captain James Morris, a U.S. Army Special Forces man, reports the aftermath of an ambush he sprang on a small enemy contingent:

> I moved from one dark shape to the other, making sure they were dead. When I moved up on the last one, he raised up, his arms extended, eyes wide. He had no weapon. Cowboy stitched him up the middle with his AR-15. He didn't even twitch. . . . *(Esquire,* August, 1965.)

Pulitzer Prize winning correspondent David Halberstam recounts the treatment accorded a group of Viet-Cong prisoners by Government forces after a "particularly bitter" battle near Bac Lieu:

> The enemy were very cocky and started shouting anti-American slogans and Vietnamese curses at their captors. The Marines . . . simply lined up the seventeen guerrillas and shot them down in cold blood. . . . *(The Making of a Quagmire* by David Halberstam. Random House, 1965.)

The treatment of Viet-Cong POWs seems to vary with the severity of American losses in the action preceding their capture. After a platoon of the U.S. 1st Air Cavalry Division was almost wiped out in a battle in the Chu Prong foothills of the Ia Drang valley, Reuters reported:

> In one place nearby the Americans found three North Vietnamese wounded. One lay huddled under a tree, a smile on his face. "You won't smile any more," said one of the American soldiers, pumping bullets into his body. The other two met the same fate. (November 18, 1965.)

Chicago Daily News correspondent Raymond R. Coffey, reporting on the same battle, accompanied U.S. relief forces to a clearing littered with dead from the previous day's fighting. He writes:

> It was almost impossible to walk twenty paces without stumbling upon a body. . . . Suddenly a few yards away a wounded enemy soldier lifted one arm weakly and an American sergeant poured a long burst of M-16 rifle bullets into him. "Was he trying to give up, Sarge?" a man asked. "I'd like to

find more of those bastards trying to give up," the sergeant
said bitterly. No one disagreed with him. . . . (Chicago *Daily
News,* November 19, 1965.)

Improper Wartime Conduct

Apart from the moral question, U.S. and South Vietnamese torture
and execution of prisoners of war is, of course, in clear violation of
international law. Both South Viet-Nam and the United States are signatories to the 1949 Geneva Conventions governing the treatment of
prisoners. Article 17 states: "No physical or mental torture, nor any
other form of coercion, may be inflicted on prisoners of war to secure
from them information of any kind whatever." In a specific provision
pertaining to undeclared or civil war, the Conventions prohibit, with
respect to prisoners of war, "violence to life and person, in particular
murder of all kinds, mutilation, cruel treatment and torture."

The International Red Cross in Geneva, to which the Conventions
assigned the right to visit POWs and insure their proper treatment,
has publicly protested U.S. treatment of prisoners in Viet-Nam. The
New York Times declared on December 1, 1965, that "the International
Committee of the Red Cross in Geneva . . . complained again that the
United States was violating an international accord on the treatment
of prisoners. . . ." An earlier dispatch reported that "The International
Red Cross Committee is dissatisfied with the way the United States
and South Vietnamese Governments observe their pledge to respect
the Geneva Conventions protecting war victims. . . . The Committee's
representative in Saigon has been unable to visit prisoners taken by
American and South Vietnamese troops despite the affirmative reply
of the two governments to its appeal for the observance of the conventions. The Saigon authorities were said to have given repeated
assurances that they intended to allow the International Red Cross to
visit the prisoners but to date have done nothing more about it."
(*New York Times,* November 26, 1965.)

If the United States is not willing to observe the Geneva Conventions itself, it is quick to point an accusing finger at others. When the
North Vietnamese Government threatened to try captured U.S. air-
men as war criminals, the United States denounced any such move as
a violation of the Geneva Conventions and appealed to the International Red Cross. Hans Henle, a former executive of the information
Service of the International Committee of the Red Cross in Geneva,
commented:

> The Viet-Cong fighters are as protected by the Geneva Con-
> ventions as the American G.I.s are. Dramatic protests against
> violations of the Geneva Conventions should have been
> made when the first Viet-Cong prisoners were shot, when
> they were tortured, when the American Army started to

destroy Viet-Cong hospitals and to cut off medical supply. . . .
It is utterly hypocritical to condone wholesale violations of
the Red Cross principles on one side and protest reprisals
against them. . . . *(New York Times,* International Edition only,
October 14, 1965.)

Human Agony Escalates

Not content with the present level of inhumanity, some agencies of
the United States Government are attempting to turn torture from a
political liability to an asset. The Associated Press reported on October
16, 1965, that Senator Stephen Young, who had just returned from a
fact-finding mission in Viet-Nam, "says he was told by a member of
the Central Intelligence Agency in Viet-Nam that the C.I.A. committed atrocities there to discredit the Viet-Cong. Young said he was told
that the C.I.A. disguised some people as Viet-Cong and they committed atrocities. . . ." (Philadelphia *Inquirer,* October 20, 1965.) Young's
revelations landed like a bombshell on official Washington. "The
C.I.A. and the State Department went into an uproar," the *Herald Tribune* reported. "There was deep distress among State Department officials who feared his reported remarks would have disastrous repercussions abroad." (New York *Herald Tribune,* October 21, 1965.) But
Young refused to back down. "The C.I.A. has employed some South
Vietnamese," he reiterated, "and they have been instructed to claim
they are Viet-Cong and to work accordingly . . . several of these executed two village leaders and raped some women. I know such men
have been employed, and I question the wisdom of that."

So, as the war escalates, does the human agony in its wake. The
prospect is for more, not less, torture and shooting of POWs. "There
comes a time in every war," James Reston writes from Saigon, "when
men tend to become indifferent to human suffering, even to unnecessary brutality, and we may be reaching that point in Viet-Nam." (*New
York Times,* September 5, 1965.) Frustrated and bitter, U.S. forces in
Viet-Nam have dehumanized their enemy, and anaesthetized their
own consciences. . . .

The New York *Herald Tribune* reported on May 23, 1965, that "Near
the big coastal city of Hue, U.S. Marines set crops on fire and burned
or dynamited huts. . . . In July, 1965, U.S. Marines fought a Viet-Cong
force which had landed in sampans on the island of An Hoa and
attacked a Vietnamese navy post there. The two major towns on the
island, Longthanh and Xuanmy, had been occupied by the guerrillas.
Together the towns had about 1,500 inhabitants. After the Viet-Cong
retreated, "the Marines were ordered to burn Longthanh and Xuanmy
to prevent the Viet-Cong from reoccupying them. . . ." (*New York
Times,* July 11, 1965.) Few Viet-Cong had been killed or captured, but
two prosperous villages were razed and, according to U.S. sources,
about 100 civilians died from U.S. fire. An A.P. dispatch from the

island on July 11, 1965, reported that Americans had called An Hoa "Little Hawaii" because "of its rolling surf and happy people. In one day An Hoa became a little hell."

Tactics Against Peace

The two nearby villages of Chan Son and Camne in the Mekong Delta felt the brunt of U.S. "pacification" in August, 1965. Marine patrols near the villages had received light sniper fire from Viet-Cong guerrillas. What happened next was described by U.S. newsmen accompanying the Marines into the villages.

> A Marine shouted, "Kill them! I don't want anyone moving! . . . The Marines burned huts they believed were the sites of sniper fire. A sergeant said orders called for this. . . . [After the firing died down] U.S. Marines found a woman and two children among 25 persons they killed. . . . The woman died of a wound in the side, perhaps from one of the 1,000 artillery shells poured into the area. A wailing child beside her had an arm injury. A grenade hurled by a Marine blasted two children to death in an air-raid shelter. (*New York Times,* August 3, 1965.)

How the Marines reacted to their "victory" was described by a U.P.I. dispatch from Chan Son:

> "I got me a VC, man. I got at least two of them bastards."
>
> The exultant cry followed a 10-second burst of automatic weapons fire yesterday, and the dull crump of a grenade exploding underground.
>
> The Marines ordered a Vietnamese corporal to go down into the grenade-blasted hole to pull out their victims.
>
> The victims were three children between 11 and 14—two boys and a girl. Their bodies were riddled with bullets.
>
> Their father was still suffering from shock. A husky Marine lifted him on his shoulder and carried him off.
>
> "Oh, my God," a young Marine exclaimed. "They're all kids."
>
> A moment earlier, six children nearby watched their mother die. Her blood left a dark trail in the "air-raid shelter," where the family fled when the Marines attacked. A wrinkled grandmother had pulled her into a more comfortable position to let her die.
>
> The terrified face of a 60-year-old man looked up from a hole; his wailing mingled with the crying of the village children.
>
> In the village, a little boy displayed his sister who was no more than four. She had been shot through the arm.
>
> The Marines had received a few sniper rounds from Chan Son village. . . .

The sniper fire was enough for the Marines to open up with everything they had: rifle fire, automatic fire and grenades. A number of women and children were caught in the fire. Five of them were killed and five others wounded.

Shortly before the Marines moved in, a helicopter had flown over the area warning the villagers to stay in their homes. (New York *Herald Tribune,* August 3, 1965.)

. . . The Vietnamese peasant is caught in a vicious vise by U.S. "pacification" tactics. If he stays in his village he may die under U.S. fire; if he flees before the advancing troops he may still be rounded up, and shot on the spot as an "escaping Viet-Cong."

The Victims Are Doomed

Murders of such terrified peasants are a daily occurrence in Viet-Nam, and American G.I.'s are bagging their share of the game. A typical instance was reported by the A.P. from the town of Hoi Vuc, scene of a Marine "search-and-destroy" operation:

> "The sweat-soaked young Leatherneck stood over the torn body of a Viet-Cong guerrilla with mixed emotions flitting over his face. For Cpl. Pleas David of Tuscaloosa, Alabama, it was a day he would never forget. David had just killed his first man. 'I felt kind of sorry for him as I stood there,' said David, a lanky 17-year-old. 'And he didn't even have a weapon.'. . ." The unarmed "Viet-Cong" was walking along a paddy dike when the four Marines approached him with leveled guns. The frightened Vietnamese saw the guns and threw himself on the ground. As the Marines ran towards him he jumped up and tried to escape. "I let him get 250 yards away and then dropped him with two shots from my M-1," the A.P. quotes the young Marine, adding "The man had been hit squarely in the back. No weapons were found with him. . . ." The Marine was congratulated by his buddies. "Maybe the Viet-Cong will learn some respect for marksmanship. When we see them we hit them," one boasted. Another declared that "David is a good example. . . . Don't think we are killers. We are Marines." (New York *Post,* April 30, 1965.)

It is official U.S. military policy to shoot and ask questions later. Thus, in an operation thirty-five miles outside of Saigon, U.S. troops rushed a peasant shack believed to harbor Viet-Cong. One U.S. Lieutenant hurled a grenade through the door but the inhabitants tossed it back out. According to the A.P., "Another American soldier charged the shack, pulled the pin on a grenade and gave the fuse a few seconds count-down before pitching it in. Following the explosion the G.I. leaped into the shack with his M-14 rifle blazing. Three men and a baby died. Two women were wounded. Shrapnel took off the lower half of one woman's leg." (November 16, 1965.)

A Tragic Legacy

Not all G.I.'s enjoy making war on women and children. Some have written agonized letters home. Marine Cpl. Ronnie Wilson, 20, of Wichita, Kansas, wrote the following letter to his mother:

> Mom, I had to kill a woman and a baby. . . . We were searching the dead Cong when the wife of the one I was checking ran out of a cave. . . . I shot her and my rifle is automatic so before I knew it I had shot about six rounds. Four of them hit her and the others went into the cave and must have bounced off the rock wall and hit the baby. Mom, for the first time I felt really sick to my stomach. The baby was about two months old. I swear to God this place is worse than hell. Why must I kill women and kids? Who knows who's right? They think they are and we think we are. Both sides are losing men. I wish to God this was over.

But those American G.I.s who react with shock and horror to their bloody mission are a distinct minority. Most American soldiers in Viet-Nam do not question the orders that lead them to raze villages and wipe out men, women and children for the "crime" of living in Viet-Cong-controlled or infiltrated areas. Extermination of the (non-white) enemy is to them a dirty but necessary job, and few grumble about it. Some have even come to enjoy it. Warren Rogers, Chief Correspondent in Viet-Nam for the Hearst syndicate, reports that:

> There is a new breed of Americans that most of us don't know about and it is time we got used to it. The 18- and 19-year-olds, fashionably referred to as high-school dropouts, have steel in their backbones and maybe too much of what prize fighters call the killer instinct. These kids seem to enjoy killing Viet-Cong. . . . (New York *Journal-American,* September 16, 1965.)

To many critics of the war this "new breed of Americans" bears a disquieting resemblance to an old breed of Germans.

Senseless Air Raids

As the United States build-up has grown, there has been an increasing reliance on air attack. Any village in "VC territory" (which now comprises most of the country outside of the big cities) is considered a "free strike" area. U.S. planes rain death over vast areas of the countryside, killing Viet-Cong guerrillas and innocent peasants alike. No attempt is made to discriminate between military and civilian targets. American pilots, the Washington *Post* reported, "are given a square marked on a map and told to hit every hamlet within the area. The pilots know they sometimes are bombing women and children." (March 13, 1965.) Supersonic jets and B-52 bombers blanket vast areas of the countryside with 1,000-pound bombs, napalm and white phosphorus. According to *New York Times'* Saigon Correspondent, Charles Mohr,

> This is strategic bombing in a friendly, allied country. Since the Viet-Cong doctrine is to insulate themselves among the population and the population is largely powerless to prevent their presence, no one here seriously doubts that significant numbers of innocent civilians are dying every day in South Viet-Nam. (*New York Times,* September 5, 1965.)

The victims of such raids are always reported in the official U.S. enemy casualty lists as "dead Viet-Cong.". . .

Quangngai province has been the scene of some of the heaviest fighting of the war. When U.S. and Vietnamese troops could not dislodge the Viet-Cong from their positions it was decided to destroy all villages in the province which were not garrisoned by U.S. or Vietnamese forces. The fate of Duchai, a complex of five fishing villages on the coast, is typical. Neil Sheehan told the story of Duchai in a dispatch to the *New York Times:*

> In mid-August United States and Vietnamese military officials decided the Communists were using Duchai as a base for their operations in the area and that it should be destroyed. For the next two months . . . it was periodically and ferociously bombed by Vietnamese and American planes. . . . At least 184 civilians died during Duchai's two months of agony. Some reasonable estimates run as high as 600. . . . When an American visits Duchai these days, villagers . . . tell him horror stories of how many of the 15,000 former inhabitants were killed by bombs and shells. "There," said a fisherman pointing to a bomb crater beside a ruined house, "a woman and her six children were killed in a bomb shelter when it got a direct hit." Duchai's solid brick and stucco houses, the product of generations of hard-earned savings by its fishermen, were reduced to rubble or blasted into skeletons. Five-inch naval shells tore gaping holes in walls, and bombs of 750 to 1,000 pounds plunged through roofs, shattering interiors and scattering red rooftiles over the landscape. . . . Here and there napalm blackened the ruins. (November 30, 1965.)

Sheehan reported that at least ten other villages in the province had "been destroyed as thoroughly as the five in Duchai" and another twenty-five nearly as badly damaged. Four hundred and fifty other villages have been under intermittent attack by U.S. and Vietnamese planes. "Each month," Sheehan writes, "600 to 1,000 civilians wounded by bombs, shells, bullets and napalm are brought to the provincial hospital in Quangngai town. Officials say that about thirty percent of these cases require major surgery. A recent visitor to the hospital found several children lying on cots, their bodies horribly burned by napalm." (*Ibid.*)

Protests

An American doctor in the Quangngai hospital, J. David Kinzie, was moved to protest the horrors of the war in a letter to a U.S. magazine:

> I have been in Quang Ngai for six months in general practice at a civilian provincial hospital, and I can remain silent no longer.
>
> There comes a time in a doctor's life, no matter how hardened he has become, and perhaps in every man's life, no matter how cynical he may be, when he must protest as effectively as he can about the suffering of his fellow man. When one's own country is involved in the inhumanity, the responsibility becomes greater. Thus I add my belated voice.
>
> The civilian hospital in our province in central Viet-Nam is good by Vietnamese standards. The patients, already diseased by tuberculosis, anemia, and malnutrition in many cases, are now entering more frequently from direct effects of the war. For example, a pregnant woman demonstrator with a bullet hole in her abdomen, whose fetus died later; a twelve-year-old boy brought in unconscious by relatives who described how artillery blasted their village the night before; a fifty-year-old woman, accused of being Viet-Cong, who had been beaten, electrically shocked, and had her hands punctured for three days to extort information; three other civilians also accused of supporting the Viet-Cong were released to the hospital after severe beatings and their innocence determined. Many of the victims' "crimes" consisted merely in living in an area the Viet-Cong had overrun the night before. . . .
>
> Of course, war has always been described as evil, but does this mean that America must add to it? Our military advisers teach Vietnamese modern techniques of killing each other. Our weapons aid in more thorough destruction of themselves. Rather than liberating a people, it seems that these techniques and weapons result in innocent civilians, women, and children being beaten, burned and murdered. . . .
>
> Is America to survive on the blood of Vietnamese civilians? Does this make us great? (*Progressive*, March 1965.)

Thousands of children are dying as a result of United States air strikes. Charles Mohr writes in the *New York Times:*

> In [a] delta province there is a woman—who has both arms

burned off by napalm and her eyelids so badly burned that she cannot close them. When it is time for her to sleep her family puts a blanket over her head. The woman had two of her children killed in the air strike which maimed her last April and she saw five other children die. She was quite dispassionate when she told an American "more children were killed because the children do not have so much experience and do not know how to lie down behind the paddy dikes." (September 5, 1965.)

Bombs and Executions

Vietnamese villagers, driven to desperation, have occasionally descended *en masse* on U.S. bases to protest the bombings of their villages. Such demonstrations have been violently repressed. In early September 1965 a group of villagers marched on the U.S. air base at Danang demanding an end to air attacks on their villages. The demonstration was dispersed and five participants, selected at random, were arrested. Their punishment was swift. The Chicago *Daily News* reported from Saigon, "At Danang, three persons were executed by a South Vietnamese firing squad. The execution, held in a soccer stadium, was postponed at the last minute until midnight . . . because news photographers refused to obey an order that no pictures be taken until the final shot had been fired. The three were among five persons arrested Monday during a demonstration by about 200 persons in downtown Danang. They were protesting crop damage from artillery fire and air attacks by U.S. forces." (Chicago *Daily News,* September 23, 1965.) . . .

The essence of U.S. bombing policy was expressed with unusual frankness by a U.S. officer serving with a helicopter unit in the Mekong Delta. Jack Langguth asked the officer what the answer was to Viet-Cong activity. "'Terror,' he said pleasantly. 'The Viet-Cong have terrorized the peasants to get their cooperation, or at least to stop their opposition. We must terrorize the villagers even more, so they see that their real self-interest lies with us. . . . Terror is what it takes.'" (*New York Times* Magazine, September 19, 1965.)

But in the long run, the bombing only helps the National Liberation Front. According to Senator George McGovern: "To bomb [the Viet-Cong] is to bomb the women and children, the villages and the peasants with whom they are intermingled. Our bombing attacks turn the people against us and feed the fires of rebellion." (*Congressional Record,* June 17, 1965.) Robert Taber, an authority on guerrilla warfare, writes in his book *The War of the Flea* [published by Lyle Stuart, 1965]: "The indiscriminate use of air power against presumed Viet-Cong targets does much to explain the alienation of the rural population from the Saigon Government. Country people whose only contact with the government comes in the form of napalm and rocket attacks can scarcely be expected to feel sympathetic to the government cause, whatever it may be. On the other hand, they have every reason to feel solidarity with the guerrillas, usually recruited from their villages, who share their peril and their hardships."

More than any other single factor, our air war in Viet-Nam is turning the rest of the world against the United States.

Entreaty for Cessation

All war, of course, is hell. There is no such thing as a "clean war," in Viet-Nam or anywhere else. But even in warfare there are certain observable norms of decency which cannot be disregarded. These were laid down after World War Two in the Charter of the International Military Tribunal, under which the Nuremberg Trials of top Nazi civilian and military leaders were held. Our actions in Viet-Nam fall within the prohibited classifications of warfare set down at Nuremberg under Article 6 which reads:

> . . . The following acts, or any of them, are crimes coming within the jurisdiction of the Tribunal for which there shall be individual responsibility:
>
> a) Crimes against peace: namely, planning, preparation, initiation or waging of a war of aggression, or a war in violation of international treaties, agreements, or assurances, or participation in a common plan or conspiracy for the accomplishment of any of the foregoing.
>
> b) War crimes: namely, violations of the laws or customs of war . . . plunder of public property, wanton destruction of cities, towns or villages, or devastation not justified by military necessity.
>
> c) Crimes against humanity: namely, murder, extermination, enslavement, deportation, and other inhumane acts committed against any civilian population, before, or during the war. . . .

Under the provisions of Article 6 the United States is clearly guilty of "War Crimes," "Crimes against Peace" and "Crimes against Humanity," crimes for which the top German leaders were either imprisoned or executed. If we agree with Hermann Goering's defense at Nuremberg that "In a life and death struggle there is no legality," then no action can or should be taken against the government leaders responsible for the war in Viet-Nam. But if Americans still believe that there is a higher law than that of the jungle, we should call our leaders to account. Otherwise we shall have proved Albert Schweitzer correct when he wrote:

> It is clear now to everyone that the suicide of civilization is in progress. . . . Wherever there is lost the consciousness that

every man is an object of concern for us just because he is a man, civilization and morals are shaken, and the advance to fully developed inhumanity is only a question of time. . . . We have talked for decades with ever increasing lightmindedness about war and conquest, as if these were merely operations on a chessboard; how was this possible save as the result of a tone of mind which no longer pictured to itself the fate of individuals, but thought of them only as figures or objects belonging to the material world? (*The Philosophy of Civilization.*)

The issue at stake in Viet-Nam is not, as President Johnson constantly claims, what will happen if we leave. It is what will happen to us as a people, and to our judgment in history, if we stay.

WAR CRIMES ON TRIAL

Neil J. Kritz

In the following essay, Neil J. Kritz discusses the legacy of the Nuremberg Trials, which has made it possible to hold war criminals accountable for their crimes. For instance, he writes, an international war crimes tribunal was created in 1993 to address the horrors of "ethnic cleansing" in the former Yugoslavia, while another tribunal was formed in the following year to deal with genocidal activity in Rwanda. Both tribunals have faced considerable setbacks because of varying political interests and legal complications, Kritz notes, but in view of ongoing atrocities, the international community feels an obligation to lend its support. According to Kritz, these two tribunals have been highly significant in establishing legal precedents regarding international laws and domestic handling of war criminals. Kritz is a scholar at the United States Institute of Peace in Washington, D.C., which is an independent federal institution that promotes the peaceful resolution of international conflict.

Emsud Bahonjic and Fidele Kayabugoyi never met. They came from very different backgrounds and cultures, and were separated by more than 3,500 miles. History will remember them, however, for what they have in common: both were brutally and sadistically killed because of their respective Bosnian Moslem and Rwandan Tutsi ethnicity, victims of genocide, "ethnic cleansing," and related mass crimes in their countries. How their respective societies and the world deal with the killers of these two men, and with the many other perpetrators of these odious crimes in the former Yugoslavia and Rwanda, may have significant consequences for the long-term peace of their ravaged lands.

How can peace and reconciliation be achieved after atrocities such as these? What role, constructive or otherwise, might prosecution of war crimes play in putting these societies back together? Some would suggest that the best way to reconcile is to leave the past in the past. They argue that war crimes prosecutions will most likely be show trials unbefitting a sincere effort to establish peace and democracy, that

Reprinted from "War Crimes on Trial," by Neil J. Kritz, *Issues of Democracy*, May 1996.

a public review of wartime atrocities will inflame passions and hatreds rather than calming them, that shattered societies should focus their limited human and material resources on the urgent task of economic reconstruction—building a brighter tomorrow—rather than diverting those limited resources to dwell on the sins of yesterday.

The Need for Closure

If the goal in these countries, however, is something more than a tenuous, temporary pause in the violence, dealing in a clear and determined manner with war crimes and genocide is essential. To assume that individuals and groups who have been the victims of hideous atrocities will simply forget about them or expunge their feelings without some form of accounting, some semblance of justice, is to misunderstand human psychology and to leave in place the seeds of future conflict. What is true of individuals emerging from massive abuse and trauma is no less true of nations: mechanisms are needed to confront and reckon with that past, facilitating closure rather than repression. Otherwise, the past can be expected to haunt and infect the present and future. Victims may harbor deep resentments that, if not addressed through a process of justice, may ultimately be dealt with through one of vengeance. A public airing and condemnation of these crimes may be the best way to draw a line between times past and present, lest the public perceive the new order as simply more of the same. Dealing with the grievances and the grieving, accountability and forgiveness, and the rehabilitation of victims and perpetrators will be a painful and delicate process. It will take time—certainly longer than the time allotted for technical tasks like the separation and reduction of military forces. But doing nothing in response to war crimes and related atrocities adds to the injury of victims, perpetuates a culture of impunity that can only encourage future abuses, and contributes to the likelihood of vigilante justice and retribution.

In this context, war crimes prosecutions can serve several functions. They provide victims with a sense of justice and catharsis—a sense that their grievances have been addressed and can more easily be put to rest, rather than smoldering in anticipation of the next round of conflict. In addition, they can establish a new dynamic in society, an understanding that aggressors and those who attempt to abuse the rights of others will henceforth be held accountable. Perhaps most importantly for purposes of long-term reconciliation, this approach makes the statement that specific individuals—not entire ethnic or religious or political groups—committed atrocities for which they need to be held accountable. In so doing, it rejects the dangerous culture of collective guilt and retribution that often produces further cycles of resentment and violence.

In both Rwanda and Bosnia, the repatriation of massive numbers of refugees is integrally related to the question of justice and accountability. Nearly two years after the 1994 genocide in Rwanda, close to two million Hutus, the ethnic group identified with initiating the killings, remain in refugee camps in neighboring countries. Interviews in those camps confirm that the primary obstacle to their return home is the refugees' fear as to what kind of justice will greet their return.

International Prosecution of War Crimes

When war crimes trials are undertaken, are they better conducted by an international tribunal—like those in Nuremberg and Tokyo—or those for the former Yugoslavia and Rwanda—or by the local courts of the country concerned? There are sound policy reasons for each approach.

An international tribunal is better positioned to convey a clear message that the international community will not tolerate such atrocities, hopefully deterring future carnage of this sort both in the country in question and worldwide. It is more likely to be staffed by experts able to apply and interpret evolving international standards in a sometimes murky field of the law. It can do more to advance the development and enforcement of international criminal norms. Relative to the often shattered judicial system of a country emerging from genocide or other mass atrocities, an international tribunal is more likely to have the necessary human and material resources at its disposal. It can more readily function—and be perceived as functioning—on the basis of independence and impartiality rather than retribution. Finally, where the majority of senior planners and perpetrators of these atrocities have left the territory where the crimes were committed (as is the case in both Rwanda and Bosnia), an international tribunal stands a greater chance than local courts of obtaining their physical custody and extradition.

The most important precedent for international treatment of war crimes is, of course, the post–World War II trials at Nuremberg. The prosecution of Nazi atrocities before the International Military Tribunal and the subsequent Nuremberg tribunals established several key principles which continue to influence international conduct. Among these are the notions that the human rights of individuals and groups are a matter of international concern; that the international community's interest in preventing or punishing offenses against humanity committed within states qualifies any concept of national sovereignty; that not just states but individuals can be held accountable under international law for their role in genocide and other atrocities; and that "following orders" is no defense to such accountability.

Many expected the momentum generated by Nuremberg to result in the prompt creation of a more permanent international court for the prosecution of war crimes and related atrocities. The 1948 Genocide Convention reflected this assumption, providing for trials "by such international penal tribunal as may have jurisdiction." The immediate entry into the Cold War, however, froze any prospects for such a development for the next four decades.

In May 1993, responding to overwhelming evidence of "ethnic cleansing" and genocidal activity in the ongoing war in the former Yugoslavia, the United Nations Security Council voted to create the first international war crimes tribunal since those at Nuremberg and Tokyo. The Security Council established the "International Tribunal for the Prosecution of Persons Responsible for Serious Violations of International Humanitarian Law Committed in the Territory of the Former Yugoslavia since 1991" in the explicit belief that accountability would "contribute to the restoration and maintenance of peace." The tribunal has its seat in the Hague. It is comprised of eleven judges from as many countries, divided into two trial chambers and an appellate chamber.

The Yugoslavia tribunal is in several ways an improvement on the Nuremberg model. Its rules of procedure incorporate positive developments over the past 50 years with respect to the rights of criminal defendants under international law. To the extent that Nuremberg was perceived as a prosecution of World War II's losing parties by the victors, the current tribunal is nothing of the sort. As noted above, it is a truly international exercise, and the countries which supply its judges, prosecutors, and staff are not parties to the conflict. In addition, it is committed to the investigation and prosecution of war crimes committed by persons from each side in the war.

Considering that almost 50 years passed between the Nuremberg and Yugoslavia tribunals, the next major institutional development occurred in rapid succession. In November 1994, "convinced that in the particular circumstances of Rwanda, the prosecution of persons responsible for serious violations of international humanitarian law would . . . contribute to the process of national reconciliation and to the restoration and maintenance of peace," the Security Council voted to create an International Criminal Tribunal for Rwanda. Not surprisingly, the structure and mandate of the new tribunal closely tracked that of its counterpart for the former Yugoslavia. To maximize the efficient sharing of resources, avoid conflicting legal approaches, and minimize start-up time, the two tribunals share their chief prosecutor and their appellate chamber; their respective rules of evidence and procedure are virtually identical. A deputy prosecutor directs a small team of investigators and criminal attorneys in the Rwandan capital of Kigali; the actual trials will take place at the tribunal's seat in Arusha, Tanzania.

Obstacles Keep Mounting

These two tribunals are playing a truly historic role, expanding the horizons for the international treatment of war crimes and establishing important precedents. They have been functioning from the outset under significant constraints.

In his final report to the Secretary of the Army on the Nuremberg proceedings, chief prosecutor Telford Taylor noted that after the initial military tribunal trial, the need to organize new structures, administration, and staffing for the twelve trials to follow delayed the war crimes program by almost a year. The delay had its cost. "If the trials . . . had started and been finished a year earlier," observed Taylor, "it might well have been possible to bring their lessons home to the public at large far more effectively." These words still ring true half a century later. Delays in funding, staffing and organization of the two international tribunals for the former Yugoslavia and Rwanda have undercut their impact to date—it took a year and a half for the Yugoslavia tribunal to issue its first indictment.

This will hopefully change as the first trials get underway. In the period following the Dayton Peace Agreement [which the Serbs, the Bosnians, and the Croats initialed in Dayton, Ohio, on November 21, 1995], the Yugoslav tribunal has garnered increased public support and attention and has made some impressive gains.

The end of the Cold War, combined with the establishment of the two ad hoc tribunals, provided significant impetus for resurrecting the long-dormant discussion regarding creation of a permanent international criminal authority. In 1993, at the request of the UN General Assembly, the International Law Commission produced a detailed draft statute for such a court, which it further refined in 1994. A preparatory committee established by the General Assembly completed a three-week consideration of the issue, and resumed its deliberations in August 1996. While there are a number of important issues still to be ironed out—e.g., the role of the Security Council as a gatekeeper for referral of cases to the court; possible jurisdiction over such crimes as terrorism, aggression, and drug-trafficking; the authority of the prosecutor to initiate investigations; and questions of extradition and of procedure—there is a broad consensus that the court would have jurisdiction over individuals for the core crimes of genocide, war crimes, and crimes against humanity. Establishment of this body would, of course, obviate the need for further ad hoc tribunals and would significantly reduce the delays which have hampered the commencement of these tribunals. In 1998, the process moved to the next stage: a plenipotentiary conference for the final drafting and adoption of a treaty establishing this international criminal court.

The Domestic Component

Prosecution of war crimes before domestic courts can also serve some important purposes. It can enhance the legitimacy and credibility of a fragile new government, demonstrating its determination to hold individuals accountable for their crimes. Because these trials tend to be high profile proceedings which receive significant attention from the local population and foreign observers, they can provide an important focus for rebuilding the domestic judiciary and criminal justice system, establishing the courts as a credible forum for the redress of grievances in a nonviolent manner. Finally, as noted in 1994 by the UN Commission of Experts appointed to investigate the Rwandan genocide, domestic courts can be more sensitive to the nuances of local culture and resulting decisions "could be of greater and more immediate symbolic force because verdicts would be rendered by courts familiar to the local community."

In addition, not all cases of war crimes will result in the creation of another international judicial entity. Atrocities committed by the Mengistu regime in Ethiopia, for example, are being handled by a Special Prosecutor's Office established for this purpose by the new government. Various countries have provided technical and financial assistance to this process, but a separate international body was not deemed necessary.

Finally, even where an international tribunal has been established to prosecute war crimes, an additional factor motivating separate local efforts at justice is the sheer pressure of numbers. For reasons of both practicality and policy, the international tribunals for Rwanda and the former Yugoslavia can be expected to limit their prosecutions to a relatively small number of people. By way of contrast, the Nuremberg operation had vastly more substantial resources than its two contemporary progenies. At peak staffing in 1947, for example, the Nuremberg proceedings employed the services of nearly 900 allied personnel and about an equal number of Germans.

Other Influences

The authorities at Nuremberg had virtual control of the field of operations and sources of evidence, and the prosecution team had the benefit of paper trails not matched in the Yugoslav and Rwandan cases. Even with these advantages, the Nuremberg trials ultimately involved the prosecution of some 200 defendants, grouped into thirteen cases and lasting four years. If the two current international tribunals combined ultimately prosecute this many cases, it will be an enormous success.

This means that, even if the international bodies achieve their maximum effectiveness, thousands of additional cases of war crimes and related atrocities will be left untouched. In the case of the former Yugoslavia, the Bosnian state commission on war crimes currently has some 20,000 cases in its files, and various Bosnian officials suggested to the author in recent interviews that as many as 5,000 may be appropriate for domestic prosecution. Croat and Serb authorities each have their war crimes cases as well. After the foreign troops are gone, after the international tribunals have completed their operations, local government, judiciary, and society will still need to deal with this legacy and these people—whether by prosecution or otherwise.

The charters of the two international tribunals recognize this domestic component, providing that they share concurrent jurisdiction with national courts over the crimes in question. (It is worth noting that the draft statute for the permanent international criminal court also stresses this domestic component, declaring the international body to be "complementary to national criminal justice systems in cases where such trial procedures may not be available or may be ineffective.") The Bosnian government has already designated six special judicial panels around the country, and one appellate panel in Sarajevo, to deal exclusively with war crimes and genocide cases. The Rwandan challenge has been more complicated, as explained below. In each of the countries involved, implementation of their national war crimes program will be influenced by their perception of the degree to which the international community is serious and committed to supporting the work of the international tribunals. In each case, how they handle the question will have significant consequences for the viability of both peace and the rule of law.

Managing the Numbers

Where prosecutions are undertaken, how widely should the net be cast? There is a growing consensus in international law that, at least for the most heinous violations of human rights and international humanitarian law, a sweeping amnesty is impermissible. International law does not, however, demand the prosecution of every individual implicated in the atrocities. A symbolic or representative number of prosecutions of those most culpable may satisfy international obligations, especially where an overly extensive trial program will threaten the stability of the country. This approach has been adopted, for example, in Argentina, Ethiopia, and in some of the countries of Central and Eastern Europe in dealing with the legacy of massive human rights abuses by their ousted regimes.

In several cases ranging from Nuremberg to Ethiopia, given the large number of potential defendants, an effort has been made to distinguish three categories of culpability and design different approaches for each. Roughly, these classifications break down into (a) the leaders, those who gave the orders to commit war crimes, and those who actually carried out the worst offenses (inevitably the smallest category numerically); (b) those who perpetrated abuses not rising to the first category; and (c) those whose offenses were minimal. The severity of treatment follows accordingly. The Dayton Accords concluding the war in the former Yugoslavia more or less adopt this approach. In the first category, the warring parties commit themselves to provide full cooperation and assistance to the international tribunal as it prosecutes those who perpetrated the most heinous offenses. In the second tier of culpability, the accords characterize as a confidence-building measure the obligation of the parties to immediately undertake "the prosecution, dismissal or transfer, as appropriate, of persons in military, paramilitary, and police forces, and other public servants, responsible for serious violations of the basic rights of persons belonging to ethnic or minority groups." Finally, those charged with any crime related to the conflict "other than a serious violation of international humanitarian law" are guaranteed amnesty for their offenses. While the early post-war period has exhibited some serious challenges in the implementation of these provisions, the basic framework they create is a sound one.

Rwanda's Situation

The Rwandan case demonstrates the need for pragmatism to temper an absolutist approach to prosecution. In one of the most horrific genocidal massacres in recent memory, up to one million Rwandan Tutsis and moderate Hutus were brutally slaughtered in just 14 weeks in 1994. Throughout their first year in office, many senior members of the new government insisted that every person who participated in the atrocities should be prosecuted and punished. This approach, however, would put more than 100,000 Rwandans in the dock, a situation that would be wholly unmanageable and certainly destabilizing to the transition. As of April 1996, although no formal charges have yet been filed, some 70,000 Rwandans are detained in prisons built to house a fraction of that number on allegations of involvement in the genocide. To compound the problem, the criminal justice system of Rwanda was decimated during the genocide, with some 95% of the country's lawyers and judges either killed or currently in exile, or prison. Justice for war crimes in Rwanda requires a creative approach that takes into account the staggeringly large number of potential cases and the overwhelmingly small number of available personnel to process them.

Legislation presently under consideration by the Rwandan government would create four levels of culpability for the genocide: (1) the planners and leaders of the genocide, those in positions of authority who fostered these crimes, and killers of more than 50 people—all subject to full prosecution and punishment; (2) others who killed; (3) those who committed other crimes against the person, such as rape; and (4) those who committed offenses against property. Persons in categories (2) and (3) who voluntarily provide a full confession of their crimes, information on accomplices or co-conspirators, and, importantly, an apology to the victims of their crimes will benefit from an expedited process and a significantly reduced schedule of penalties. Those in category (4) will not be subject to any criminal penalties.

Other Alternatives

Criminal trials are the most obvious way of reckoning with genocide and similar atrocities. Depending on the particular conditions in a country, however, justice for these crimes may entail a variety of alternative or supplemental approaches. In Spain, both sides fully acknowledged their sins (no one has done so in Bosnia) and then granted each other a mutual amnesty. In Greece, hundreds of soldiers and officers were prosecuted for torture of former prisoners. In South Africa, amnesty will be granted on a case-by-case basis to those who committed abuses, but only after the individual offenders apply for that amnesty and provide detailed confessions of their crimes. In countries like Chile and El Salvador, "truth commissions" have produced a national historical accounting as a form of justice. In the Czech Republic, Lithuania and post-communist Germany, administrative purges have temporarily removed those affiliated with past abuses from positions in the public sector. An effort at justice may also involve official recognition and rehabilitation of victims.

The way accountability for mass atrocities is handled may be relevant beyond the borders of the country in question; it may also have consequences for future, seemingly unrelated conflicts in other parts of the world. When asked whether he was concerned about the international community holding him accountable for his diabolical campaign of genocide, Adolph Hitler infamously scoffed, "Who remembers the Armenians?" referring to the victims of a genocide only 25 years earlier for which no one had been brought to book. In pursuing their campaign of ethnic cleansing and genocide, Bosnian Serb leaders were asked the same question, and more than once pointed to the fact that the Khmer Rouge leadership has never been prosecuted or punished for the atrocities they committed in Cambodia in the 1970s.

One of the many reasons advanced for creation of the Rwanda tribunal was the need to demonstrate that the international community would not tolerate such atrocities, deterring future carnage not only in Rwanda but notably in Burundi, where renewed ethnic violence was beginning to escalate. If the international community had promptly established the Rwanda tribunal and provided it with adequate personnel and resources—if the tribunal had been born as a robust entity with the wherewithal to aggressively pursue its mandate—it would almost certainly have given pause to those inclined toward extremist violence in neighboring Burundi. Unfortunately, the message of warning to Rwanda's southern twin has been relatively anemic. Rwandans and Burundians have each taken note of the enormous delays in getting the tribunal even partially staffed, financed, and operational, and Burundi has sadly slipped deeper into violence and chaos. The UN Secretary-General urges preparations for intervention by a multilateral military force. When the international community now asks what could have been done to avoid this slide, a close look at the adequacy of support for the Rwanda tribunal provides at least part of the answer. Hopefully, as the tribunal's first trials finally get underway, they will still be able to serve a constructive role in the Burundian context.

Some analysts and diplomats will no doubt continue to suggest that justice for genocide and other mass abuses is a luxury that post-traumatic societies can ill afford; they will still argue that peace is best achieved by simply closing the door on past wrongs. But there were thousands and thousands like Emsud Bahonjic and Fidele Kayabu-goyi, and they are survived by millions of relatives and friends who will tell you otherwise. They will demand justice sooner or later; the challenge is to achieve that justice in a manner that best facilitates a durable peace.

CHAPTER 3

PERSONAL REFLECTIONS ON WAR CRIMES

THE PRISON CAMPS

Peter Maass

From 1992 to 1996, Bosnia and other territories of the former Yugoslavia were the sites of mass killings and other atrocities at the hands of the ruling Serbs. The Serbs' campaign for "ethnic cleansing" included placing non-Serbs in prison camps, where they were subjected to torture, rape, maiming, and death. In August 1992, a small group of journalists were allowed to visit three prison camps that held non-Serbs in Prijedor, Bosnia. Peter Maass was one of those journalists. In the following excerpt from his book, *Love Thy Neighbor: A Story of War*, Maass recounts the horrors he witnessed in the Bosnian prison camps. He reports that the prison guards held complete power over the lives of the non-Serb prisoners and engaged in sadistic games of torture and murder. Maass describes the prisoners as walking skeletons, close to death from being deprived of basic human needs and yet somehow still able to endure unspeakable brutalities.

Go back in time. It is 1992. After cleansing one-third of Croatia, Serb militias are cleansing Bosnia. They have odd names, these death squads, names such as "Arkan's Tigers" and "the White Eagles," and their commanders have odd names too, such as "Major Mauser" and "the Duke." Stage Two in the creation of Greater Serbia—an age-old nationalistic dream of extending Serb control into large parts of Croatia and Bosnia—is different from Stage One. The campaign in Bosnia is far bloodier, as though the efforts in Croatia were a mere warm-up for the main event. Mass torture. Mass executions. Mass rapes. By the time the cleansing in Bosnia is finished, by the time Bosnia itself is finished, at least 200,000 people will be dead, several million will be homeless, and the world will be at a loss to understand what happened or what should have been done to stop it.

In 1996, after a peace treaty has been signed and half of Bosnia has been awarded to the Serbs, more than 20,000 U.S. troops are on the ground to make sure the fighting does not break out again. "We cannot stop war for all time," President Bill Clinton said in his November 27, 1995, speech to the nation. "But we can stop some wars."

The U.S. troops are to come home in 1997. No one knows whether they will leave behind a country rebuilding itself or a country preparing for more war. When they return to America, it is unlikely they will have any answers to the fundamental question raised by the conflict, a question that has stumped philosophers and statesmen through the ages. It is a simple question, and does not apply solely to Bosnia: Why?

A war is like an explosion or a fire; to understand its causes, you must find its ground zero. In Bosnia, ground zero was the Serb prison camps. It is in large part because of the slaughter that occurred there in the summer of 1992, and our horror over it, and our guilt for not stopping it sooner, that we belatedly stepped into Bosnia with our army and our treasure (the peacekeeping mission will cost tax payers at least $2 billion, and reconstruction may cost several billion dollars more). The essence of the war—a hideous mix of madness and violence and hate—existed in its purest form in those camps. . . .

Too Close to Death

I had never thought that one day I would talk to a skeleton, but that's what I did at Trnopolje. I walked through the gates and couldn't quite believe what I saw. There, right in front of me, were men who looked like survivors of Auschwitz. I remember thinking that they walked surprisingly well for people without muscle or flesh. I was surprised at the mere fact that they could still talk. Imagine, talking skeletons! As I spoke to one of them, I looked at his arm and realized that I could have grabbed hold of it and snapped it into two pieces like a brittle twig. I could have done the same with his legs.

Since leaving Bosnia, I have often been asked the same questions: Did you visit those camps? Were they really so bad? I still find it hard to believe that Americans and Western Europeans are confused about Bosnia and, in particular, about the camps. Yes, I visited them, and yes, they were as bad as you could imagine. Didn't you see the images on television? Don't you believe what you saw? Do you give any credence to the word of Radovan Karadžić, the indicted Bosnian Serb leader, who said the news photographs were fakes? Chico Marx had a great line in *Duck Soup* as he tried to fool an unsuspecting Margaret Dumont into believing a preposterous put-on: "Well, who you gonna believe, me or your own eyes?" It was like that with Karadžić and the camps.

Imprisoned for Safety

Trnopolje was the repository for men who had been released from the hardcore concentration camps of Omarska and Keraterm. That's where the skeletons came from. Also, women and children who had been cleansed from nearby villages came to Trnopolje voluntarily. Yes, voluntarily. It was one of the strangest situations in Bosnia—people seeking safety at a prison camp. Trnopolje was no picnic, but the known brutalities dished out there were preferable to the fates awaiting Bosnians who tried to stay in their homes. Women might be raped at Trnopolje, but they probably would not be gang-raped. They might be beaten, but they probably would not be killed. Ironically, the first television images that shocked the world came from Trnopol-je, the "best" camp. The outside world never saw the worst camps when they were at their worst.

The luckiest prisoners at Trnopolje had found a spot on the floor in the school building, which stank of urine and unwashed humanity. You could not walk inside without tripping over someone. The less fortunate inmates lived outside, baking in the August sun and shivering in the cool nights. Drljača gave us 15 minutes to wander around, and, technically speaking, we were free to talk with whomever we wished. But guards with Kalashnikov assault rifles and Ray-Ban sunglasses sauntered through the grounds, and I could talk for no more than a minute or so before one of them would creep up behind me and start listening.

A few guards had slung their rifles across their backs and started snapping pictures of us as we talked with prisoners. They were not subtle: they were in charge, and they wanted us to know it. One skeletal prisoner had just enough time to unbutton his shirt, showing off a mutilated chest with a few dozen fresh scars from God knows what torture, before a look of horror came over his face. He was staring, like a deer caught in a car's headlights, at a spot just above the top of my head. I looked around. A guard stood behind me.

Wounds from Beatings

I walked on. A prisoner tugged at my sleeve. *Follow me.* I followed, trying to look as though I weren't following. He led me to the side of the school building and, after glancing around, darted through a door. I followed. Where was he taking me? Why? I feared not only the trouble that I might be getting into but also the trouble that he might be getting into. The door closed behind me. The room was small, dark. My eyes took a moment to adjust. People were whispering beside me. I looked at the floor. Two bodies on the ground. Corpses? Not yet. I was in the infirmary, the sorriest infirmary you could imagine. No medicine, no beds. I was not supposed to be there.

The doctor, also a prisoner, motioned for me to crouch down so that guards could not see me through the window. He began peeling off a filthy bandage from the leg of one of the two men. Puss oozed out. The man had an infected hole the size of a baseball just under his knee, the result of a bone-crushing blow from a rifle butt. In a few days, the leg would turn gangrenous, and the man would die. The doctor whispered his explanations to Vlatka, my interpreter, who whispered them to me.

I looked at the other body. The man seemed to be in his late 30s or early 40s. It was hard to tell. His face was cut and bruised, colored black and red, and swollen like the grossly expanded reflection you see in a trick mirror at a circus. I looked at his naked torso—more bruises, more swelling, more open wounds. He didn't move. I didn't need to ask what had happened to this poor man, or what was going to happen to him. His agony would be over soon, for if his wounds didn't finish him off in the next 24 hours, then the guards would. As I learned later, guards routinely killed prisoners who could not recover quickly from the beatings.

Painful Departures

We slipped out after several minutes. Vlatka first, me a few seconds later. An 18-year-old youth came up to us. He had just arrived at Trnopolje after two months at Omarska, the worst camp of all. His skin was stretched like a transparent scarf over his ribs and shoulder bones. "It was horrible," he whispered. "Just look at me. For beatings, the guards used hands, bars, whips, belts, chains—anything. A normal person cannot imagine the methods they used. I am sorry to say that it was good when new prisoners came. The guards beat them instead of us."

I slipped into his hand a sandwich from my shoulder bag. It was a ham sandwich.

"I'm sorry, it's all I have," I said. "Will you eat it?"

He stared at me, as though I were a naked fool. Of course he would eat it. It was food. Allah would look the other way as he devoured the forbidden pork.

I approached another skeleton, this one too afraid to talk, who turned away after whispering a single word, "Dachau."

It was time to go. The guards started rounding up the journalists. We boarded the van. I forget my parting words as I broke off my conversation with the last prisoner. What do you say in a situation like that? See you later? Good luck? You are leaving the condemned, the half-dead, and the fact that you have spoken to him probably puts him in even greater peril. You had a good breakfast that morning, a couple of eggs, some toast, lots of jam. He had half a slice of stale bread, if he was lucky. Your money belt contains $5,000, and there is always more where it came from. He has nothing. You have an American passport that allows you to walk into the camp and walk out unmolested. He has no passport, only two eyes that watch you perform this miracle of getting out alive. You have a home somewhere that has not been dynamited. You have a girlfriend who has not been raped. You have a father who has not been killed in front of your eyes.

Whenever I returned to a normal place after an assignment in Bosnia, friends would ask me what it was like to suddenly leave a war zone and then be in a place where bombs are not falling. I would say that it was no big deal, which was the truth. Going from Sarajevo to London in a day is a piece of cake in psychological terms. I would feel relief, splendid relief. It didn't compare to the experience of mixing with death-camp inmates and then walking away, a free man with a future. The misery of Bosnia is staring right at you, less than a foot away, watching you as you get into a van and drive off, and it notices that you don't look back.

Facing Brutality

The next stop was Omarska. I was to have the privilege, if you can call it that, of meeting some of the worst torturers of the 20th century.

During its heyday, in the summer of 1992, Omarska was the principal killing field. After the existence of the camp and of the horrors there had become known, the Serbs began playing a shell game: most prisoners were shipped off to other locations or executed; the camp was cleaned up; food rations were improved for those left behind.

When we pulled up to the camp gates, no more than 250 prisoners remained of the thousands who had been there, and those on display were recent arrivals, not yet emaciated or bloodied. Omarska was going out of business, but one thing was unaltered, the terror in the prisoners' eyes. They had plenty of reason to be afraid.

Every imaginable degradation had been played out at Omarska during the previous months. It was not a death camp on the order of Auschwitz. There was no gas chamber to which the prisoners were marched off every day. What happened at Omarska was dirtier, messier. The death toll never approached Nazi levels, but the brutality was comparable or, in some cases, superior, if that word can be used. The Nazis were interested in killing as many Jews as possible, and doing it as quickly as possible. The Serbs, however, wanted to interrogate their Bosnian prisoners, have sadistic fun by torturing them in the cruelest of ways, and then kill them with whatever implement was most convenient, perhaps a gun, perhaps a knife or scissors, perhaps a pair of strong hands wrapped around an emaciated neck. If the Germans had used the same approach, they would have needed decades to kill six million Jews.

Death Camp

Omarska was an abandoned mining compound. The prisoners were kept primarily in two places—an open-pit mine and a huge storage shed. Many interrogations ended with execution in a building the prisoners called "the White House." There was another building, known as "the Red House," where, in addition to more executions taking place, the torn corpses were kept until being buried outside Omarska or thrown down a disused mine shaft. On a daily basis, between 25 and 50 people were killed. Some prisoners never made it as far as the White or Red House, dying of thirst or starvation or asphyxiation (because they were crowded so tightly) while awaiting their formal torture, or dying when they made the mistake of asking a guard for water and received a bullet in the head instead. In a way, they were the lucky ones, for whom death came quickly and painlessly.

Our van halted on a strip of asphalt next to the White House. A group of about 50 prisoners were washing themselves at an open spigot at a side of the building. They were surrounded by guards with submachine guns. It is a neutral term, "guards," and it implies a certain amount of discipline, a sense that the camp had rules, and that these men whom we called "guards" enforced the rules. Nothing could be further from the truth. There were no rules at Omarska except for one: The guards were omnipotent. It might be accurate therefore to refer to them as gods rather than guards. They could kill as they pleased, pardon as they pleased, rape as they pleased. Their subjects, the prisoners, prayed to them for forgiveness, for a favor, for life.

What They Claimed

We were marched into the building and up a dark stairwell to the second floor. "Into that room," our escort Simo Drljača told us, motioning toward a door at the end of the hallway. We went. It was a stuffy office, with stacks of papers in the corners, a few books on a shelf, a table, chairs, a desk. A calendar hung behind the desk. It showed a half-nude woman with a huge pair of breasts.

The camp's "chief investigator" was sitting behind the desk. I had brought an Instamatic camera on this trip, an idiot-proof apparatus, and during the half-hour that the "chief investigator" talked to us, I tried to line up a picture that would show him and the nude woman in the background. The interview was a piece of obscenity, so what could be better than a visual touch of obscenity to go with it?

The session was forgettable, and so I have forgotten much of it. That sounds strange, because it's not often that you get to question a man who, in all probability, spent the previous months overseeing a frenzy of cruelty. Imagine, how could an interview with Dr. Josef Mengele be forgettable? But this man, like dozens of war criminals whom I interviewed during my time in Bosnia, was not going to pour his heart out to us. Of course not. He said that the prisoners were interrogated to learn what role they had played in "the Islamic insurrection," and that they were released if the investigators decided they had played no role. The ones who were involved in the fabled insurrection were transferred to "other facilities" for trial. Torture? He laughed. Of course not.

"Interrogation is being done in the same way as it is done in America and England," he said.

I looked up from my notebook. The nude woman on the calendar was smiling.

What I find most remarkable about the session is that I cannot recall the chief investigator's face. It is a total blank, gone from my memory, or sealed in a corner I cannot reach, no matter how long and hard I think about Omarska, no matter how firmly I close my eyes and try to recall. It is as though my subconscious were playing a trick on me, perhaps trying to send me a message that the man's identity is not important: he is just another human being, faceless. He is you, he is my friend, he is me.

Allowed to Ask Questions

It was showtime. We were led downstairs to the cafeteria, a small one of the institutional, stainless-steel variety. Bean soup was being served. Inmates were shepherded into the room in groups of two dozen, heads bent in supplication, shuffling one after another, hunched over. They knew the drill. After getting their lunchtime soup and piece of bread— the only meal of the day—they shuffled to the few tables and spooned the muck into their mouths as quickly as possible. They had about a minute or two before one of the guards said a word and they jumped out of their chairs, shuffling to the exit and handing their bowls and spoons to the next group. There was none of the dawdling or yawning that you would see at normal prisons. There was only fear and power, awesome power.

We were allowed to meander around the room and ask questions. It was another act of humiliation for the prisoners and, this time, for the journalists too. Perhaps that's why it was done. The guards were never more than a few feet away, and there was no outdoor breeze to carry a prisoner's voice out of snooping range. Words bounced off the walls like those tiny, transparent "superballs" that I played with as a child. I bent over to a few prisoners and asked questions, but I never got a real response. They bowed their heads lower, noses virtually in the bowls. This was a place where words, any words, could kill them.

"Please, don't ask me questions," one of them begged in a whisper.

A Different Tactic

The visit of journalists was just another form of torture. I tried to turn the tables a bit, to interview one of the guards. I settled on a massive oaf who, like the other guards, was in need of a shave. His height seemed somewhere between six and seven feet. Dressed in a dark combat outfit, he had the physique of a steroid-pumped linebacker and was packing enough weapons to arm a platoon: a pistol on either hip, a compact AK-47 assault rifle hanging by a strap from his right shoulder, and a foot-long bowie knife dangling from his belt. His hands were covered to the knuckles by black leather gloves. He wore reflector sunglasses. We were indoors.

I tipped my head toward the ceiling and tried to soften him up. The only thing we seemed to have in common was that we were sweating a lot.

"Hot in here, isn't it?" I suggested. He peered down at me for a second or two. He didn't respond. I tried again.

"How long have you worked here?" No response. Vlatka gave me a look that said, *Forget about it.* I gave it one last try.

"Is it true that you torture the prisoners?"

I had gotten his attention. He glanced down at me, and his lips arched into the kind of thin smile that fails to make you smile in return.

"Why would we want to beat them?" he said.

Feeble Reports

The show continued. We were led to a dormitory room filled with about 40 bunk beds. It wasn't such a bad place, but of course it was created for our benefit. A guard shadowed me all the time, so trying to talk to the prisoners was more fruitless than ever. I decided to go outside, in the hope the guard would follow me, leaving Vlatka free to ask a few questions. As I headed for the exit, I passed the television crew. The reporter was interviewing a feverish inmate lying on a bunk bed. The television light was shining right on the poor fellow, and several guards were hovering around the bed. The inmate was shaking, his blankets moving up and down with the furious heavings of his chest.

"Are you being treated well?" the reporter asked. The prisoner's look of terror tightened a few notches more, and he glanced at one of the guards, not knowing how to respond. Obviously he could not speak honestly, but the guard might get mad if he was too fulsome in his praise. The truth would kill, and even the wrong lie would kill.

"*Dobro, dobro,*" he gasped. Good, good.

I left the room, feeling sad for the prisoner and angry at the TV crew, which seemed to have crossed a boundary by getting involved in this game. It was a sort of Russian roulette. Five empty chambers in the gun, one filled with a bullet. The reporter was handing the gun to the prisoner when he turned the camera on. *Speak*, the reporter urged. *Pull the trigger*. The prisoner was safe while we were around, but what would happen when we left?

The Real Story

The whole truth emerged as journalists and diplomats interviewed Bosnians who had gotten out of the camps and reached safety in Croatia, where they could speak freely. I questioned several dozen survivors in Croatia and read the written testimony of scores of others. The best overall picture was drawn, belatedly, by the State Department, which had far greater resources than any single journalist, in a series of reports sent to the United Nations Security Council. The reports amount to a catalogue of the unimaginable and the unbearable. One of the most chilling passages is in an October 22, 1992, report under the heading "Abuse of Civilians in Detention Centers." This is how it summarizes the experience of one ex-prisoner from Omarska:

"The witness stated that a young Muslim man from Kozarac who had owned a Suzuki motorcycle was tortured in front of the other prisoners. He was severely beaten all over his body and his teeth were knocked out. The guards then tied one end of a wire tightly around his testicles and tied the other end to the victim's motorcycle. A guard got on the motorcycle and sped off."

Unbelievable Horrors

Do you believe that Europeans did this at the end of the 20th century? Excuse me, the question should be rephrased. Europeans, as Bosnia reminds us, do not have an inside track on virtue. Ugandans, Germans, Cambodians—there is no difference in the cruelty sweepstakes, it is a dead heat. Here's the question again: Do you believe humans can do this at the end of the 20th century? I find it hard to believe that a man can get on a motorcycle and ride off with another man's testicles attached to the tailpipe. Yet the testimony from camp survivors is consistent. It gnaws away at me.

One survivor, Emin Jakubović, told journalists he was ordered by his Omarska jailers to castrate three prisoners. "They forced me to tear off their testicles, with my teeth, so I tore off their testicles with my teeth. They were screaming with pain." Impossible? At a refugee center in Croatia, I interviewed a man who said he witnessed the episode. It was wintertime and we were sitting in a bare, unheated room littered with cigarette butts and trampled-on newspapers. My overcoat was buttoned up against the cold, and the ink in my pen was freezing, as was my right hand, which became too stiff to write legibly. I had been interviewing prison survivors for several hours, and I was tired, fed up with it all.

I looked at the man, whose name was Ibrahim, still half emaciated from his ordeal, and shook my head. Even though I had heard of such things before, I could not believe it. No, I told him, I do not believe your story. *I do not believe it.* Even among torturers, there is a line beyond which they do not go, such as castration. I asked Ibrahim, Would you believe someone who said the things you have just said? He stared back at me.

"I know," he replied. "I wouldn't believe it unless I had seen it."

More than two years later, on February 13, 1995, in its first batch of indictments, the United Nations War Crimes Tribunal issued international arrest warrants for 21 Serbs on charges of committing war crimes and crimes against humanity. The indicted men included Dušan Tadić, who, according to the tribunal, forced a Muslim prisoner to bite off the testicles of another prisoner.

Thoughts Too Overwhelming

Bosnia makes you question basic assumptions about humanity, and one of the questions concerns torture. Why, after all, should there be any limit? For a person capable of torture, no form of it is out of bounds. The big moral leap backward has already been taken once the door marked Torture has been opened and the first cut made in the prisoner's skin, or the first butt blow landed to the prisoner's face. Suddenly, the torturer realizes that he, or she, has entered a new universe of sadistic pleasures. The wild beast has been set free and taken up residence in his soul.

What's the moral difference between slitting a man's throat and slicing off his testicles? Please tell me, anyone. There is none. If you have the stomach to crush a man's head under your boots, then you probably have the stomach to cut off a woman's breasts. Will God treat you better because you killed but refrained from mutilating? No. You can do as you please and you have nothing to fear.

You can, for example, barge into a house and put a gun to a father's head and tell him that you will pull the trigger unless he rapes his daughter or at least simulates the rape. (I heard of such things in Bosnia.) The father will refuse and say, I will die before doing that. You shrug your shoulders and reply, O.K., old man, I won't shoot you, but I will shoot your daughter. What does the father do now, dear reader? He pleads, he begs, but then you, the man with the gun, put the gun to the daughter's head, you pull back the hammer, and you shout, *Now!* Do it! Or I shoot! The father starts weeping, yet slowly he unties his belt, moving like a dazed zombie; he can't believe what he must do. You laugh and say, That's right, old man, pull down those pants, pull up your daughter's dress, *and do it!*

You are the law, and you feel divine.

What People Might Do

Prison survivors describe an odd enthusiasm on the part of their torturers, who laughed, sang, and got drunk while committing their crimes. They weren't just doing a job, they were doing something they enjoyed. They felt liberated. They could smash every crystal glass in the shop and break every taboo in the book, and no law could touch them. Torture became entertainment.

"After beating us for a while one night, the guards got tired," Ibrahim told me. "They decided it would be a good idea to have the prisoners fight each other. A guard singled out me and another prisoner. He told the other prisoner to stand still and he told me to punch the prisoner as hard as possible in the face. I did it. But the guard said I wasn't doing it hard enough, and so he hit me in the back of my head with the butt of his gun. He kept hitting me until I was covered in blood. And then he took another prisoner out of the line and told him to hit me."

I talked to an American diplomat who debriefed prisoners freed from Omarska. "It was like [the] Roman Colosseum," she said. "You have to hit the other guy as hard as you can if you want to stay alive. If you don't hit hard enough, then you get shot."

The guards even opened the camp gates and allowed their friends to share in the fun. Civilians came from the outside and would spend a night beating or killing or raping. What's extraordinary is the reasons these Serbs entered the gates of hell for a night of twisted pleasure. They wanted to settle old scores. Survivors told me of hiding behind the backs of other prisoners when Serbs they knew suddenly showed up on the campgrounds. A poor Serb might search for the wealthy Muslim who had refused to give him a job five years earlier; a farmer might try to find the Croat who, a decade before, had refused to lend his tractor for a day; a middle-aged man might look around for the Muslim who, 25 years ago, stole away his high-school sweetheart. Petty quarrels were settled with major crimes.

It sounds unbelievable, yet it happened. It makes me wonder what would happen if half the population of Peoria were put into a prison camp, and the other half were told that it could go into the camp and do whatever it wanted to whomever it wanted, and that no punishment need be feared, because any violent or sexual act committed against a prisoner would be an act of patriotism. How many citizens of Peoria would yield to the temptation? How many would resist?

WAR CRIMES INFLICT PERMANENT DAMAGE

Lisa Chiu

While on an exchange program at the National University in Vietnam, Lisa Chiu interviewed two of the five remaining survivors of the 1968 My Lai massacre. She describes their ordeal in the following selection. The massacre occurred during the Vietnam War, Chiu writes, when U.S. soldiers tortured and brutally murdered over five hundred Vietnamese civilians within a four-hour period. Thirty years after the event, the two survivors Chiu interviewed still had vivid memories of the terror they endured. Both women survived by being buried alive under the bodies of other villagers, and both bear permanent emotional wounds from their experiences. Chiu notes that the soldiers who instigated the carnage received little punishment and that the U.S. government has tried to ignore the event in subsequent years. However, she maintains, the survivors will never be able to forget the atrocities they lived through. Chiu has written for the *Nation*, the *Philadelphia Inquirer*, and the *Union News* of Springfield, Massachusetts.

When the US Army gave Hugh Thompson Jr., Lawrence Colburn and the family of Glenn Andreotta the Soldier's Medal—the highest medal for bravery not involving enemy conflict—in 1998, many Americans believed the country was finally coming to terms with the My Lai massacre of 1968.

The award ceremony made many Americans remember something that was thirty years forgotten. But the reality is that most young Americans have never heard of My Lai. Nor do they have any comprehension of what it revealed—an unjust war in Vietnam and sole responsibility for one of the world's most brutal war crimes.

The accolades given to Andreotta's family, Thompson and Colburn were long overdue for the three soldiers who attempted to put an end to the murders at My Lai. In many ways it represented the one honorable act in a sea of senseless ones.

But at Son My, the village where the bloodshed took place, two of

Reprinted, with permission, from "My Lai Revisited," by Lisa Chiu, *Philadelphia Inquirer*, March 15, 1998.

the five remaining survivors are still asking questions that no medal, however belated, can answer. For Ha Thi Quy and Pham Thi Thuan, who both still reside in Son My, their lives are a constant reminder of what happened in their village.

Unimaginable Atrocities

"When the GIs came here . . . I was preparing breakfast," said Thuan. "It was just before sunrise. . . . They started shooting. People ran into bomb shelters and hootches. The GIs just came into their homes and killed them."

The 150 soldiers from Task Force Barker's Charlie Company landed in My Lai on the morning of March 16, 1968. In the course of three hours—encountering no return fire, meeting no opposition—they leveled the settlement.

The largest mass killing took place at the village irrigation ditch, where 170 civilians were rounded up and shot. Both Thuan and Quy were hauled there for execution. The order was given by the only soldier to be convicted in a court-martial for the massacre, Lieut. William Calley. Calley was later paroled after spending only four and a half months in jail.

"They gathered all the people to stand at the bank of the irrigation ditch," said Quy. "Then they took a monk and shot him before all the villagers. We were so terrified and prayed to him. We tried to revive him but he didn't survive. Then they shot all the people with machine guns."

Quy survived by the deaths of others. As the weight of the dead bodies piled on top of her, she lost consciousness. When she awoke hours later, she was wounded in her lower back. She ran to a neighboring village to receive food, shelter and clothing. She lost her mother, brother, grandchild and her son.

Horrible Images Survive

Thuan also survived because of the numerous bodies that fell on her. She was able to feign death, hoping that the American soldiers would leave without discovering her.

"I was frightened. I couldn't sigh, cry or shout. . . . When I saw that no GIs were there, I ran out at night. Some people in the village came back and brought me to safety to the next village," said Thuan.

Images of the massacre were brought to life by military reporter Ronald Haeberle, whose pictures would later shock an entire nation. The same images are forever etched in Quy's memory.

"There was a child dead near the guard tower. He still had his mouth on his mother's breast. They both died that way," said Quy. "The GIs came in and shot all the women and children. . . . We couldn't understand why the GIs were so selfish. They became like animals."

Gross sexual atrocities went hand in hand with the carnage. According to journalists Michael Bilton and Kevin Sim, in the book *Four Hours in My Lai*, one soldier was reported to have forced a woman to perform oral sex while holding a gun to her child's head. Another woman was said to have died when a rifle barrel was inserted into her vagina and the trigger was pulled.

Forgetting Is Impossible for Some

The total death count, according to the Son My museum, was 504. Of that figure, 182 of the victims were women, 17 of them pregnant, and 173 were children, 56 of them less than 5 months old.

The victims were all buried, scattered throughout the rice fields that were once their village. No marker commemorates where they actually perished. Only the foundations of their homes and places of mass execution mark their names. Apart from the museum, the site at Son My is essentially a graveyard.

"I want the Americans who fought in Vietnam to remember that if they have children and grandchildren, to teach them about this for the next generation," Thuan says, urgency in her voice. "They must do everything to prevent this event from happening again."

Quy reminds us that after the massacre, for many of the survivors, life has been filled with challenges, first to move on after the horror and second to survive in one of the poorest provinces in Vietnam.

"I'll never forget this. I will remember it always. . . . I know that not all Americans condoned this act . . . but I will always remain with hatred in my heart. How a child who was just born had to die . . . and women who didn't know anything about fighting or guns had to die," said Quy. "I just have one question: Why did the GIs shoot innocent civilians who just worked in the rice fields?"

There is no choice for Quy and Thuan and the other survivors but constantly to be reminded of the horrific events that tore their whole village apart and forever changed their lives, memories that are now thirty years old.

For Americans, however, forgetting seems to be all too easy.

Perpetrating the Crimes

Yuasa Ken, as told to Haruko Tayo Cook and Theodore F. Cook

Yuasa Ken was a doctor in the Japanese army during the Japanese occupation of China (1931 to 1945), in which over 30 million Chinese civilians, including women and children, were brutally murdered. Yuasa describes the common practice of using Chinese prisoners to train Japanese doctors in medical skills essential in wartime. These prisoners would be forced to undergo unnecessary operations, such as amputations of arms, and would then be summarily executed, according to Yuasa. He explains that the atrocious acts in which he played a key role were considered his duties as an army officer and patriotic citizen. Imprisoned in China as a war criminal until 1956, Yuasa relates that although he has confessed and acknowledged his horrible crimes, most of his colleagues pretend as though they never took part in such gruesome incidents. Haruko Tayo Cook is a linguistics professor at the University of Hawaii at Manoa, and Theodore Cook is a history professor at the William Paterson College of New Jersey. They are the authors of *Japan at War: An Oral History*, from which the following selection is taken.

My father had his own practice in Shitamachi, the old district of Tokyo. I became a doctor myself in March 1941. I took the exam to become a short-term army doctor in the fall. Everyone passed. You can't fight a war without doctors. In December 1941, I entered the Twenty-Sixth Regiment in Asahikawa, Hokkaido, and within two months was promoted to first lieutenant. We were a privileged elite, treated as if we were different from the rest of the people.

I was soon dispatched to a city hospital in the southern part of Shansi province in China. I arrived there January 1, 1942. It was still bitterly cold that day in the middle of March when, just after lunch, the director of the hospital, Lieutenant Colonel Nishimura, summoned everyone together. Seven or eight MDs, an accounting officer, a pharmacist, and a dentist. All officers. He excused the housekeeper and other women. After they'd left, he said, "We'll be carrying out an

From "Army Doctor," by Yuasa Ken, in *Japan at War: An Oral History*, edited by Haruko Tayo Cook and Theodore F. Cook. Copyright ©1992. Reprinted by permission of The New Press.

operation exercise. Assemble again at one o'clock." I was chilled to the bone, but it wasn't the weather. I'd heard before I went that they did vivisections there.

The hospital building adjoined a courtyard and a requisitioned middle-school building. Our patients were in there. There were nearly a hundred employees. Ten nurses, fifty to sixty technicians, some non-coms, too. I'm the kind of man who usually agrees to whatever I'm told to do. A "yes man," you could say. I remember that first time clearly. I arrived a little late; my excuse was that I had some other duties. . . .

Circumstances of the Crime

A solitary sentry stood guard. He saluted me the moment I opened the door. I then saw Medical Service Colonel Kotake and Hospital Director Nishimura, so I snapped to attention and saluted. They returned my salute calmly. I approached Hirano, my direct superior. That's when I noticed two Chinese close to the director. One was a sturdy, broadchested man, about thirty, calm and apparently fearless, standing immobile. I thought immediately, that man's a Communist. Next to him was a farmer about forty years old. He was dressed as if he had just been dragged in from his field. His eyes raced desperately about the room. Three medics were there, holding rifles. Nurses were adjusting the surgical instruments by the autopsy tables. There were some fifteen or sixteen doctors present.

You might imagine this as a ghastly or gruesome scene, but that's not how it was. It was just the same as any other routine operation. I was still new to it. I thought there must be a reason for killing those people. I asked Hirano, but he just answered, "We're going to kill the whole Eighth Route Army."' I pretended to know what he meant. The nurses were all smiling. They were from the Japanese Red Cross.

The director said, "Let's begin." A medic pushed the steadfast man forward. He lay down calmly. I thought he'd resigned himself to it. That was completely wrong. As a rule, Chinese don't glare at you. He had come prepared to die, confident in China's ultimate victory and revenge over a cruel, unjust Japan. He didn't say that aloud, but going to his death as he did spoke for itself. I didn't see that back then.

I was in the group assigned to the other fellow. A medic ordered him forward. He shouted, "No! No!" and tried to flee. The medic, who was holding a rifle, couldn't move as fast as the farmer, and I was a new officer, just arrived in the command. I was very conscious of my dignity as a military man. The hospital director was watching. I never really thought, if this man dies, what will happen to his family? All I thought was, it will be terribly embarrassing if I end up in a brawl, this man in farmer's rags and me dressed so correctly. I wanted to show off. I pushed that farmer and said, "Go forward!" He seemed to lose heart, maybe because I'd spoken up. I was very proud of myself. Yet when he sat on the table, he refused to lie down. He shouted "Ai-ya-a! Ai-ya-a!" as if he knew that if he lay down he was going to be murdered. But a nurse then said, in Chinese, "Sleep, sleep." She went on, "Sleep, sleep. Drug give"—Japanese-style Chinese. The Chinese of the oppressor always bears that tone, as if to say, "There's no possibility you will fail to understand what I'm saying." He lay down. She was even prouder than me. She giggled. The demon's face is not a fearful face. It's a face wreathed in smiles.

Gruesome Techniques

I asked the doctor who was about to administer lumbar anesthesia if he wasn't going to disinfect the point of injection. "What are you talking about? We're going to kill him," he replied. After a while, a nurse struck the man's legs and asked him if it hurt. He said it didn't, but when they tried to get him to inhale chloroform, he began to struggle. We all had to hold him down.

First was practice in removing an appendix. That was carried out by two doctors. When a man has appendicitis, his appendix swells and grows very hard. But there was nothing wrong with this man, so it was hard to locate. They made an incision, but had to cut in another place and search until they finally found it. I remember that.

Next a doctor removed one of his arms. You must know how to do this when a man has shrapnel imbedded in his arm. You have to apply a tourniquet, to stanch the flow of blood. Then two doctors practiced sewing the intestines. If the intestine or stomach is pierced by bullets, that kind of surgery is a necessity. Next was the opening of the pharynx. When soldiers are wounded in the throat, blood gathers there and blocks the trachea, so you need to open it up. There is a special hook-shaped instrument for field use for cutting into the trachea. You drive it in, hook it open, then remove it, leaving only a tube behind. The blood drains out. It all took almost two hours. You remember the first time.

Eventually, all the doctors from the divisions left. Then the nurses departed. Only the director, the medics, and those of us from the hospital remained. The one I did, small-framed and old, was already dead. But from the sturdy man's mouth came, "Heh. Heh. Heh." One's last gasps are still strong. It gave us pause to think of throwing him, still breathing, into the hole out back, so the director injected air into his heart with a syringe. Another doctor—he's alive today—and I then had to try to strangle him with string. Still he wouldn't die. Finally, an old noncom said, "Honorable Doctor, he'll die if you give him a shot of anesthesia." Afterwards we threw him into the hole. This was the first time.

Duties of War

Japan's occupation of China was no more than a collection of dots and lines in a vast theater of operations. When a man suffered from appendicitis, you couldn't bring him to a hospital. His appendix had to be removed right there at the front line. But there weren't enough surgeons available. Even ophthalmologists or pediatricians had to be able to do it, and they didn't know how, so they practiced. Doctors weren't in China primarily to cure illness. No, we were there so that when units clashed, the leaders could give orders to the soldiers and say, "We have doctors to take care of you. Charge on!" We were part of the military's fighting capability. It was easier to get men to fight if they thought there was a doctor to treat them when they were hit.

The next time we did it, we were practicing sewing up intestines for bullet wounds that had passed through the stomach. I remember the dentist was there, too, saying, "Oh, I've got his teeth!" The urologist removed the testicles. The hospital director said, "I will instruct you myself in this technique." He cut into the intestine and then sewed it back up. At that moment a phone call came for him, and he left the room to take it. One doctor observed the director's work and noticed something wrong: "It's sewed up backwards!" We all laughed. When the director returned, we were still snickering, but when he asked "What is it? What's the matter?" we just couldn't tell him. I remember fragments like this.

Orders for such exercises went from First Army headquarters, through the army hospital, and out to the divisions and brigades. In the beginning, exercises were conducted only twice, in the spring and the autumn. But by the end, we were getting doctors who couldn't do a thing, couldn't even handle instruments. Old men. I felt, we have to do this much more often. We should do it six times a year. I took the initiative and sought permission from the hospital. It was necessary to improve the technique of the army doctors. I did that as a loyal servant of the Japanese military. I felt I was willing to do anything to win. Doctor Ishii Shiro, the director of Unit 731, came to our hospital many times for education. "If the only way to win a war against America is bacterial warfare, I am ready. I will do anything," I thought. "This is war."

A Sick Education

Besides training, I also treated patients. Sometimes they were wounded soldiers, but half suffered from tuberculosis. Infectious diseases, malaria, typhoid, dysentery, and liver diseases were common. I really enjoyed my work. When I went out to town, I could swagger, you know, swing my shoulders as a Japanese officer, feeling I was serving the nation, and watch people treat me well because they were afraid of me. Everybody saluted an officer. All the girls addressed me as "Honorable Military Doctor." If anybody showed even a trace of resistance, we could send him directly to the front. It was easy at the hospital. We had no worries about being killed. We had plenty of sake. Anything we wanted. I felt I ruled the whole country. At morning roll call, they saluted me. I had only to say, straighten up that line, and they'd do it. They'd move back and forth until I told them to stop. I did it only for the sake of my own ego.

In late 1942, at the time of the battle for Guadalcanal, we realized things weren't going to be too easy. About forty doctors were gathered in the city of Taiyuan for a meeting. We were told to assemble at Taiyuan Prison, where I ended up myself a few years later. There, two men from the judicial corps brought out a couple of blindfolded Chinese. They then asked the doctor in charge of the meeting if everything was set. At his nod, they suddenly shot the Chinese, right in their stomachs, four or five times each. We then had to remove the bullets. That was our challenge. Could we remove them while they were still alive? That was how they measured the success or failure of the operation. When asked, "Want to do it?" I said, "No. I do this all the time." But eventually everyone got in on it, helping to control the bleeding or whatever. They both died.

We also carried out medic training. It was in 1944, at a time when we already knew we were going to lose. Those soldiers! Skinny and hardly able to write at all. I was in charge of education by then. I decided there was no way to teach them except by practical experience. I went to the Kempeitai and asked them to give us one of their prisoners. We practiced leg amputation. The one I got bore no traces of torture. I remember how surprised I was. "This one's real clean," I thought. I remember one soldier fainted.

Another time they sent us two for educational purposes. We didn't have many doctors at the time, so we were able to do all we had to do on just one of them. But we really couldn't send the other one back. So the director chopped his head off. He wanted to test the strength of his sword.

We received requests from a Japanese pharmaceutical company for brain-cortex tissue. They were making adrenocortical hormones. We cut tissue from the brains and sent it along. We sent one bottle. Then a second request came from the company for ten bottles, which we filled. This was a "private route." Everybody was involved. . . .

Unable to Acknowledge Wrongdoing

I was imprisoned until 1956. That's when I returned to Japan.

All the doctors and the nurses who had been with me at that hospital in Shansi came to Shinagawa station to welcome me when I returned to Tokyo. The nurses said to me, "Doctor, you had such a hard time. We're so sorry for you." One man said, "Doctor Yuasa, I hope you did your best to assert your Emperor's policy was just and Communism was wrong." That's what they said! I told them, "Don't you remember? I did those things with you. You did them, too." The man I said that to seemed to shudder. Suddenly, for the first time, he recalled that he was a murderer!

It is scary. It's outrageous to murder a person. Yet it's far worse to forget that you've done it. That's the most horrible thing imaginable!

I did about ten men in three and a half years. Six times, all together, I took part in exercises to improve the technique of medical doctors. Removed brains, testicles. Most doctors did that, in the divisions, or in hospitals, all over China. Yet all keep quiet! Why do they forget? Everybody did it. At that time we were doing something good. That's what we let ourselves believe. But they still keep their mouths shut. If they were to recall it, it would be unbearable. That's why they are silent. It was "because of the war." That's enough for them.

CHAPTER 4

HOW SHOULD WAR CRIMES BE ADDRESSED?

WAR CRIMES MUST BE CONFRONTED IMMEDIATELY

Ed Vulliamy

In 1992, Serb forces attacked Muslim and Croat population centers in Bosnia-Herzegovina, forcing most Muslims and Croats from their homes and holding thousands in the Omarska concentration camp. During his coverage of the conflict in the former Yugoslavia, Ed Vulliamy, a correspondent for the London *Guardian* newspaper, discovered the Omarska concentration camp and exposed it to the outside world. At the time, according to Vulliamy, politicians and diplomats took little action concerning the camp. He writes that the international community did not begin to address the problem of the concentration camp until the Dayton Peace Agreement was signed in November 1995 and the North Atlantic Treaty Organization (NATO) began to make its presence felt in Omarska. In Vulliamy's opinion, this attention came far too late to help the victims. He argues that if action against war crimes is to be effective, it must be immediate; without immediate action, war criminals will deny their crimes while committing further atrocities.

In 1992, a television reporter and I stumbled into a place that bewildered and outraged the world. Omarska was a concentration camp in northwestern Bosnia run by Bosnian Serbs and dedicated to the humiliation and murder of Muslims and Croats. It seemed unbelievable that a network of such camps—with their echo of the Third Reich—could have existed in the heart of Europe, hidden from view for three months while thousands were slaughtered and those who remained were kept skeletal, bloodied by torture and living in abject, desolate terror.

With Bosnia's guns at least temporarily silenced, the bitter reckoning [has started]. On May 7, 1996, one of Omarska's most notorious alleged torturers and killers, Dusko Tadic, took his place in the dock at the war crimes tribunal in The Hague, standing where no man has stood since Hermann Göring and Rudolf Hess, charged with crimes

Reprinted, with permission, from "Middle Manager of Genocide," by Ed Vulliamy, *The Nation*, June 10, 1996.

against humanity. (I am obliged to testify at the trial as a witness for the prosecution.) But the reckoning is more than a judicial matter. It is an attempt to try to understand the most ferocious carnage to blight Europe in fifty years. To understand the war, I had to return to the iron-ore mine that had housed the accursed concentration camp.

Denial

In 1992 it took five putrid summer days to argue our way into the camp. But now the road is empty at the turnoff for Omarska. Flakes of snow, which mute all sound and drape the mine in virgin white, have overlaid what happened here. It is seven below zero, but our shivers are not from the cold. Children play with sleds in the yard behind the gate. A couple of stray mongrels now frolic in and out of the jaw of a hydraulic door.

In 1992, this tarmac was a killing yard, the bodies loaded onto trucks by bulldozer. Omarska was a place where cruelty and mass murder had become a form of recreation. The guards were often drunk and singing while they tortured. A prisoner called Fikret Harambasic was castrated by one of his fellow inmates before being beaten to death. One inmate was made to bark like a dog and lap at a puddle of motor oil while a guard and his mates from the village jumped up and down on his back until he was dead. The guards would make videos of this butchery for their home entertainment. But the most extraordinary hallmark of the carnage was its grotesque intimacy. People knew their torturers, and had often grown up alongside them.

The mine installations have become emblems of evil: Rusty boxcars sit along the railway tracks leading out of the complex. In 1992, this rolling stock was loaded with Muslim deportees. Spidery iron tentacles, conveyor belts and limbs of machinery link one shed to another, silent and skeletal like the inmates that were packed inside.

Now, three sentries stop us. Two of these lads are from the village of Omarska itself, and had worked at the mine. "Nothing happened here," asserts a bright-eyed 28-year-old who was employed as a mine technician and has stayed on with the security staff, now in military uniform. Iron ore was processed here, he says, up until the end of 1992. "So how can it have been any kind of camp in August that year? We are from Omarska, we would have known." He elaborates: "They came here recently, the Americans, looking for mass graves, but they didn't find any. There are no mass graves here. There was no camp—ever." The technician's friend and co-sentry is only 24, from the village but "too young to have worked at the mine." He says: "I blame the journalists. The Muslims paid the media, and the television pictures were forged." There is a fascination with deception. "Anyone could do that," says the 28-year-old.

We ask them their names. The answer from the technician, suddenly harsh, is unexpected. "We had a nice chat, but names are a secret. The Muslims know me, and I know them. But they have to produce evidence of what I did. These days, they can just come up to you in the street and take you to The Hague. That's how they work."

"Did you know Dusko Tadic?" I ask. They shrug and mumble. "Not well. He had a nice cafe in Kozarac. . . . There was no camp here. . . ."

One Leader's Development

At the briefing in August 1992 at the Prijedor town hall, from where Omarska was administered, the authorities insisted that there was no camp, only an "investigation center." (It was in the town hall that I briefly met Tadic that year.) The figure responsible for day-to-day administration of the camp was Milan Kovacevic, a man with a swashbuckling mustache and a "US Marines" T-shirt. He decreed then that there was nothing the world could teach the Serbs about concentration camps, since he had been raised in one—Jasenovac, where the Croatian Nazi-puppet regime imprisoned and killed thousands of Serbs, Jews and Croatian dissidents between 1941 and 1945. After our discovery of Omarska, the media circus descended and the camp was hastily closed. Kovacevic was assigned the task of explaining to the world's cameras what an "investigation center" is.

In 1992, Kovacevic's eyes were fiery with enthusiasm for what he called "a great moment in the history of the Serbs." They are still fiery now, but from some other emotion. He has a taste for homemade plum brandy, and he extracts some from his cupboard at 9 A.M. It's been a good year for plums, he explains, but the jam factories are all shut. Shame to let the fruit go to waste.

Kovacevic is also a medical man, now director of the town hospital of Prijedor. Despite growing up "to learn that all Germans were killers," he elected to go to Germany to study anesthesiology. He is still a proud nationalist who "wanted to make this a Serb land, without Muslims." But his certainty about the ends conceals doubt about the means. What about burning the Muslim houses along the road? Was that necessary, or a moment of madness? Kovacevic proceeds cautiously, accompanied by a second glass of brandy: "Both things. A necessary fight and a moment of madness. The houses were burned at the beginning, when people were losing control. People weren't behaving normally." This comes as a surprise. Was it all a terrible mistake? "To be sure, it was a terrible mistake." A third glass, and suddenly, unprompted: "We knew very well what happened at Auschwitz and Dachau, and we knew very well how it started and how it was done. What we did was not the same as Auschwitz or Dachau, but it was a mistake. It was planned to have a camp, but not a concentration camp."

Usually it is only "enemies of the Serbian people" who invoke Auschwitz when talking about Omarska. But the anesthetist plows boldly on. He has never had this conversation before, he says. In fact, no one in Bosnia has had this conversation before. "Omarska," he continues, "was planned as a camp, but was turned into something else because of this loss of control. I cannot explain the loss of control. You could call it collective madness."

Reluctance to Admit Wrongdoing

Another glass of brandy to steel the spirit, and for reasons not hard to guess, his childhood in Jasenovac comes to mind. "Six hundred thousand were killed in Jasenovac," he muses. "I was taken there as a baby, by my aunt. My mother was in the mountains, hiding. We remember everything. History is made that way." But Jasenovac was run by Croats; why did the Serbs turn on the Muslims? Kovacevic straightens himself. "There is a direct connection between what happened to the Muslims in our camps and the fact that there had been some Muslim soldiers in the [pro-Nazi] Greater Croatia. They committed war crimes, and now it is the other way round."

In Omarska, he says, "there were not more than 100 killed, whereas Jasenovac was a killing factory." Only 100 killed at Omarska? He blushes. "I said there were 100 *killed*, not died." Then Kovacevic loses his way and throws off caution: "Oh, I don't know how many were killed in there; God knows. It's a wind tunnel, this part of the world, a hurricane blowing to and fro. . . ."

By now the cheaply paneled room is steaming with the exhaled fumes of fast-disappearing cigarettes, a fifth glass and talk of death. So, Doctor, who planned this madness? "It all looks very well planned if your view is from New York," he says. He edges forward on his low chair, as if to whisper some personal advice. "But here, when everything is burning, and breaking apart inside people's heads—this was something for the psychiatrists. These people should all have been taken to the psychiatrist, but there wasn't enough time."

In 1992, Kovacevic did not hide his role in operating the camp, but now The Hague is becoming serious. Were you part of this insanity, Doctor? "If someone acquitted me, saying that I was not part of that collective madness, then I would admit that this was not true. . . . If things go wrong in the hospital, then I am guilty. If you have to do things by killing people, well—that is my personal secret. Now my hair is white. I don't sleep so well."

Further Fabricating

Kovacevic's boss was the mayor of Prijedor, Milomir Stakic. I remember him barking in 1992 about an armed Islamic conspiracy against the Serbs, coordinated by the United States. At the time he was the man with the authority to grant or refuse access to Omarska. When I meet Stakic again, I find out he is also a medical man, director of the daycare health center in Prijedor, not too far from Omarska. His specialization in neuropsychiatry was interrupted by war and political office. Dr. Stakic introduces a fellow with a menacing air, Viktor Kondic, whom he calls his deputy at the health center.

Stakic swivels back and forth in his chair as he speaks. "As a doctor," he says, "I saw many wounded and mutilated people. The question was: Do the Serbs stay on their knees, or go back to Jasenovac a second time?" If there was a threat to the Serbs, was the reaction perhaps a little too much? "No," he snaps. What about Omarska? Kondic intervenes quickly and disagreeably. "Omarska was a mine. An iron-ore mine. That is all." The reports, the television pictures? Dr. Stakic clarifies: "They were pictures of Serbs in Muslim camps. There were no prisoners there."

Then comes an immediate negation: "Omarska was for Muslims with illegal weapons. Omarska was not a hotel"—he manages his only smile, and it is not an agreeable one—"but Omarska was not a concentration camp."

"The Serbs go to extremes only when their freedom is threatened," says Stakic, suddenly and oddly. "Unfortunately," chimes in Kondic, who now describes himself as "a lawyer" (we later find out he is a secret policeman) and whose eyes roll skyward, "we learned to defend our freedom in concentration camps." There ensues a long, torturous conversation not about Omarska but about Jasenovac. The wintry night has fallen, the streets outside are still, Prijedor is wrapped in fog. Within there is a leaden silence, until Stakic volunteers a strange remark: "It is very brave of you to be sitting here like this, with us so late in the evening."

Distortions and History

The journey to Omarska in 1992 began and ended in the Serbian capital of Belgrade. Upon arrival, we were welcomed by a senior middle manager of the proclaimed Serbian Republic of Bosnia-Herzegovina, Professor Nikola Koljevic. He was to supervise our access to Omarska.

An expert on Shakespeare, the impish Koljevic has seduced many Westerners with his ample quoting of the Bard and command of English. The day after we finally found the camps, his invitation to tea and cakes at a smart hotel back in Belgrade was irresistible. "So you found them," he said sardonically, "congratulations!" And then, in a piquant voice that evoked his favorite Shakespearean character, Iago, he embarked on a double-edged reproach: "It took you a long time to find them, didn't it? Three months! And so near *Venice*! All you people could think about was poor, sophisticated Sarajevo. Ha-ha!" And then, with a chill in his voice: "None of you ever had your holidays at Omarska, did you? No Olympic games in Prijedor!"

I find him again, in wintry Banja Luka, in 1996. Koljevic walks over to the window and stares down at the people trudging through the slush. This miserable place has achieved what it wanted; it has "won" its war: every Muslim gone, every mosque disappeared without a trace.

Koljevic, transfixed, loses his flow and begins to talk to himself: "Bones," he mutters. "Bones, we were digging up the bones." His eyes widen unpleasantly; he appears hypnotized, his imagination ambushed. "The bones of our dead from 1941. We dug them up to give them proper burial on Serbian land. . . . We found shoes. Children's shoes. How much more alive a shoe is than bones. . . ." (This was a macabre prologue to the war, in the late eighties: a Serbian cult of exhuming their World War II dead.) Then the professor suddenly comes to his senses. "Er . . . I'm just trying to illustrate the psychology." Finally, I feel, we are approaching an answer to the question: How did Omarska happen?

What the Serbs have done is to project their own obsessive and disastrous "racial memory" (Koljevic's term) onto their perceived enemies. The Serbs' inimitable cult of the victim demanded that they create victims. Their experience of concentration camps demanded that they create concentration camps. They lie and manipulate, but insist on a conspiracy of lies and manipulation against them. When they look into the mirror they see someone they must call their enemy, so as not to see themselves. When they look at history they must contort it, lest they see what they do. They must rewrite the history they defile.

And then there is the psychodrama of the restless dead, of Professor Koljevic's bones. The Serbs exhumed the bones of their own dead from World War II, only to bury their enemies in mass graves. Now they exhume those victims and move them away from the glare of the Hague investigations, meanwhile disinterring their own relatives for reburial on "Serbian" soil. The joke is that the only people enjoying freedom of movement under the Dayton plan [a peace treaty signed in Dayton, Ohio] are the dead.

Too Many Victims

Professor Koljevic is fascinated by victims and masters. "The basic problem with Muslims," he says, "is their problem with equality. Psychologically, historically, they are either masters or servants. Now they want to be masters again." It is a description not of the Muslims but of the Serbs. By way of farewell, the professor produces his current reading, Daniel Boorstin's *The Image*. He reads aloud from the foreword: "This book is about our art of self-deception. How we hide reality from ourselves." For the perpetrators of Bosnia's carnage, the reckoning is an opportunity to confront what they have done and exorcise it—much as the Germans did out of the ashes of the Third Reich. But, undefeated, the Serbs choose to "hide reality from themselves." They think they were right, and they can think it again.

Thousands of miles away in the spring of 1998, a book is published—Daniel Goldhagen's *Hitler's Willing Executioners*—positing the terrifying notion that it was a whole society that unleashed the Nazi Holocaust, not an elite that poisoned the minds of an otherwise innocent people. We had the same argument here, over and over again:

Can such a whirlwind of violence be dictated by an elite that dupes an otherwise kindly, boozy folk?

Here at the village of Omarska, in the shadow of the accursed mine, everyone knew and nobody objected. There are soldiers and pretty girls sipping coffee at the Wiski Bar where the main street meets the railway sidings that run into the mine. For four months, as they freebooted around the scrappy streets, these people were yards away from the screaming and the mutilation. They would have watched the "ethnic cleansing" convoys pass, out on the road to nowhere. I was part of such a convoy of 1,600 wretched Muslim deportees myself; we were herded over the mountains at gunpoint, through a terrifying gantlet of hatred and spitting, or else cold nonchalance, by the Serbs who beheld us from the roadside.

These people in Omarska's Wiski Bar, listening to Madonna on the jukebox, would have watched the trucks enter Camp Omarska full of people, only to come out empty. Perhaps they spat then, too. But now, in the frozen village, we are told, "There was no camp here—ever."

Meanwhile, the outside world, as Professor Koljevic rightly mocked, failed to uncover Omarska, "so near Venice." The media and the politicians cared for a few days once Omarska was forced into the spotlight, but then the world did as little as possible about it. A few bloody years later, NATO's commanding admiral, Leighton Smith, is breaking through Omarska, leading platoons of writers from glossy magazines and experts from the human rights industry in a search for buried bones. When there was everything to be done, we pretended to know nothing. Today, when there is so little left to do, we want to know everything. Such is the dark triumph of the middle managers of genocide.

INTERNATIONAL WAR CRIMES TRIALS ARE NECESSARY

Gary Jonathan Bass

In the following selection, Gary Jonathan Bass defends the importance of international war crimes trials and tribunals. Bass concedes the tribunals have not been altogether successful historically, noting that political interests often impede human interests, resulting in the failure to capture war criminals or even to conduct trials. However, despite the obstacles to trying war criminals, he asserts, the absolute necessity of such trials still exists. Not only do war crime trials offer the possibility of international justice, says Bass, but they also serve the important function of documenting the crimes for posterity. Ultimately, he concludes, the laborious and painful process of examining and trying crimes of war is the best method of deterring further atrocities. Bass is a writer for the *Economist* and a fellow at Harvard's Center for International Affairs in Cambridge, Massachusetts.

The international war crimes tribunal for ex-Yugoslavia, once written off even by some of its supporters as a well-intentioned but ineffectual experiment, has made remarkable strides in 1998. Since the summer of 1997, NATO has conducted three raids to arrest indicted war criminals in Bosnia; this has evidently scared some other suspects into turning themselves in. Four suspects, all Bosnian Serbs, have surrendered to the tribunal since mid-January. For years, the tribunal's 24-cell prison, mostly empty, was a symbol of the tribunal's powerlessness; on March 4, 1998, Dragoljub Kunarac became the twenty-fourth suspect in custody.

But the tribunal is still far from being an unqualified success. The most important accused war criminals—Radovan Karadzic, the wartime Bosnian Serb leader, and Ratko Mladic, his military chief—remain at large. Snaring the rest of the suspects on the tribunal's list is a major challenge for NATO, and many skeptics remain. The same people in Congress who never wanted to use military force to help Bosnia during the war don't want to use it to arrest war criminals; the Pentagon doesn't want to risk soldiers in raids or subsequent reprisals;

Reprinted by permission of *The New Republic* from "Due Process," by Gary Jonathan Bass, *The New Republic*, March 30, 1998. Copyright ©1998 by The New Republic, Inc.

and Bill Clinton recently suggested that if Karadzic is "deep enough underground, if he can't have any impact on it, we might make the peace process work anyway."

It is up to advocates like Secretary of State Madeleine Albright to make a persuasive case for international justice—and it is not, alas, a simple case to make. Men like Karadzic richly deserve criminal prosecution, and one would like to think doing the decent thing would automatically be good strategy, too. But an examination of a century's worth of international efforts at prosecuting war criminals suggests a muddier picture. In the end, war crimes trials are worthwhile, not because they represent an ideal solution, but because they are the least unappealing of several problematic alternatives for dealing with atrocities.

Too Much Time

One drawback to tribunals is that it takes time—and patience—for trials to bring reconciliation. Take the best-case scenario: post–World War II West Germany, the country with the best record of coming to grips with its criminal past. The spectacle of Nuremberg initially had an impressive impact, according to polls in the U.S.-occupied zone of Germany. But, as trials for lesser Nazis dragged on, many Germans turned against the proceedings. In 1949, Konrad Adenauer, West Germany's postwar chancellor, followed public opinion and asked the Allies for clemency for Nazi war criminals. It took time and patience to remake Germany. Things went worse in Japan, where the Allied international military tribunal at Tokyo—a sibling court to Nuremberg—is publicly scorned to this day, and where there's still a depressing amount of sympathy for those Japanese the Allies branded war criminals.

In Germany and Japan, at least, there was little chance for a destabilizing backlash against the war crimes tribunals, because both countries were firmly under Allied occupation. But resentment of foreign-imposed war crimes trials can be much more dangerous when there's less military commitment. The best examples come from the aftermath of World War I, when the Allies imposed war crimes trials in Germany and Ottoman Turkey. In 1920, the British Embassy in Berlin reported nervously that Allied demand for the trial of German war criminals, including men as popular as Paul von Hindenburg, "arouses passionate resentment amongst all classes," and it worried that such policies might topple the shaky German government. The Allies' efforts galvanized right-wing nationalists who were significantly more dangerous than the [royal family] Hohenzollerns' loyalists. Hermann Göring first encountered Hitler at one of the many rallies held across Germany to protest French demands that the Weimar government turn over accused German war criminals.

There was the same kind of backlash in the crumbling Ottoman Empire. By March 1919, a new Ottoman government eager to mollify the Allies had arrested a huge group of prominent wartime Ottoman leaders, including Said Halim Pasha, the grand vizier during the 1915 Armenian massacres. They went on trial in April 1919 before a special Turkish court martial. But the court's first death sentence brought mobs into the streets. Britain's efforts to punish war criminals became a rallying cry for Young Turk nationalists and for Atatürk's successful drive to expel the British from Turkey.

It's not so different today. Milorad Dodik, the relatively moderate prime minister of the Serb entity in Bosnia, known as Republika Srpska, faces roughly the same dilemma the Ottoman sultanate did. His uncertain grip on power is threatened by Karadzic, but also by any impression he's cooperating with Western efforts to arrest Karadzic. (One way to help Dodik: the West could make more of an effort to explain to Bosnian Serbs that, contrary to years of nationalist propaganda, the tribunal isn't an unfair anti-Serb court.)

Few Are Ever Punished

Another problem with tribunals is that justice is often symbolic: there's no chance of putting anything close to all of the guilty parties on trial. Daniel Jonah Goldhagen estimates that there were at least 100,000 perpetrators of the Holocaust, and perhaps as many as 500,000. But, according to Nuremberg prosecutor Telford Taylor, only about 3,500 Germans had been tried by 1948. Gérard Prunier, a Rwanda expert, estimates that there were between 80,000 and 100,000 murderers in the 1994 Rwanda genocide. But the U.N.'s Rwanda tribunal has indicted just 35 people (although among the 23 suspects in custody are some of the most important men in Rwanda's old Hutu-led regime). The ex-Yugoslavia tribunal has publicly indicted only 74 men. (There are an undisclosed number of secret indictments.) Of the 24 in custody, only a few, like Bosnian Croat leader Dario Kordic and his Gen. Tihomir Blaskic, are high-ranking.

Yet another worry: Although supporters of tribunals usually claim such courts deter war crimes, the war criminals are all too often unimpressed. In May 1915, for example, while Ottoman Turkey was massacring about a million Armenians, the Allies issued a direct threat to Constantinople: "The Allied governments announce publicly to the Sublime Porte that they will hold personally responsible [for] these crimes all members of the Ottoman government and those of their agents who are implicated in such massacres." Talaat Pasha, the Ottoman minister of the interior, and Enver Pasha, the minister of war, were unfazed. As Henry Morgenthau Sr., the American ambassador in Constantinople, reported back to Washington, the Ottomans "refused to modify even when Russia, France, and Great Britain threatened Ottoman Cabinet ministers with personal responsibility." Sometimes, it's the lower-level perpetrators who aren't deterred, even when their leaders are. In May 1945, Heinrich Himmler tried to ingratiate himself with the Allies by ordering an end to the "death marches" of Jews; his men continued their killings.

True, international pressure has occasionally yielded results in the Bosnian conflict. Peter Galbraith, until recently the American ambassador to Croatia, says that berating Mate Boban, a Bosnian Croat leader, made the Croats shut down some camps. Some senior American officials say the tribunal's indictment of Serb rebel leader Milan Martic for ordering rocket attacks on Zagreb helped deter similar attacks later on. But such successes pale next to the tribunal's failure to deter the single worst war crime in Europe since World War II. In July 1995, two years after the creation of the feeble ex-Yugoslavia tribunal in The Hague, Mladic's Bosnian Serb army slaughtered 7,000 Bosnian Muslim men and boys at Srebrenica. The tribunal sent new investigators and issued new indictments for Karadzic and Mladic, but the Bosnian Serbs simply defied the United Nations, the world community, and the tribunal. And, in March 1998, Serbian units carried out vicious reprisals against Albanian rebel supporters in Kosovo despite the example of recent trials in The Hague.

Necessary Measures

So why bother setting up tribunals? Because they still serve some vital functions. Although it may seem elementary, it's critically important to record what crimes actually happened. The Nuremberg court assembled a definitive record of Nazi criminality—a record that, even today, arms historians against would-be deniers. Conversely, the failure of the Constantinople trials has made it easier for successive Turkish regimes to deny the Armenian massacres. Lies like that pave the way to future violence. Such records are vital today, when Hutu *génocidaires* [killers] deny there was any unusual violence in Rwanda and when Karadzic claims that the Bosnian government faked several massacres.

Even if war crimes tribunals don't bring near-term reconciliation, they are still better than the usual alternative: vengeance. Near the end of World War II, the first American and British plan for dealing with top Nazi war criminals was simple: summary execution. In September 1944, the Treasury Department was considering shooting as many as 2,500 Germans. That was less than the 50,000 or 100,000 Stalin suggested killing, but it's likely even the Anglo-American plans would have gotten bloodily out of control. If many Germans came to resent the Allies' war crimes trials, they would have resented such executions even more. It was surely wiser to use judicial mechanisms, like Nuremberg, to restrain and focus Allied revenge.

Also, if the international community does not bring perpetrators to justice, vigilantes may just kill them instead. In 1919, the British high commissioner in Constantinople warned that, if the punishment of the Young Turks was ignored, "it may safely be predicted that the question of retribution for the deportations and massacres will be an element of venomous trouble in the life of each of the countries concerned." Sure enough, in 1921, Talaat Pasha, a mastermind of the Armenian massacres who had fled to Germany, was shot to death on a Berlin street by a revenge-minded Armenian. Said Halim Pasha, the former grand vizier, was gunned down in Rome the same year.

Continued Responsibility

Even without such dire scenarios, an impartial tribunal is a useful way of defusing the inevitable tensions when old victims and perpetrators run into one another. The feebleness of international efforts at justice so far has left a vacuum that's filled by even more disruptive local Balkan legal and quasi-legal processes. Croatian courts, for example, are full of extremely dubious cases against Serbs. Franjo Tudjman's regime issued a general amnesty for the Serbs who rebelled against Croatian control in the border region called the Krajina, but Croatia keeps its Serbs off balance by not letting them know who's safe and who's still suspected of war crimes that go beyond the amnesty. As of October 1997, the court in Zadar said it still had to look at approximately 10,000 cases against Serb rebels. Some of these trials prove provocative. In April 1997, a local Croatian court in Zadar tried Momcilo Perisic, the chief of staff of the Yugoslav National Army (JNA) and 18 other JNA officers in absentia, sentencing Perisic to 20 years in jail for ordering artillery attacks on Zadar in 1991. This, predictably, infuriated Serbia.

Understandably, considering the horrific losses suffered by Bosnians, the Muslim-Croat Federation in Bosnia has its own war crimes prosecutions, too, which can also inflame local tensions. The federation trials are almost all against low-level Bosnian Serbs who fought against the Bosnians. Some are basically fair, but, according to the Office of the High Representative's monitors who follow the Bosnian trials, there are a lot of flaws: excessively tough sentencing, judges who are still used to old Yugoslav jurisprudence, a lack of space for an effective defense, and an inability to get to witnesses from Republika Srpska. And sometimes the trials go blatantly awry: just consider the case of Sretko Damjanovic, a Bosnian Serb convicted in 1993 of killing a group of Muslims, two of whom turned up alive in 1996.

Some high-profile cases have sparked crises. On February 6, 1998, Bosnian intelligence agents in Sarajevo captured a Bosnian Serb soldier accused of shooting Bosnia's deputy prime minister in 1993; in a tense standoff, Serbs took Muslim hostages in reprisal. On January 30, 1996, Djordje Djukic, a Bosnian Serb army general and Mladic crony, blundered into Bosnian government custody. The Bosnian government held Djukic as a major war criminal. After a nerve-wracking standoff between NATO and the Bosnian Serbs, America had Djukic flown to The Hague, where the tribunal decided there was enough evidence to indict him. (In a bizarre twist, he soon died of cancer.)

Bosnian Serbs may scorn the tribunal, but they would have been even angrier to see Djukic in a Bosnian government court.

Do war crimes tribunals work? The only serious response is: Compared to what? War crimes tribunals have clear *potential* to work, and to work much better than anything else statesmen have come up with at the end of a war. A well-run legal process is superior, both practically and morally, to apathy or vengeance. True, the track record of international war crimes tribunals so far has often been underwhelming. Hamstrung for almost all of its existence by a lack of serious Western political support, The Hague tribunal has often looked like a failure, along the lines of Constantinople, rather than a heady success, along the lines of Nuremberg. But the lesson should be to do a better job from now on. If at first you don't succeed, try again.

MILITARY FORCE IS A MORE EFFECTIVE DETERRENT THAN INTERNATIONAL TRIALS

David Rieff

In July 1998, an International Criminal Court was created to serve as a permanent tribunal for war crimes, with the hopes that its existence will deter such crimes. According to David Rieff, however, the court will not be effective in reducing war crimes. Rieff points out that the court's jurisdiction is in fact very limited. Furthermore, he maintains, an international community within which all members can be expected to obey the laws simply does not exist. He argues that the prospect of facing criminal trial will do little to deter leaders of warring nations from violating the international laws of war. Ultimately, the application of force by more powerful nations is the most effective means of putting an end to war crimes, he concludes. Rieff is a frequent contributor to magazines and newspapers, including the *New Yorker, Esquire*, and the *London Sunday Independent*. He is the author of *Los Angeles: Capital of the Third World* and *The Exile: Cuba in the Heart of Miami*.

Among most of those who have been horrified by genocide in Rwanda, ethnic cleansing in Bosnia, and all the other crimes of war since the cold war, an ironclad consensus seems to have developed that an International Criminal Court (ICC) is the best, and perhaps only, hope for bringing the architects of such horrors to account. Thus, while the court that was actually created by the treaty signed in Rome on July 17, 1998—a court with sharply circumscribed powers—did not meet its proponents' highest expectations, the fact of its creation is being hailed as a great victory for humanity. Even before the treaty's formal signing, Aryeh Neier, president of the Soros Foundation and its Open Society Institute and one of the animating spirits behind the creation of the court, declared: "For the first time in human history, those committing war crimes, crimes against humanity, or the ultimate crime, genocide, [will] have to reckon seriously with the possi-

Reprinted with the permission of The Wylie Agency, Inc., from "Court of Dreams," by David Rieff, *The New Republic*, September 7, 1998. Copyright ©1998 by David Rieff.

bility that they [will] be brought before the international bar to face truth, be held accountable, and serve justice." Neier and distinguished organizations such as Human Rights Watch and Doctors Without Borders argue that the court, whatever its limitations (above all, that it will not have jurisdiction over war crimes committed in internal armed conflicts by states that have not signed the treaty), is an invaluable first step toward what *Le Monde* called "the prevention of conflicts through judicial dissuasion."

Given the impressive experience and undeniable goodwill of the court's advocates, critics need to proceed with great caution. Nonetheless, it is anything but clear that the current enthusiasm for the ICC is warranted. Indeed, it may very well be the wrong answer to the moral and political challenges posed by the world of genocide and ethnic cleansing in which we find ourselves. Far from ushering in a new era of certain punishment for war criminals, it may prove to be an exemplary case of good intentions gone awry and lead to less respect for international law rather than more.

The first set of objections is practical. As designed by the treaty-drafters in Rome, the court is probably too weak to bring wrongdoers to justice. Indeed, since most of the greatest crimes committed in contemporary wars go on during internal conflicts outside the purview of the Rome treaty, it is not clear what abuses the court will actually address. It would not have had jurisdiction over Saddam Hussein's war against the Kurds, Pol Pot's reign of terror in Cambodia, or the Rwandan genocide of 1994—much less the slow extermination of the animist peoples currently taking place in southern Sudan.

To the extent that such horrors can be prevented, they will be stopped by the use of force by outside powers, which, in practical terms, usually means the United States. This brings us to the second pragmatic objection: The court is just strong enough to impinge upon the sovereignty of individual states and thus will further inflame isolationist and, above all, anti-multilateralist feeling in the United States—both in the U.S. military and in the general public.

Proponents of the court wager that the long-term benefits (they would say necessity) of taking this first step far outweigh the meager practical results that can be expected from the court as it is now constituted. But, after Bosnia and Rwanda, it may well be that more such idealistic initiatives are exactly what we don't need—that, in fact, initiatives should be judged by the actions they are likely to engender in the here and now—not by the better world they may, in some indeterminate future, help to usher in. In the absence of a world government, or of a United Nations army, such strong action, of course, can only be undertaken by states. Utopianism can be a fine thing, but not if it is based on a misperception of the world as it actually exists. And that misperception seems to have bedazzled the decent people who have campaigned for the court.

Taking Lessons from History

The deeper argument that didn't quite take place before the Rome treaty was signed would have revolved around the relation of law and politics. Advocates of the court never really ask what law can honestly be expected to accomplish in what is still very much a lawless world, no matter how many nations have signed up for how many international covenants and conventions. People today rightly mock the 1928 Kellogg-Briand pact, which, among its other provisions, "outlawed" war. If the idea that the likes of Ratko Mladic will really be dissuaded by the existence of a court in The Hague is not equally preposterous, then surely the advocates of the court must meet the burden of proving that the world has changed in fundamental ways since 1928. The experience of the past 60 years should be enough to demonstrate that they can do no such thing. What was needed in the 1930s was not pacifism but a war against fascism. What will be needed to stop the next Bosnia or the next Rwanda will be force, not the prospect that, somewhere down the line, the criminals may find themselves indicted for war crimes. Imagining otherwise is like supposing that street thugs will decide not to commit a mugging or a rape because of the distant possibility they may go to jail.

There is something hubristic about the effort to graft a system of international law onto the tragedies of faraway peoples. I say faraway because, of course, none of the main nations backing the International Court, U.S. anxieties to the contrary notwithstanding, really imagines that its own citizens will ever stand in the dock. Would an international legal system have been the right response to the American Civil War, to use an obvious example, at least to those who believe Lincoln's war was a just one? And, if the answer is that Sherman's war crimes in Georgia (and that, by today's standards, is what they were) were of secondary importance to the need to break the will of the Confederacy, then why should the same defense not be available to the Rwandan Patriotic Front, which committed war crimes in a just war against its genocidal enemies?

It is as if the advocates of the court have all concluded that history is at an end, or at least that they can interrupt history's tragic march and replace it with international legal norms and the moral convictions of human rights activists, international lawyers, and humanitarian aid workers. Were there really such a thing as the international community, such assumptions might be warranted. But, as anyone who has been in a place like Rwanda—or watched how decisions are made at the U.N., NATO, or the European Union—knows, the international community does not exist. What exist, for better or worse, are tribes, peoples, nation states, and international alliances. It's rank wishful thinking to pretend otherwise.

Law proceeds out of civilizational change; it can never prefigure it. Nor can it be expected to do for the people of Rwanda, or Bosnia, or

Sudan what they cannot do for themselves. Some, of course, argue that, in places where ordinary people can do nothing to resist their oppressors, only some form of protectorate imposed by a supranational organization like the U.N. can help them. This may be so. Certainly, it is difficult to imagine a place like Cambodia recovering without some period of benign external rule. But so long as world government, or, for that matter, the more modest goal of U.N. protectorates in so-called failed states, is not in the offing, instituting an International Criminal Court amounts to trying to construct an international legal structure for an international political structure that does not yet exist.

The view of the civilizing process as a top-down one, imperial in nature, may be effective in certain contexts. But, in the case of a court with, literally, global reach, it is one that fundamentally evades the question of the court's legitimacy. The presumption is of a consensus that does not exist. (Even the judicial norms the court will use will have to be cobbled out of various legal systems whose assumptions are, in crucial ways, very different from one another.) But laws work when legal bodies are deemed legitimate by those over whom they have authority. If the civil rights movement was successful in the United States, this was in large measure because most American citizens, including those in the South, accepted that the decisions of American courts were binding, whatever their private feelings. And even then troops had to be sent to certain places to enforce the law.

An Unrealistic Proposal

Advocates of the court will argue that to oppose the court is to surrender to despair. Leaving aside the fact that there are times when it is right and proper to despair, the issue is not one of forswearing hope for a better world. It is one of not fostering false, illusory hope. To some extent, even the court's strongest proponents know this. Aryeh Neier in the preface to his book, *War Crimes*, concludes that "the heart says civilized men and women with respect for the rule of law cannot permit [crimes like those that occurred in Bosnia] to happen again. The mind, sadly, sends a different message." Knowing this, Neier still believes in the court. Others may wonder if, in doing so, he is not letting his heart get the better of his head—if he is not trying to do something, anything, rather than sit idly by and watch the next Radovan Karadzic, the next Interhamwe militia, start a murderous assault.

In reality, it is the court that is the counsel of despair. Its real rationale derives from the hope that, somehow, the law can rescue us from situations from which politics and statecraft have failed to deliver us. But the law can never do this, and this time will be no exception. With the best intentions in the world, we are creating one more institution that, like the United Nations itself, is sure to be unable to meet the high hopes that attended its creation and is bound to create, as the U.N. itself has done, not hope but disillusion.

A STRONGER UNITED NATIONS CAN PREVENT WAR CRIMES

Robert C. Johansen

In the following selection, Robert C. Johansen calls for changes in the United Nations that would effectively prevent genocide and other war crimes. The United Nations should establish not only an international criminal court, argues Johansen, but also a permanent body of trained volunteers who would investigate, police, and enforce international laws in a timely manner. These volunteers would especially work to prevent armed conflict, he states, thus reducing the possibility that war crimes would occur. He also suggests that the UN Security Council be revamped so that it fairly represents all the world's nations, not just the most powerful ones. These and other measures designed to strengthen the United Nations' ability to respond to armed conflicts would greatly decrease the incidence of war crimes and genocide, Johansen asserts. Johansen is a professor of government and international studies at the University of Notre Dame and director of graduate studies at the Kroc Institute for International Peace Studies in Notre Dame, Indiana.

Despite sharp disagreements among people in the United States, Europe and elsewhere over what went wrong in the former Yugoslavia and Rwanda, everyone agrees that when tragedies engulfed these lands the international community was sadly unprepared to halt "ethnic cleansing" and mass killings. Because these conclusions seem so familiar and unexceptional, we overlook their profound significance for the future of world peace, and for our own moral integrity.

It is too late to erase the disasters suffered by people in Yugoslavia and Rwanda; it is not too late to prevent future Rwandas and Yugoslavias. Communal conflict is smoldering from Sri Lanka to Chechnya, from Georgia to Mexico, from Sudan to the Philippines, from India to Burundi, and from Iraq and Turkey to Kosovo, Macedonia and Moldova. Unless we act now to discourage conditions that

Reprinted, with permission, from "Will We Do Nothing?" by Robert C. Johansen, *The Christian Century*, March 20–27, 1996. Copyright 1996 Christian Century Foundation.

will give rise to violent bigotry and genocidal slaughters, we cannot claim to be morally responsible.

Practical Measures Exist

Many people do nothing to prevent future genocides because they believe nothing can be done: they argue that the people of the Balkans can be expected to inflict cruelty on one another from time to time, as can Hutus and Tutsis, and that the international community can provide no antidote at an acceptable cost. These are false assumptions. It is not difficult to imagine practical measures that could be taken to prevent genocide. Five deficiencies, clearly identified in the Rwandan and Yugoslavian cases, come to mind:

- The United Nations does not have highly developed early warning and conflict prevention systems.
- The United Nations does not possess constabulary forces of sufficient size, appropriate training, preparedness and financial backing to discourage "ethnic cleansing" and genocidal killings.
- The Security Council has not been able to act decisively or with sufficient legitimacy and political support to prevent genocide.
- The world community lacks adequate international institutions for holding individuals accountable to the internationally established rules designed to prohibit genocide and crimes against the peace.
- The financial resources available for protecting succeeding generations from the scourges of genocide and war are grossly inadequate.

With these problems in mind, citizens and governments should cooperate with the UN secretary-general in developing a long-term plan to guide the UN Secretariat, the Security Council, the General Assembly and other relevant organs of the UN in addressing these deficiencies.

Prevention Is a Goal

The plan should include the creation of a UN Dispute Settlement Service that would provide the timely dispatch of trained and experienced UN fact-finders, conciliators and mediators when a conflict threatens to turn violent. When disputes prove to be intractable, these representatives would have the authority to recommend legally binding arbitration or advisory opinions from the International Court of Justice.

Preventing genocide or war almost always entails lower costs than paying for the consequences of violence. Because the UN could provide professional services in early stages of conflicts, its permanent dispute settlement machinery would have many advantages over ad hoc diplomatic initiatives.

The plan would entail the establishment of a permanent UN constabulary force of from 10,000 to 100,000 personnel, carefully selected and trained by the UN from among men and women of all nations who volunteer to aid in policing, peacekeeping and enforcement. A well-trained, highly motivated and sophisticated force cannot result from ad hoc arrangements such as those used in past peacekeeping forces. The UN was unwilling to send ad hoc forces to Rwanda in 1994, in part because no member wanted to place its forces immediately under UN command and send them into high-risk environments. UN members expressed similar reservations about sending their forces to protect Bosnian areas designated as "safe" by the Security Council. Because governments may not feel that their own national interests are sufficiently at stake to send their forces into high-risk operations, it is essential to have a permanent UN force that can respond quickly and skillfully.

Moreover, if a sufficient number of UN personnel are sent into a conflict early enough, they can often take actions more characteristic of police upholding order than of soldiers embarking on major military combat. During debate on Rwanda, a high-ranking UN official said that one brigade "deployed in Kigali within seven to 14 days might have stabilized the situation." These early, strong measures are essential in preventing a spiral toward genocide.

Equal Representation

With a moderate expansion of council membership and democratization of procedures, the Security Council could more fairly represent all peoples of the world and make decisions that would not be subject to veto by any one member. The council's legitimacy is dwindling because it does not fairly represent the world's people. It gives disproportionate weight to those who dominated diplomacy at the time the United Nations was founded at the end of World War II. The societies that were defeated in World War II and the regions that were underrepresented now deserve equitable representation. This could be achieved by giving permanent seats to Japan, Germany, India, Brazil, and South Africa or Nigeria.

In addition, no country should exercise a veto power that allows it to be judge in its own case. No nation can safely demilitarize its own society or rely on the council to act impartially in behalf of its security if some council members can immobilize the council when they, their allies or their friends are guilty of aggression. The veto should be gradually phased out.

Of course, the Permanent Five [England, France, Russia, the United States, and China] object strongly to qualifying the veto, even though their size and strength give them ample means with which to protect their interests. Yet because they will obstruct any plan to remove the veto altogether, the veto must be qualified in a more modest and palatable way.

Timely Investigations

Without any Charter revision, the council could decide that the proposed International Criminal Court should function automatically, without any further council votes, to investigate and prosecute alleged war crimes and crimes against humanity wherever convincing allegations arise. The council could also agree that the secretary-general could automatically send his emissaries and conflict resolution teams to any trouble spot in the world when he deems their services essential to prevent genocide. The secretary-general could even be empowered to deploy the proposed UN Peace Force whenever a straw vote showed that two-thirds of the council members, and four-fifths of the permanent members, favored sending the Peace Force to emergencies in which genocide threatens, but in a police rather than a military mode of operations. These cautious innovations would protect the legitimate interests of UN members large and small; they also would enable the UN to respond more quickly and effectively.

To enforce norms against genocide and aggression effectively and at a politically acceptable cost, the Security Council needs to move as quickly as possible toward holding individuals accountable to the law. Laws must be enforced on the individuals who commit misdeeds rather than on entire societies in which many people are innocent of any wrongdoing. Enforcement must be strictly impartial. Once established, a permanent International Criminal Court and a mechanism for prosecution would systematically gather information about alleged crimes, prepare indictments, issue international warrants for arrest and hold impartial trials under due-process procedures. The temporary nature of the existing ad hoc tribunals inevitably gives the impression that the law against genocide will be applied in some cases but not in others. The international community can no longer tolerate this practice. The proposed court should act automatically; it should not be required to wait for special authorization from the Security Council, as the United States now insists, or be subject to political decisions by the council.

The presence of a court and indictment procedure would help deter crimes against the peace, war crimes and crimes against humanity. To reinforce this deterrent, the Security Council should request that all members include in their military training a clear exposition of the precedents set in the Nuremberg and Tokyo war crimes tribunals, whose standards and purposes have been overwhelmingly endorsed by the UN membership. A government's refusal to do so should be considered a threat to international peace and grounds for Security Council sanctions against the delinquent government. These legal precedents stipulate that no commander or officer may use as a justifiable defense the claim that he or she was acting under orders from superiors while committing war crimes. In its November 1994 report the International Law Commission drew up draft articles that can serve as a basis for establishing the court.

Gathering Monetary Support

To make enforcement effective and to protect UN personnel, UN forces engaged in upholding the peace must have the right to arrest anyone committing aggression or violent acts, including violence against UN personnel themselves. The Security Council should also impose sanctions or take other action to dissuade any society from shielding or refusing to extradite persons for whom an international arrest warrant has been issued by the court.

No threatened people or government will take seriously the existing international prohibitions of genocide and aggression unless a Peace Force and International Criminal Court have sufficient financial backing to make them effective in action. Perhaps the most equitable and practical way to generate revenue is to charge an extremely modest fee of, say, five-hundredths of 1 percent (0.05 percent) on the world's international currency exchanges. Such a small levy would not overburden anyone. In addition to discouraging currency speculations that can cause economic havoc, such a fee is a fair strategy. It would generate over $150 billion per year which could be divided among these essential functions: peace operations (preventive diplomacy, monitoring, peacekeeping and enforcement), establishment and operation of an International Criminal Court, preventive development and peace-building activities to promote social integration and eliminate conditions giving rise to violence, and programs for environmental sustainability that would alleviate disputes over water, food and land that might erupt into violence. Other approaches to generating revenue should also be considered, including fees imposed on arms production and transfers or on commercial and military uses of the global commons.

Most of the world's people stand united in opposing genocide, yet they have felt powerless to prevent mass killings in Cambodia, the former Yugoslavia, Rwanda and elsewhere. By mandating a plan to stop genocide, officials in Washington and other capitals can respond to the people's just demand for an end to the killing. The scourge of genocide and aggression can be lifted if the UN members are prompted to act forcefully. Although some governments may feel that such a plan of action is too dramatic, nothing less can ensure that we will discharge our responsibility to protect innocent people against unjustifiable violence.

POWERFUL GOVERNMENTS SHOULD BE HELD ACCOUNTABLE FOR THEIR WAR CRIMES

Ramsey Clark

In the following excerpt from *The Fire This Time: U.S. War Crimes in the Gulf*, Ramsey Clark asserts that all too often, powerful nations and the victors in wars are never held accountable for the war crimes they commit. He contends that all nations—not only weak or defeated countries—should be punished for violating the laws of war. In particular, Clark charges that the U.S. government has repeatedly committed war crimes for which American leaders have flagrantly denied responsibility. While the U.S. government may support punishment of war crimes by other nations, it has thwarted attempts to bring American war criminals to justice, Clark maintains. He argues that all nations must willingly comply to international law if war crimes are to be prevented. Clark is a former U.S. Attorney General and the author of *Challenge to Genocide: Let Iraq Live*.

War is the most violent crime that humanity inflicts upon itself. Other conduct does not approach its horror. History leaves no doubt of this.

Law reaches its highest potential for good when it addresses crimes against peace and war crimes. The very names of the places associated with the major conventions addressing war and its conduct fill us with both hope and dread—The Hague, Geneva, Nuremberg. We know those statutes were written with the blood of millions who died in the wars from which these lessons were learned. The highest commitment of law to peace must be in their faithful, equal, and fair enforcement.

If society wants to prevent war, control and punish those who cause it, address its excesses, and avoid its consequences, then it must take action to enforce laws designed for such purposes. Until the most powerful military forces and their highest officers are held equally accountable with the powerless for crimes related to war, the rule of force will remain paramount. And the world will remain, as the Athenians said it was, a place where the powerful do as they will and the weak suffer as they must.

The Reign of Force

The concept of war crimes presents the choice between the rule of law and the reign of force. When principle is chosen, all are equally accountable. If we are to live in a world of principle, then we must apply those principles to all, including our own country.

In an interview during the Nuremberg trials, Hermann Goering, the highest-ranking Nazi defendant, said of war crimes trials, "The victors will always be the judges, the accused the vanquished." At Nuremberg, defendants shouted, "What about Dresden? What about Hiroshima?" Yet despite the universal principles of the Nuremberg Charter, and the assurance of the Chief Prosecutor for the United States, Robert H. Jackson, that it would apply to all including those sitting in judgment, the Nuremberg court accused only the vanquished and only the victors sat in judgment.

Tragically, the victors in World War II did not submit themselves to the rule of law, or even maintain the Nuremberg Tribunal they had created and under whose mandate enemy leaders were put to death. Had they done so, nuclear proliferation, the arms race, and military conflict which dominated life on the planet for the next generation might have been limited. Instead, immediately after the worst war ever, the victorious nations quickly began the Cold War, which caused an arms race, spawned armed conflicts around the world, was responsible for the deaths of millions, and resulted in the impoverishment of hundreds of millions by the displacement of people, destruction of property, consumption of wealth, and glorification of violence. This is the greatest crime against humanity yet committed.

Organized Societies Need Laws

Effective enforcement of international principles preventing and controlling war is as essential to peace and human survival as effective enforcement of domestic criminal codes is to the prevention and control of crime in neighborhoods where people live. For over 200 years, the people of the United States have acted on the assumption that the rule of law is essential to insure domestic tranquility. Indeed, all people living in politically organized societies have shared that assumption for several thousand years. Common experience has suggested to most that personal safety depends on the enforcement of principles designed to protect individuals from the violence, lust, greed, and cunning of others.

Nearly all who live in the United States believe their lives, their fortunes, and their sacred honor depend on the police department, the criminal courts, and the district attorney. Americans believe the rule of law and its effective enforcement is essential to their physical safety. They would be terrified at the prospect of a society without police, prisons, and criminal laws. A large part of popular dissatisfaction is with the assumed failure of these institutions to protect society.

Experience shows that international tranquility depends on the enforcement of an international rule of law. More than 700 years ago, Thomas Aquinas wrote, "War is inevitable among sovereign nations not governed by positive law," and the observation has been around for several millennia. War and lesser forms of international violence and coercion have been the dominant experience of nearly every generation in nearly every society on the planet throughout recorded history.

In this last generation, the technology of war and the expanding capacity for mass destruction have become so horrific that assured peace is no mere amenity, but necessary for moral, mental, economic, and physical survival. The need for international law and its enforcement is as urgent for the world community to prevent omnicide as local law and police are to a family whose home is surrounded by a mob bent on arson and murder.

Ignoring World Laws

Yet in the face of this inescapably dangerous environment, the public overwhelmingly yawns, shrugs, or blinks at the suggestion of world law as a means to peace. They have accepted nuclear arms as their protector. Lawyers themselves consider the subject of international law as too exotic, if not embarrassing, to contemplate. Powerful national governments proclaim it unpatriotic or treasonous.

Discussions about domestic law and order fill the electronic and print media, as well as daily conversations among friends, family, and casual acquaintances. Rarely is any notion of world law mentioned; and when it is, it is usually derided as the province of dreamers. The courts, our citadels of law, are worse. A U.S. court of appeals which addressed the argument that international law is part of the supreme law of the land in 1989 found it "fanciful," "idiosyncratic," "far-fetched." Most courts decline to consider the argument at all.

However, this attitude simply ignores the incontestable fact that international law is woven into the fabric of American law. Article VI of the U.S. Constitution includes international treaties in the supreme law of the land. Common law processes absorb customary international law into the domestic corpus juris [body of the law]. Yet the courts, legislatures, government executives, and lawyers relegate issues of war and peace that threaten all life to international anarchy.

Law in theory has always recognized and often glorified its role in the quest for peace. The Pax Romana [Roman peace] was said to be founded on Roman law. Hugo Grotius, in his great work on international law, *The Law of War and Peace* (*De Jure Belli ac Paces*), first published in 1625, wrote, "This care to preserve society, which we have here roughly outlined, and which is characteristic of human intelligence, is the source of all law which is properly so called." The very purpose of law is peace. A major international lawyers' association created during the early years of the Cold War calls itself World Peace Through Law. Literally hundreds of organizations seek to create systems of laws they believe will bring peace.

Acting Above the Law

Those who wield power naturally oppose international law because such law would impose limits on the use of power and require peaceful resolution of disputes. Power prefers to have its way. In reality, the media in the United States is an instrument of power: while the media may preach principles and occasionally even the rule of international law, it urges the exercise of power in practice. When international law challenges the privileges of power the media overwhelmingly derides the law and justifies force.

That the American people acquiesce in this rejection of international law exposes a failure of our democratic institutions. Surely a knowledgeable people guiding their own destiny through democratic processes based on principles of law would wrest power from such governance as a preliminary act toward self-preservation.

Unwilling to assert outright that there is no international public law binding the United States, federal courts often invoke the "political question" doctrine when confronted with international issues. This doctrine holds that courts are not competent to judge questions of war and peace. It finds that the political branches, the Congress and the President, are delegated authority by the Constitution over activity involving foreign relations. This is tantamount to declaring the absence of law in the crucial area of war and peace, or at least an absence of law that can be enforced against the political branches by the courts. Such a doctrine places the executive above the law when it acts in the foreign policy area, even if the result is the slaughter of hundreds of thousands, assassination of foreign leaders, invasion of foreign countries, or military raids without authority of domestic or international law, treaty, or declaration of war.

The position U.S. policy makers take is that Congress can alter, amend, repeal, or ignore any international law. This is a declaration of independence from the world community and a warning that the United States will not be bound by any international rule not to the liking of Congress. Little wonder then that few lawyers are willing to spend much time or thought on international law, since however important we say international law is, in action it is near impotent. It may be a helpful political argument, and it may even reinforce public opinion outraged by despicable acts. But it has little power to fulfill its promise against the will and force of the nations involved in a controversy.

Refusals to Abide by the Laws

While nations do abide by decisions of the International Court of Justice, which was established by the UN Charter, such obedience is largely a matter of choice, at least for the powerful nations. A prime example of this was the U.S. refusal to acknowledge the Court's jurisdiction when the Sandinista government of Nicaragua claimed damages for U.S. military aggression against it. The United States had battered Nicaragua with direct attacks, Contra warfare, and severe economic sanctions, and had spent close to $48 million to create an artificial unified opposition political party, stealing an election in utter contempt of democratic principles. A first act of the Chamorro government after its election in Nicaragua ousted the Sandinista government was dismissal of the suit against the United States. Its reward was the further debilitation of international law and democracy.

Another international court is the Inter-American Court for Human Rights at San Jose, Costa Rica. It has a history of inaction and little power to enforce any disputed decision. Its major weakness stems from the lack of participation of the United States, the region's preeminent power. One consequence of this is widespread human rights violations throughout the hemisphere. In contrast, the European Court at Strasbourg is a highly effective tribunal for the enforcement of international human rights principles within Europe. It has successfully ordered Germany, France, Italy, Spain, and the United Kingdom, among others, to stop violating human rights.

Few national courts have considered enforcing international principles concerning war and peace against their own governments. Until they do, national courts cannot restrain militarism. The history of litigation in the United States courts seeking enforcement of international public law principles against the government is spotty and ambiguous. While there are a few heroic court decisions over the years, the most recent growing out of the Korean War, U.S. legal history contains huge voids because claims are not asserted against the government in spite of terrible injuries inflicted by war crimes. The law is undeveloped, and few layers are willing to mount serious lawsuits in the face of the bleak prospects for success.

Facing Powerful Opponents

An illustration of the difficulties facing suits against the United States based largely on international law involves claims arising from the U.S. bombing of Libya in April 1986. I brought suit in federal district court in Washington, D.C. for hundreds of civilians injured by this attack and the families of those killed. The suit alleged that the bombing was an attempt to assassinate a foreign leader and randomly kill civilians to terrorize the people into overthrowing their government. The claims were based upon international law, U.S. constitutional and statutory law, the laws of armed conflict, and U.S. criminal law.

Motions to dismiss on behalf of the United States, the United Kingdom, Margaret Thatcher, and the chain of command from President Ronald Reagan to the pilots of the assaulting aircraft were filed. The court accepted the allegations of the complaint as true, thus conceding the attempts to assassinate Colonel Qaddafi and to kill civilians. Yet it dismissed the claims—being later affirmed by the court of appeals—on the basis of sovereign immunity, ignoring all arguments based on international law. The court added, "the case offered no hope whatsoever of success, and plaintiff's attorneys surely knew it." The United States and the United Kingdom both sought monetary sanctions against my law office for daring to bring the action. The court called the action "not so much frivolous as audacious," and refused to punish counsel. The court of appeals reversed without opinion on the merits and ordered sanctions. The sanctions issue remains in the courts. The chilling effects on future claims will further diminish the role of law in war.

Meanwhile, the United States demanded and Iraq paid $36 million in damages to families of U.S. servicemen killed and injured when the U.S.S. *Stark* was torpedoed by an Iraqi jet in the Persian Gulf during the Iran-Iraq War. The United States paid nothing in reparations to the families of people killed in its invasions of Grenada and Panama, or to the 270 families of persons killed on an Iranian commercial airliner shot down by the U.S. while on a scheduled flight from Shiraz to Bahrain in 1987. Power prevailed, and as a result, in the very field of most urgent need and greatest importance, positive international law seems largely dormant, if not dead, at the hands of military supremacy.

No Accountability

International law, as practiced by American foreign policy makers, is not a coherent set of principles and procedures. Instead, it is what these policy makers will accept—principles that are thoroughly politicized, then savaged by discretionary actions. Enforceability of international rules against the United States is not even contemplated by its foreign policy establishment, or presently imaginable to its courts. The position of the U.S. government reflects the determination of power not to be accountable. Therefore, true international law, applied equally to the entire world community as it must be, offers slender hope for the establishment of a peaceful world order.

And for those who believe that law is what the courts say it is, the problem with international public law is clear. For most questions, there is no court to say what the law is. The International Court of Justice can decide only a narrow range of cases between nations. Individuals and organizations have no standing. Few cases are brought and the issues are rarely of great importance. There is no substantial body of international case law creating patterns of principles to guide conduct and future decision making. And no court has the power to enforce its order.

With an imperial President uncontrolled by domestic law or public opinion and free to interpret international law as he chooses, there is little limitation on his arbitrary decision to go to war, or the arbitrary use of military force to destroy an enemy.

Few presidential acts in American history have been as dangerous, unreasoning, or arbitrary as President George Bush's decision to send troops to the Persian Gulf. In August 1990 he abandoned all pretense of constitutional authority, made no gesture to obtain approval of the Congress, offered no explanation of the source of his power to unilaterally commit American military forces to foreign territory half a world away. A military dictator could not have been less restrained.

Acting Against Standard Procedures

The question of constitutionality, of law and democratic institutions, does not seem to arise when the President wants war. President Bush did not even deem it necessary to invoke the usual and usually false justification that military action was necessary to protect American citizens. The depth of the administration's commitment to that canard is revealed by its failure to take steps to protect the several thousand Americans in Iraq and Kuwait before acts were committed that might—and did—put them in jeopardy.

The Constitution delegated war powers to the Congress. Its authors were aware of the consequences to the lives of citizens who lived under a monarch capable of committing a country to war at his will. Despite the clarity of the Constitution and the known importance of placing such crucial power in the legislative branch, President Bush claimed power to act alone without congressional or UN authority. He restated his views as late as January 9, 1991, a week before the bombing began.

The fig leaf of UN approval was a fraud. The Security Council resolutions were secured by what would constitute criminal bribes, coercion, and extortion in any system of government desiring integrity in voting. The delegation of authority to unnamed nations to use any means necessary is as lawless as legislation can be. It was no ordinary discretion that was delegated by the Security Council. It was undefined, unlimited, and unsupervised. The United States misused that mandate to kill civilians, cripple Iraq, and destroy most of Iraq's military power. Yet not a word of the resolution authorized any attack on Iraq itself.

Even if the President had been empowered under the Constitution and authorized by the UN to attack Iraq, there can be no claim that war crimes were, or could have been, authorized by the Congress or the UN. Nor can there be any doubt that specific and binding international laws applied directly to military acts committed under the orders of President Bush. As the Supreme Court noted in a famous case protecting Confederate property from superior Union force after the Civil War, "No man in this country is so high that he is above the law."

That President Bush thought he was above the law was revealed in many ways. A sad illustration was when the press reported Pentagon sources saying Bush had ordered General Colin Powell to target Saddam Hussein for assassination shortly after August 2, 1990. We now know that an attempt to carry out this order was made by dropping "super bombs" on a command shelter in February 1991, and we may never know what other efforts were made. Of course, the assassination of a foreign head of state, even in time of war, is prohibited by laws. Article 23 of the Hague Regulations, the Convention on the Prevention and Punishment of Crimes Against Internationally Protected Persons, and even U.S. Presidential Executive Order 12333 prohibit assassinations. . . .

Leaders Commit Grave Crimes

War inherently knows no principle. Still, societies have struggled for generations to place limits on how commanders conduct war. In the destruction of Iraq, the U.S. military placed no limits on bombing civilians or soldiers. Its purpose was the destruction of the Iraqi military and crippling of the economy of the whole society. Its means were the measured death and destruction of civilians and their life-support systems.

The slaughter of Iraqi civilians and soldiers was a continuing war crime from the first bomb on the morning of January 17 through the last destructive assault on a retreating army division 48 hours after the ceasefire on March 3. The crimes took the lives of tens of thousands of defenseless people by direct violence and more than that number by the foreseeable consequences of destroying facilities essential to human life and the embargo on the importation of necessary food, medicines, and parts and equipment for restoration of facilities and health delivery systems.

Even greater than war crimes are crimes against peace, for if there are no crimes against peace, there is no war. U.S. crimes against peace began no later than 1989, with the planning of the assault on Iraq, and continued until the bombing began in January 1991. The United States planned to destroy Iraq and worked to avoid any negotiation that would prevent its purpose.

For such acts there must be accountability if the world is to know justice and peace.

DIFFICULT QUESTIONS ABOUT APPROPRIATE PUNISHMENT

David Fromkin

In the following piece, David Fromkin poses many questions about the proper or effective means of addressing war crimes and punishing perpetrators. Fromkin posits that the Nuremberg trials provide a poor example of handling war crimes trials because the clear distinction made between "evil" Nazi leaders and "good" accusers has not been possible since World War II. For example, he writes, it is virtually impossible to decide who should be tried for the atrocities in Cambodia because many people claim to have committed these crimes in fear for their own lives. Another consideration, according to Fromkin, is whether war crimes trials are worth the destabilizing effect they might have on nations just beginning to recover from war or civil unrest. Fromkin is the author of several books, including The Way of the World: From the Dawn of Civilizations to the Eve of the Twenty-First Century.

Should murderers be punished? Yes, if the crime is private, but no if it is in the public service: such is the contradictory and morally unsatisfying answer society has always given. Soldiers in wartime, like the fictitious James Bond and his fellow double-o's, are licensed to kill the enemy. In the performance of their duties, the police enjoy similar, though more circumscribed, rights.

The laws of war, spelled out in the relevant Hague and Geneva Conventions, impose limits and restrictions. So do the constitutions and statutes of countries, which also impose penalties. But these are ineffective in restraining or punishing a murderous government. Individuals in government are legally shielded in their official performance, while governments themselves cannot be sued without their consent. Is nobody to be held responsible for a country's crimes? Do governments have a permit?

What Does History Prove?

In this century of mass murders, a body of opinion has come into being that will not accept the validity of licenses to kill—not, at least,

Reprinted, with permission, from "Egregious Crimes, Elusive Punishment," by David Fromkin, *The New York Times*, Op-Ed section, January 25, 1999. Copyright ©1999 by The New York Times.

in all cases. When human rights violations are exceptionally vicious—when crimes against humanity, however defined, are committed, when there is aggression or massacre or genocide—we question the immunity both of the individuals who gave the orders and of those who carried out the orders.

The judgments at Nuremberg were a landmark in this respect. However, they also gave rise to concerns that are still with us. The Nazi war criminals who were on trial there were guilty. Yet Soviet representatives were among those sitting in judgment, and Joseph Stalin was guilty of many of the same deeds as Hitler and on the same scale. Soviet leaders were among the punishers when they should have been among the punished.

A trial in which the accusers, the prosecutors and the judges were on one side, the accused on the other, was inherently flawed: thou shalt not judge in thine own cause. Only if the vanquished could have convicted the victors as well would the Nuremberg proceedings have expressed our sense of due process.

So as a precedent Nuremberg is dangerous; as a practical proposition, it stands for the rule that after a war the leaders of the losing side will be taken out and executed. And the defeated who are thus condemned may be innocent and indeed virtuous. It should be remembered that in this imperfect world it is not always the children of light who win wars, or the children of darkness who lose them.

Nuremberg should be regarded as sui generis [altogether unique]. The Nazi leaders were evil in a way and on a scale unique to the human race. It was right that in this one case we should have disregarded restraints and punished them as national leaders had never been punished before. Nuremberg provided us with an exception. It should not provide us with a rule.

Who Can Be Tried?
Ever since Nuremberg, all around the world questions have arisen, and continue to arise, as to the morals of how to deal judicially with mass wickedness. And these complex questions yield unsatisfactory answers. It is not at all clear what we should think, for example, of war crimes trials in the former Yugoslavia. If atrocities were committed by 100,000 people (to pick a figure at random), and if in the end 100 (let us suppose) are brought to trial and imprisoned, is it a step forward—because a few of the guilty were brought to justice? Or is it a fiasco, because almost all of the guilty go free? And is it right or wrong to punish one person who is guilty if you can't punish everybody who is guilty?

The current debate in Cambodia raises other issues. The Khmer Rouge leaders who ruled the country in the 1970's were responsible for the deaths of more than a million people. Speculation continues as to whether the surviving leaders will be put on trial for mass murder. But what about the Khmer Rouge functionaries accused of having been members of the killing squads but who claim to have acted in fear for their own lives? Are they guilty nonetheless? And if tens of thousands of these people are guilty, how, as a practical matter, can so large a number be tried and punished?

In Cambodia, at least, there are no distracting questions of jurisdiction, of the competent court and the applicable law. The crimes were committed in Cambodia by Cambodians against Cambodians; the Cambodian Government and courts have the right to deal with them as they see fit.

For the Living or the Dead?

Questions of jurisdiction, however, continue to vex proceedings taking place on the other side of Eurasia, in the British House of Lords, where the question of the responsibility of Augusto Pinochet for the actions of his regime in Chile is entangled in prior questions of sovereign immunity and of the forum in which the case should be tried.

But one issue that runs through both the Chilean and Cambodian situations is moral and political rather than moral and judicial. It was raised by reports from Chile that, if accounts with Mr. Pinochet were settled abroad, the delicate political balance within the country would be upset. Terrible things were done in the Pinochet years. This is a reason for punishing him according to some, but for leaving him alone according to others, who fear a return to the dark days if the ex-dictator is harmed.

The editor of a Cambodian newspaper recently wrote an article on the Khmer Rouge that made a similar argument. To safeguard the living, he wrote, "It is better not to find justice for the dead." One might well counter that justice is something that is owed not only to the dead, but to the living.

Whether or not one agrees with the Cambodian editor, he is surely right to remind us of two important things: that in dealing with the Khmer Rouge, his country is faced with questions not only of law and morals but also of politics; and that the welfare of the Cambodian people might take priority over other considerations.

So, should murderers be punished? Surprisingly, the answer is much less clear and unequivocal than one might think.

THE EVIL THAT PERPETUATES WAR CRIMES SHOULD BE STUDIED

Paul Shore

Paul Shore is an assistant professor in education and American studies at Saint Louis University in Missouri. According to Shore, history has provided a multitude of instances of evil displayed through war crimes. People typically try to distance themselves from such atrocities, Shore ventures, by placing the blame on a few highly visible leaders and by objectifying war criminals as subhuman monsters. In truth, he says, evil is not limited to a few monstrous individuals; the potential for evil exists in every human being. Instead of avoiding or ignoring the existence of evil, Shore argues that addressing it directly, studying its appearance, and examining its occurrence are effective ways to combat and prevent the further spread of atrocities.

There are many troubling lessons to be learned from the continuing horror in Bosnia, some more obvious than others. The more easily grasped lessons have to do with the inability of the world community, despite its revulsion at the unending cycle of atrocity and reprisal, to stop the violence. Beyond this sad truth lie other disturbing realities concerning the motivations of those engaged in "ethnic cleansing" and other acts of savagery.

The most pertinent for Americans is the absence of a single individual or group of individuals who can definitively be blamed for the violence. This is hard for us to accept, since for over a century our government and media have encouraged the demonization of highly visible leaders to explain and simplify complex circumstances resulting in violence. King George III, rather than the British parliament, was blamed for the estrangement that led to the American Revolution. Before the Spanish-American War, it was "Butcher Weyler" whom we learned to hate in Cuba. In World War I, "Kaiser Bill" was the object of our enmity. And in World War II, Adolf Hitler, Benito Mussolini, and Hideki Tojo were the personifications of our enemies. More recently, a demonic Saddam Hussein has been cast in the role of the evil leader responsible for the wrongs we were to right.

Reprinted, with permission, from "The Time Has Come to Study the Face of Evil," by Paul Shore, *The Humanist*, November/December 1995.

Reaching Past the Surface

Whatever the pluses and minuses of this approach in the past, it won't work in the case of Bosnia. The politicians and generals who nominally lead the various warring groups are no saints, but they are not solely to blame for what has happened. Something far deeper than a *generalissimo's* bluster has driven both Croats and Serbs to murder children, the elderly, and the mentally handicapped. Historical enmity and differences of religion, ethnic affiliation, and language are contributing factors but do not always provide a completely adequate explanation.

Nor is it simply that those committing the atrocities lack proper education or have not been adequately informed about the rules of civilized behavior as set forth by the United Nations and other bodies. They know better but choose to do otherwise. This is another bitter pill for Americans to swallow, since it goes against our notions both that human beings can improve and that education promotes this improvement. Like many others who have committed atrocities, the killers in Bosnia cannot be objectified as subhuman monsters. In fact, the killers come from rich and highly developed cultural traditions where literacy is the norm and education is valued.

Let us be honest and say that the criminals of Bihac, Srbrnica, and a hundred other nameless places are what they are: men who have chosen to do evil. By evil, I mean not simply the Aristotelian notion of the absence of good, or the lack of knowledge as to what the good might be. Instead let us call evil an active, dynamic capacity for harming others gratuitously, which understands consequences and recognizes but ignores the disapproval of others. The word *evil* is certainly politically incorrect, with its biblical overtones and judgmental quality. Yet no other word or concept will do. Evil exists, and the time has come to talk about it frankly.

Unpleasant Truths

The problem of human evil should not be left just to the theologians and the criminologists to debate. We are aware of and justly celebrate the human capacity to do good, but we must at the same time be willing to examine the human capacity to deliberately do wrong. Atrocities—whether they claim Chinese students, Hutu villagers, or old Bosnian women trying to flee into the woods—should be labeled for the unspeakable evil which they are and, most importantly, should be made the subject of deliberate study in schools. As important as the currently expanding study of such events as the Holocaust is, it is not enough to examine isolated instances of evil. The potential for human beings to commit terrible crimes against one another should itself be the focus of study—for evil is a universal and complex phenomenon, knowing no political, cultural, or religious boundaries.

This points to another uncomfortable truth about the Bosnian catastrophe. Because they are happening in Europe, these atrocities are most often compared to the crimes of Nazi Germany. Such a comparison is understandable and valid but allows Americans some distance and potential moral superiority toward the horrors taking place. Isn't there something disturbingly familiar about the litany of villages destroyed, promises to keep the peace broken, noncombatants massacred, and refugees forced to flee in long caravans? If you can't seem to make a connection closer to home, talk to a Cherokee, a Lakota Sioux, or a Nez Perce. In a time not so long ago, Americans too exhibited the same face of evil which now shows itself on the evening news from Bosnia. Again, our schools' exploration of the genocide practiced on Native Americans understandably tends to focus on the specifics of particular historical occurrences. If we are ever to grasp the true significance of these events, however, we must be prepared to recognize the commonalities between distant and very recent exhibitions of evil—even if it means acknowledging some unpleasant truths about our own heritage.

Examining Real Evil

Some will object that many events in history cannot be labeled *good* or *evil*, that many apparent misdeeds are filled with moral ambiguity, that honest mistakes and misjudged motives have contributed to much of the world's suffering. True enough, but this does not reduce the reality of those unambiguously evil acts associated with the names Auschwitz, Babi Yar, Sand Creek, Bataan, My Lai, and many others. Refusing to call a spade a spade also prolongs the denial of crimes committed, as is evidenced by the waffling of the Japanese government regarding that country's conduct during World War II.

In fact, a study of those cases where controversy continues concerning the moral quality of the act committed (such as the United States dropping atomic bombs on Japan) can and should include discussion of the human potential for evil. Examinations of the moral quality of these controversial acts should not be limited to the typical classroom question "What would you have done?" but must expand to include the possibility of motives difficult for most of us to grasp who are not spectacularly evil on a day-to-day basis. What are the common features of various expressions of evil? How far can hatred blind an individual? Is the hundredth murder easier than the first? How do people come to enjoy committing atrocities? Where does individual and collective responsibility lie for crimes against the innocent? What, if anything, can be done to prevent these actions?

Evil studies—the phrase has a distasteful ring to it. But human evil undoubtedly exists, and it is high time to investigate the problem for what it is: something which the advance of technology, science, and even formal schooling has done nothing to curb. Perhaps with greater understanding of its origins and limits, our children will have better luck than we have had.

Appendix

The Nuremberg Principles

As a result of the post–World War II trials of Nazi leaders, the International Law Commission formulated the Nuremberg Principles, establishing guidelines for wartime conduct to be honored by all nations. Although other laws of war have since been established, the Nuremberg Principles are still regarded as highly significant for their historic and humanitarian value.

Principles of International Law Recognized in the
Charter of the Nuremberg Tribunal and in the
Judgment of the Tribunal
As formulated by the International Law Commission, June–July 1950.

Principle I

Any person who commits an act which constitutes a crime under international law is responsible therefor and liable to punishment.

Principle II

The fact that internal law does not impose a penalty for an act which constitutes a crime under international law does not relieve the person who committed the act from responsibility under international law.

Principle III

The fact that a person who committed an act which constitutes a crime under international law acted as Head of State or responsible government official does not relieve him from responsibility under international law.

Principle IV

The fact that a person acted pursuant to order of his Government or of a superior does not relieve him from responsibility under international law, provided a moral choice was in fact possible to him.

Principle V

Any person charged with a crime under international law has the right to a fair trial on the facts and law.

Principle VI

The crimes hereinafter set out are punishable as crimes under international law:

a. Crimes against peace:

(i) Planning, preparation, initiation or waging of a war of aggression or a war in violation of international treaties, agreements or assurances;

(ii) Participation in a common plan or conspiracy for the accomplishment of any of the acts mentioned under (i).

b. War crimes:

Violations of the laws or customs of war which include, but are not limited to, murder, ill-treatment or deportation to slave-labour or for any other purpose of civilian population of or in occupied territory, murder or ill-treatment of prisoners of war or persons on the seas, killing of hostages, plunder of public or private property, wanton destruction of cities, towns, or villages, or devastation not justified by military necessity.

c. Crimes against humanity:

Murder, extermination, enslavement, deportation and other inhuman acts done against any civilian population, or persecutions on political, racial or religious grounds, when such acts are done or such persecutions are carried on in execution of or in connexion with any crime against peace or any war crime.

Principle VII

Complicity in the commission of a crime against peace, a war crime, or a crime against humanity as set forth in Principle VI is a crime under international law.

International Law Commission, *The Nuremberg Principles*, 1946.

The Geneva Convention

The Geneva Convention consists of four international treaties that established rules for the treatment of prisoners of war and civilians. The treaties were first formulated at an international convention held in Geneva, Switzerland, in 1864, and have been amended and expanded several times since then. The following excerpt is taken from the first and second chapters of Geneva Convention I, concerning the treatment of the sick and the wounded.

Convention (I) for the Amelioration of the Condition of the Wounded and Sick in Armed Forces in the Field

Signed at Geneva, 12 August 1949.

Entry into Force: 21 October 1950.

Draft Agreement Relating to Hospital Zones and Localities

The undersigned Plenipotentiaries of the Governments represented at the Diplomatic Conference held at Geneva from 21 April to 12 August 1949, for the purpose of revising the Geneva Convention for the Relief of the Wounded and Sick in Armies in the Field of 27 July 1929, have agreed as follows:

Chapter I

General Provisions

Article 1. The High Contracting Parties undertake to respect and to ensure respect for the present Convention in all circumstances.

Art. 2. In addition to the provisions which shall be implemented in peacetime, the present Convention shall apply to all cases of declared war or of any other armed conflict which may arise between two or more of the High Contracting Parties, even if the state of war is not recognized by one of them.

The Convention shall also apply to all cases of partial or total occupation of the territory of a High Contracting Party, even if the said occupation meets with no armed resistance.

Although one of the Powers in conflict may not be a party to the present Convention, the Powers who are parties thereto shall remain bound by it in their mutual relations. They shall furthermore be bound by the Convention in relation to the said Power, if the latter accepts and applies the provisions thereof.

Art. 3. In the case of armed conflict not of an international character occurring in the territory of one of the High Contracting Parties, each Party to the conflict shall be bound to apply, as a minimum, the following provisions:

(1) Persons taking no active part in the hostilities, including members of armed forces who have laid down their arms and those placed hors de combat by sickness, wounds, detention, or any other cause, shall in all circumstances be treated humanely, without any adverse distinction founded on race, colour, religion or faith, sex, birth or wealth, or any other similar criteria. To this end, the following acts are and shall remain prohibited at any time and in any place whatsoever with respect to the above-mentioned persons:

(a) violence to life and person, in particular murder of all kinds, mutilation, cruel treatment and torture;

(b) taking of hostages;

(c) outrages upon personal dignity, in particular humiliating and degrading treatment;

(d) the passing of sentences and the carrying out of executions without previous judgment pronounced by a regularly constituted court, affording all the judicial guarantees which are recognized as indispensable by civilized peoples.

(2) The wounded and sick shall be collected and cared for.

An impartial humanitarian body, such as the International Committee of the Red Cross, may offer its services to the Parties to the conflict.

The Parties to the conflict should further endeavour to bring into force, by means of special agreements, all or part of the other provisions of the present Convention.

The application of the preceding provisions shall not affect the legal status of the Parties to the conflict.

Art. 4. Neutral Powers shall apply by analogy the provisions of the present Convention to the wounded and sick, and to members of the medical personnel and to chaplains of the armed forces of the Parties to the conflict, received or interned in their territory, as well as to dead persons found.

Art. 5. For the protected persons who have fallen into the hands of the enemy, the present Convention shall apply until their final repatriation. . . .

Art. 8. The present Convention shall be applied with the cooperation and under the scrutiny of the Protecting Powers whose duty it is to safeguard the interests of the Parties to the conflict. For this purpose, the Protecting Powers may appoint, apart from their diplomatic or consular staff, delegates from amongst their own nationals or the nationals of other neutral Powers. The said delegates shall be subject to the approval of the Power with which they are to carry out their duties.

The Parties to the conflict shall facilitate to the greatest extent possible, the task of the representatives or delegates of the Protecting Powers.

The representatives or delegates of the Protecting Powers shall not in any case exceed their mission under the present Convention. They shall, in particular, take account of the imperative necessities of security of the State wherein they carry out their duties. Their activities shall only be restricted as an exceptional and temporary measure when this is rendered necessary by imperative military necessities.

Art. 9. The provisions of the present Convention constitute no obstacle to the humanitarian activities which the International Committee of the Red Cross or any other impartial humanitarian organization may, subject to the consent of the Parties to the conflict concerned, undertake for the protection of wounded and sick, medical personnel and chaplains, and for their relief.

Art. 10. The High Contracting Parties may at any time agree to entrust to an organization which offers all guarantees of impartiality and efficacy the duties incumbent on the Protecting Powers by virtue of the present Convention.

When wounded and sick, or medical personnel and chaplains do not benefit or cease to benefit, no matter for what reason, by the activities of a Protecting Power or of an organization provided for in the first paragraph above, the Detaining Power shall request a neutral State, or such an organization, to undertake the functions performed under the present Convention by a Protecting Power designated by the Parties to a conflict.

If protection cannot be arranged accordingly, the Detaining Power shall request or shall accept, subject to the provisions of this Article, the offer of the services of a humanitarian organization, such as the International Committee of the Red Cross, to assume the humanitarian functions performed by Protecting Powers under the present Convention.

Any neutral Power, or any organization invited by the Power concerned or offering itself for these purposes, shall be required to act with a sense of responsibility towards the Party to the conflict on which persons protected by the present Convention depend, and shall be required to furnish sufficient assurances that it is in a position to undertake the appropriate functions and to discharge them impartially.

No derogation from the preceding provisions shall be made by special agreements between Powers one of which is restricted, even temporarily, in its freedom to negotiate with the other Power or its allies by reason of military events, more particularly where the whole, or a substantial part, of the territory of the said Power is occupied.

Whenever, in the present Convention, mention is made of a Protecting Power, such mention also applies to substitute organizations in the sense of the present Article.

Art. 11. In cases where they deem it advisable in the interest of protected persons, particularly in cases of disagreement between the Parties to the conflict as to the application or interpretation of the provisions of the present Convention, the Protecting Powers shall lend their good offices with a view to settling the disagreement.

For this purpose, each of the Protecting Powers may, either at the invitation of one Party or on its own initiative, propose to the Parties to the conflict a meeting of their representatives, in particular of the authorities responsible for the wounded and sick, members of medical personnel and chaplains, possibly on neutral territory suitably chosen. The Parties to the conflict shall be bound to give effect to the proposals made to them for this purpose. The Protecting Powers may, if necessary, propose for approval by the Parties to the conflict, a person belonging to a neutral Power or delegated by the International Committee of the Red Cross, who shall be invited to take part in such a meeting.

Chapter II

Wounded and Sick

Art. 12. Members of the armed forces and other persons mentioned in the following Article, who are wounded or sick, shall be respected and protected in all circumstances.

They shall be treated humanely and cared for by the Party to the conflict in whose power they may be, without any adverse distinction founded on sex, race, nationality, religion, political opinions, or any other similar criteria. Any attempts upon their lives, or violence to their persons, shall be strictly prohibited; in particular, they shall not be murdered or exterminated, subjected to torture or to biological experiments; they shall not wilfully be left without medical assistance and care, nor shall conditions exposing them to contagion or infection be created.

Only urgent medical reasons will authorize priority in the order of treatment to be administered.

Women shall be treated with all consideration due to their sex. The Party to the conflict which is compelled to abandon wounded or sick to the enemy shall, as far as military considerations permit, leave with them a part of its medical personnel and material to assist in their care.

Art. 13. The present Convention shall apply to the wounded and sick belonging to the following categories:

(1) Members of the armed forces of a Party to the conflict, as well as members of militias or volunteer corps forming part of such armed forces. (2) Members of other militias and members of other volunteer corps, including those of organized resistance movements, belonging to a Party to the conflict and operating in or outside their own territory, even if this territory is occupied, provided that such militias or volunteer corps, including such organized resistance movements, fulfill the following conditions: (a) that of being commanded by a person responsible for his subordinates; (b) that of having a fixed distinctive sign recognizable at a distance; (c) that of carrying arms openly; (d) that of conducting their operations in accordance with the laws and customs of war. (3) Members of regular armed forces who profess allegiance to a Government or an authority not recognized by the Detaining Power. (4) Persons who accompany the armed forces without actually being members thereof, such as civil members of military aircraft crews, war correspondents, supply contractors, members of labour units or of services responsible for the welfare of the armed forces, provided that they have received authorization from the armed forces which they accompany. (5) Members of crews, including masters, pilots and apprentices, of the merchant marine and the crews of civil aircraft of the Parties to the conflict, who do not benefit by more favourable treatment under any other provisions in international law. (6) Inhabitants of a non-occupied territory, who on the approach of the enemy, spontaneously take up arms to resist the invading forces, without having had time to form themselves into regular armed units, provided they

carry arms openly and respect the laws and customs of war.

Art. 14. Subject to the provisions of Article 12, the wounded and sick of a belligerent who fall into enemy hands shall be prisoners of war, and the provisions of international law concerning prisoners of war shall apply to them.

Art. 15. At all times, and particularly after an engagement, Parties to the conflict shall, without delay, take all possible measures to search for and collect the wounded and sick, to protect them against pillage and ill-treatment, to ensure their adequate care, and to search for the dead and prevent their being despoiled.

Whenever circumstances permit, an armistice or a suspension of fire shall be arranged, or local arrangements made, to permit the removal, exchange and transport of the wounded left on the battlefield.

Likewise, local arrangements may be concluded between Parties to the conflict for the removal or exchange of wounded and sick from a besieged or encircled area, and for the passage of medical and religious personnel and equipment on their way to that area.

Art. 16. Parties to the conflict shall record as soon as possible, in respect of each wounded, sick or dead person of the adverse Party falling into their hands, any particulars which may assist in his identification. These records should if possible include: (a) designation of the Power on which he depends; (b) army, regimental, personal or serial number; (c) surname; (d) first name or names; (e) date of birth; (f) any other particulars shown on his identity card or disc; (g) date and place of capture or death; (h) particulars concerning wounds or illness, or cause of death.

As soon as possible the above mentioned information shall be forwarded to the Information Bureau described in Article 122 of the Geneva Convention relative to the Treatment of Prisoners of War of 12 August 1949, which shall transmit this information to the Power on which these persons depend through the intermediary of the Protecting Power and of the Central Prisoners of War Agency.

Parties to the conflict shall prepare and forward to each other through the same bureau, certificates of death or duly authenticated lists of the dead. They shall likewise collect and forward through the same bureau one half of a double identity disc, last wills or other documents of importance to the next of kin, money and in general all articles of an intrinsic or sentimental value, which are found on the dead. These articles, together with unidentified articles, shall be sent in sealed packets, accompanied by statements giving all particulars necessary for the identification of the deceased owners, as well as by a complete list of the contents of the parcel.

Art. 17. Parties to the conflict shall ensure that burial or cremation of the dead, carried out individually as far as circumstances permit, is preceded by a careful examination, if possible by a medical examination, of the bodies, with a view to confirming death, establishing identity and enabling a report to be made. One half of the double identity disc, or the identity disc itself if it is a single disc, should remain on the body.

Bodies shall not be cremated except for imperative reasons of hygiene or for motives based on the religion of the deceased. In case of cremation, the circumstances and reasons for cremation shall be stated in detail in the death certificate or on the authenticated list of the dead.

They shall further ensure that the dead are honourably interred, if possible according to the rites of the religion to which they belonged, that their graves are respected, grouped if possible according to the nationality of the deceased, properly maintained and marked so that they may always be found. For this purpose, they shall organize at the commencement of hostilities an Official Graves Registration Service, to allow subsequent exhumations and to ensure the identification of bodies, whatever the site of the graves, and the possible transportation to the home country. These provisions shall likewise apply to the ashes, which shall be kept by the Graves Registration Service until proper disposal thereof in accordance with the wishes of the home country.

As soon as circumstances permit, and at latest at the end of hostilities, these Services shall exchange, through the Information Bureau mentioned in the second paragraph of Article 16, lists showing the exact location and markings of the graves, together with particulars of the dead interred therein.

Art. 18. The military authorities may appeal to the charity of the inhabitants voluntarily to collect and care for, under their direction, the wounded and sick, granting persons who have responded to this appeal the necessary protection and facilities. Should the adverse Party take or retake control of the area, he shall likewise grant these persons the same protection and the same facilities.

The military authorities shall permit the inhabitants and relief societies, even in invaded or occupied areas, spontaneously to collect and care for wounded or sick of whatever nationality. The civilian population shall respect these wounded and sick, and in particular abstain from offering them violence.

No one may ever be molested or convicted for having nursed the wounded or sick.

The provisions of the present Article do not relieve the occupying Power of its obligation to give both physical and moral care to the wounded and sick.

Geneva Convention I, August 12, 1949.

ORGANIZATIONS TO CONTACT

The editors have compiled the following list of organizations concerned with the issues presented in this book. The descriptions are derived from materials provided by the organizations. All have publications or information available for interested readers. The list was compiled on the date of publication of the present volume; the information provided here may change. Be aware that many organizations take several weeks or longer to respond to inquiries, so allow as much time as possible.

Amnesty International
304 Pennsylvania Ave. SE, Washington, DC 20003
(202) 544-0200 • fax: (202) 546-7142
e-mail: %20lberg@aiusa.org • website: http://www.amnesty.org

This grassroots activist organization is centered around the conviction that governments must not deny individuals their basic human rights. Amnesty International works to free all prisoners of conscience, ensure fair and prompt trials for political prisoners, end extra-judicial executions and "disappearances," and abolish the death penalty, torture, and other cruel treatment of prisoners. The organization bases its work on the United Nations Universal Declaration of Human Rights and regularly publishes country reports and other documents on human rights issues around the world.

The Carter Center
453 Freedom Parkway, Atlanta, GA 30307
(404) 331-3900 • fax: (404) 688-1701
e-mail: carterweb@emory.edu • website: http://www.cartercenter.org

The Carter Center works in partnership with Emory University and is chaired by former President Jimmy Carter. The center is guided by a fundamental commitment to human rights and the alleviation of human suffering. It seeks to prevent and resolve conflicts, enhance freedom and democracy, and improve health. The center promotes peace by bringing warring parties to the negotiating table, monitoring elections, safeguarding human rights, and building strong democracies through economic development. The center's publications include *The United States and the Establishment of a Permanent International Criminal Court* and the annual *State of World Conflict Report*.

Coalition for International Justice
740 15th St. NW, 8th Fl., Washington, DC 20005-1009
(202) 662-1595 • fax: (202) 662-1597
e-mail: jheffernan@cij.org • website: http://www.cij.org

The coalition works to support the Yugoslavia and Rwanda war crimes tribunals through advocacy, fundraising, and technical legal assistance. It created War Criminal Watch to track and publicize the criminal acts of suspected war criminals in Rwanda and the former Yugoslavia. On its website, War Criminal Watch publishes dossiers on indicted suspects and provides links to important news articles.

Freedom House
1319 18th St. NW, Washington, DC 20036
(202) 296-5101 • fax: (202) 296-5078
e-mail: fh@freedomhouse.org • website: http://www.freedomhouse.org

This organization is a leading advocate of the world's young democracies, which are coping with the debilitating legacy of statism, dictatorship, and political repression. It conducts research, advocacy, education, and training initiatives that promote human rights, democracy, free market economics, the rule of law, independent media, and U.S. engagement in international affairs. Freedom House's publications include *Freedom in the World, Press Freedom Survey*, and *Nations in Transit*.

Human Rights Watch
350 Fifth Ave., 34th Floor, New York, NY 10118-3299
(212) 290-4700 • fax: (212) 736-1300
e-mail: hrwnyc@hrw.org • website: http://www.hrw.org

Human Rights Watch is dedicated to protecting the human rights of people around the world. It investigates and exposes human rights violations and holds abusers accountable. The organization publishes extensively researched reports concerning human rights abuses in individual countries. Other publications include *A Week of Terror in Drenica: Humanitarian Law Violations in Kosovo* and the annual *Human Rights Watch World Report*.

Initiative on Conflict Resolution and Ethnicity (INCORE)
Aberfoyle House, Northland Rd., Derry (Londonderry) BT48 7JA,
Northern Ireland
Tel: + 44 (0)1504 375500 • fax: +44 (0)1504 375510
e-mail: Cathy@incore.ulst.ac.uk • website: http://www.incore.ulst.ac.uk

As a joint initiative of the United Nations University and the University of Ulster, INCORE addresses the management and resolution of international conflicts through a combination of research, training, and other activities that inform and influence national and international organizations working in the field of conflict. Its publications include *Conflict Resolution for Military Peacekeepers, Mediation in Practice*, and *Peacekeeping, Peacemaking, and Human Rights*.

International Committee of the Red Cross (ICRC)
2100 Pennsylvania Ave. NW, Suite 545,Washington, DC 20037
e-mail: icrc_wash@msn.com • website: http://www.icrc.org

ICRC is an impartial, neutral, and independent organization whose exclusively humanitarian mission is to protect the lives and dignity of victims of war and internal violence and to provide them with assistance. It directs and coordinates international relief activities during situations of conflict. It also endeavors to prevent suffering by promoting and strengthening humanitarian law and universal humanitarian principles. The organization publishes reports, brochures, and periodicals, including the quarterlies *International Review of the Red Cross* and *Movement*.

International Peace Bureau (IPB)
41 Rue de Zurich, CH-1201 Geneva, Switzerland
Tel: + 41 (22) 731 64 29 • fax: + 41 (22) 738 94 19 e-mail: info@ipb.org
website: http://www.ipb.org

The world's oldest and most comprehensive international peace federation, IPB brings together people working for peace in many different sectors, including pacifist, women's, youth, labor, religious, political and professional organizations. IPB supports peace and disarmament initiatives taken by the United Nations, governments, and citizens. The bureau devotes its main resources to informing and servicing grassroots peace campaigns and creating international projects concerning peace. Its publications include the quarterly *IPB News* and the books *The Right to Refuse Military Orders* and *From Hiroshima to the Hague*.

Minnesota Advocates for Human Rights
310 Fourth Ave. S., Suite 1000, Minneapolis, MN 55415-1012
(612) 341-3302 • fax: (612) 341-2971
e-mail: mnadvocates@igc.apc.org
website: http://www1.umn.edu/humanrts/mnadvocates/

This volunteer-based organization is dedicated to the promotion and protection of internationally recognized human rights. Its mission is to enable individuals and communities to realize their fundamental human rights and responsibilities through programs and projects that integrate human rights, fact-finding, advocacy, and education. The organization works locally, nationally, and internationally on human rights issues impacting children, women, refugees, immigrants, and marginalized populations. Its publications include *Handbook on Human Rights in Situations of Conflict* and *The U.N. Commission on Human Rights, Its Sub-Commission, and Related Procedures: An Orientation Manual.*

Nuclear Age Peace Foundation
1187 Coast Village Rd., Suite 121, Santa Barbara, CA 93108
(805) 965-3443 • fax: (805) 568-0466
e-mail: wagingpeace@napf.org • website: http://www.wagingpeace.org

The foundation works to educate people about peace, increase public awareness about critical issues, and champion constructive public policies. It publishes the quarterly journal *Waging Peace Worldwide* and numerous booklets, including *Peace is More than the Absence of War* and *Global Governance in the Global Neighborhood*.

Peace Brigades International (PBI)
5 Caledonian Rd., London N1 9DX, United Kingdom
Tel: +44-171-713-0392 • fax: +44-171-837-2290
e-mail: pbiio@gn.apc.org • website: http://www.igc.apc.org/pbi/index.html

PBI is a grassroots organization that explores and implements nonviolent approaches to peacekeeping and support for basic human rights. By invitation, PBI sends teams of volunteers to areas of political repression and conflict. PBI also provides protective international accompaniment for individuals and organizations who have been threatened by political violence or who are otherwise at risk. The organization publishes the *PBI Monthly Project Bulletin*.

Simon Wiesenthal Center
9760 W. Pico Blvd., Los Angeles, CA 90035
(310) 553-9036 • fax: (310) 553-8007
e-mail: webmaster@wiesenthal.com • website: http://www.wiesenthal.com

The center maintains offices throughout the world in the interest of fighting against bigotry and anti-semitism. Its primary activities include Holocaust remembrance and the defense of human rights. The center's Museum of Tolerance in Los Angeles showcases multimedia exhibitions that promote tolerance and sensitivity in contemporary society. It also maintains an information resource center on the Holocaust, twentieth-century genocides, anti-semitism, racism, and related issues. The center publishes *Response* magazine quarterly.

United Nations (UN)
United Nations Publications
Two UN Plaza, DC2-856, New York, NY 10017
(212) 963-5455 • fax: (212) 963-4116
e-mail: lubomudrov@un.org • website: http://www.un.org

An organization of sovereign nations, the UN's purpose is to help find solutions to international problems and disputes. The organization works to safeguard human rights, promote protection of the environment, further the advancement of women and the rights of children, and fight epidemics, famine, and poverty. It assists refugees, delivers food aid, and provides humanitarian relief to struggling countries. The organization publishes the quarterly *UN Chronicles*, as well as numerous reports on human rights issues and books on global concerns.

United States Institute of Peace (USIP)

1200 17th St. NW, Suite 200, Washington, DC 20036-3011
(202) 457-1700 • fax: (202) 429-6063
e-mail: usip_requests@usip.org • website: http://www.usip.org

The mission of this nonpartisan federal organization is to strengthen the nation's capabilities to promote the peaceful resolution of international conflicts. The institute sponsors grants and fellowships, conducts conferences and workshops, and provides library services and other educational activities. USIP publishes the bimonthly periodical *PeaceWatch* and the monthly *Peaceworks Reports*. Its reports include *Rule of Law* and *Religion, Human Rights, and Ethnic Conflict*.

War Resisters League (WRL)

339 Lafayette St., New York, NY 10012
(212) 228-0450 • fax (212) 228-6193
e-mail: wrl@igc.apc.org • website: http://www.nonviolence.org

WRL affirms that war is a crime against humanity and strives nonviolently for the removal of all causes of war. Its emphasis is on education, action, and war resistance. WRL organizes demonstrations, cooperates in coalition with other peace and justice groups, opposes conscription and all forms of militarism, and supports men and women who resist the military at any level. WRL's primary program is YouthPeace, a war resisters' league campaign promoting nonviolence, justice, and an end to the militarization of youth. The organization publishes the bimonthly magazine *Nonviolent Activist* and the annual *Peace Calendar*.

Women for Women

1725 K St. NW, Suite 611, Washington, DC 20006
(202) 822-1391 • fax: (202) 822-1392
e-mail: wmn4wmn@aol.com
website: http://www.embassy.org/wmn4wmn/

This humanitarian organization is dedicated to the educational, economic, and interpersonal support of women who are survivors of war and genocide. It organizes and promotes sponsorship programs in which sponsors can provide economic relief to war refugees. The organization's website publishes information on the crises affecting victims of war, including those in Bosnia and Rwanda.

WorldViews

1515 Webster St., No. 305, Oakland, CA 94612
(510) 451-1742 • fax: (510) 835-9631
e-mail: worldviews@icg.org • website: http://www.igc.apc.org/worldviews/

WorldViews gathers, organizes, and publicizes information and educational resource materials that deal with issues of peace and justice in world affairs. It publicizes and promotes the print and audiovisual resources produced by writers, editors, filmmakers, and others around the world who are struggling to build just and peaceful societies. The organization also publishes *WorldViews: A Quarterly Review of Resources for Education and Action* and the *Third World Resource Directory*.

BIBLIOGRAPHY

Books

Beverly Allen — *Rape Warfare: The Hidden Genocide in Bosnia-Herzegovina and Croatia.* Minneapolis: University of Minnesota Press, 1996.

David L. Anderson — *Facing My Lai: Moving Beyond the Massacre.* Lawrence: University Press of Kansas, 1998.

Yves Beigbeder — *Judging War Criminals: The Politics of International Justice.* New York: St. Martin's Press, 1999.

David Bevan — *A Case to Answer: The Story of Australia's First European War Crimes Prosecution.* Oxford, UK: Blackwell, 1998.

Patrick Brode — *Casual Slaughters and Accidental Judgments: Canadian War Crimes Prosecutions, 1944–1948.* Buffalo, NY: University of Toronto Press, 1997.

Michael Burleigh — *Ethics and Examination: Reflections on Nazi Genocide.* New York: Cambridge University Press, 1997.

Antonio Cassese and B.V. Roling, eds. — *The Tokyo Trial and Beyond.* Oxford, UK: Blackwell, 1995.

Norman Cigar — *Genocide in Bosnia: The Policy of "Ethnic Cleansing" in Eastern Europe.* College Station: Texas A & M University Press, 1995.

Belinda Cooper, William Horne, and Richard Goldstone, eds. — *War Crimes: The Legacy of Nuremberg.* New York: TV Books, 1999.

Irwin Cotler, ed. — *Nuremberg Forty Years Later: The Struggle Against Injustice in Our Time.* Montreal: McGill-Queens University Press, 1995.

Eugene Davidson — *The Nuremberg Fallacy.* Columbia: University of Missouri Press, 1998.

Charles Freeman — *Crisis in Rwanda.* Austin, TX: Raintree Steck-Vaughn, 1998.

Henry Friedlander — *The Origins of Nazi Genocide: From Euthanasia to the Final Solution.* Chapel Hill: University of North Carolina Press, 1995.

Ina R. Friedman — *The Other Victims: First-Person Stories of Non-Jews Persecuted by the Nazis.* New York: Houghton Mifflin, 1995.

Michael J. Goodwin — *Shobun: A Forgotten War Crime in the Pacific.* Mechanicsburg, PA: Stackpole Books, 1995.

Roy Gutman and David Rieff, eds. — *Crimes of War: What the Public Should Know.* New York: Norton, 1999.

David A. Hackett — *Elusive Justice: War Crimes and the Buchenwald Trials.* Boulder, CO: Westview Press, 1998.

George Hicks   *The Comfort Women: Japan's Brutal Regime of Enforced Prostitution in the Second World War*. London: W.W. Norton, 1994.

Jan Willem Honig   *Srebrenica: Record of a War Crime*. New York: Viking
and Norbert Both   Penguin, 1997.

Matthew Jardine   *East Timor: Genocide in Paradise*. Tucson, AZ: Odonian Press, 1995.

Fergal Keane   *Season of Blood: A Rwandan Journey*. New York: Viking Penguin, 1997.

Ben Kiernan   *The Pol Pot Regime: Race, Power, and Genocide in Cambodia Under the Khmer Rouge, 1975–79*. New Haven, CT: Yale University Press, 1998.

Arieh J. Kochavi   *Prelude to Nuremberg: Allied War Crimes Policy and the Question of Punishment*. Chapel Hill: University of North Carolina Press, 1998.

Saul Littman   *War Criminal on Trial: Rauca of Kaunas*. Toronto: Key Porter Books, 1998.

Theodor Meron   *War Crimes Law Comes of Age*. London: Oxford University Press, 1998.

Martha Minow   *Between Vengeance and Forgiveness: Facing History After Genocide and Mass Violence*. Boston, MA: Beacon Press, 1998.

Aryeh Neier   *War Crimes: Brutality, Genocide, Terror, and the Struggle for Justice*. New York: Times Books, 1998.

James S. Olson and   *My Lai: A Brief History with Documents*. Boston, MA:
Randy Roberts   Bedford Books, 1998.

Mark J. Osiel   *Obeying Orders: Atrocity, Military Discipline and the Laws of War*. Somerset, NJ: Transaction, 1998.

Dith Pran and   *Children of Cambodia's Killing Fields: Memoirs by
Kim Depaul, eds.   Survivors*. New Haven, CT: Yale University Press, 1997.

Gerard Prunier   *The Rwanda Crisis: History of a Genocide*. New York: Columbia University Press, 1995.

Michael P. Scharf   *Balkan Justice: The Story Behind the First International War Crimes Trial Since Nuremberg*. Durham, NC: Carolina Academic Press, 1997.

Gary D. Solis and   *Son Thang: An American War Crime*. Washington, DC:
Edwin H. Simmons   United States Naval Institute, 1997.

Yuri Tanaka and   *Hidden Horrors: Japanese War Crimes in World War II*.
Toshiyuki Tanaka   Boulder, CO: Westview Press, 1998.

Edward Vulliamy   *Seasons in Hell*. New York: St. Martin's Press, 1994.

Periodicals

Fouad Ajami   "Beyond Words," *New Republic*, August 7, 1995.

Scott Carrier   "Pol Pot's Hand-Grenaded Mud-Fish Soup," *Esquire*, October 1998.

Jimmy Carter "For an International Criminal Court," *New Perspectives Quarterly*, Winter 1997.

John Corry "A Formula for Genocide," *American Spectator*, September 1998.

Michael Ignatieff "How Can Past Sins Be Absolved?" *World Press Review*, February 1997.

Sebastian Junger "Kosovo's Valley of Death," *Vanity Fair*, July 1998.

Nicholas D. Kristof "Japan Confronting Gruesome War Atrocity," *New York Times*, March 17, 1995.

Ronnie Landau "Never Again?" *History Today*, March 1994.

Jonathan S. Landay "Opening the Docket: Trials of a War Tribunal," *Christian Science Monitor*, November 16, 1994.

Anthony Lewis "Never Again," *New York Times*, April 3, 1995.

Donatella Lorch "As Rwanda Trials Opens, a Nation Struggles," *New York Times*, April 7, 1995.

C. Douglas Lummis "Time to Watch the Watchers," *Nation*, September 26, 1994.

Gavan McCormack "Japan's Uncomfortable Past," *History Today*, May 1998.

Theodor Meron "Answering for War Crimes," *Foreign Affairs*, January/February 1997.

Ms. "Will War Crimes Against Women Finally Count?" May/June 1996.

David D. Newsom "Justice vs. Reconciliation," *Christian Science Monitor*, November 23, 1994.

Donald Ottenhoff "Genocide in Our Time," *Christian Century*, February 21, 1996.

Howard Rosenberg "What We Continue to Miss in Bosnia," *Los Angeles Times*, June 7, 1995.

Tina Rosenberg "From Nuremberg to Bosnia," *Nation*, May 15, 1995.

Elizabeth Rubin "Our Children Are Killing Us," *New Yorker*, March 23, 1998.

David J. Scheffer "Realizing the Vision of the Universal Declaration of Human Rights," *U.S. Department of State Dispatch*, October 1998.

John Silverman "Trial and Error," *New Statesman*, January 31, 1997.

Frank Smyth "The Horror," *New Republic*, June 20, 1994.

Stephen Weissman "Living with Genocide," *Tikkun*, July/August 1997.

INDEX

African Americans, 29, 30
Albright, Madeleine, 37, 38, 130
Algeria, 33
amnesty, 96, 97, 98, 133
Amritsar massacre, 44
Aquinas, Thomas, 19, 146
Armenian massacre, 52, 98, 131, 132, 133
Auschwitz concentration camp, 62, 65, 157

Backward Look, A (Lang), 57
Bahonjic, Emsud, 90, 99
Bass, Gary Jonathan, 129
Belgium, 51–52, 55
Bergen-Belsen concentration camp, 69
Bernays, Murray, 66–67
Birkenau concentration camp, 65
Bonaparte, Napoleon, 19, 48
Bormann, Martin, 22, 67
Bosnia, 91–92, 94
   assessment of blame in, 155–56
   compared to Nazi Germany, 156–57
   ethnic cleansing in, 26, 90, 101–11, 122–28
      media coverage of, 29
      rape as, 33
   UN response to, 141
   U.S. response to, 26, 28
   war crimes cases in, 95, 96, 129, 133
Britain, 52–53, 55, 149
   and Augusto Pinochet, 154
   helped to establish Nuremberg tribunal, 22
   at Munich conference, 69
   in Turkey, 131
   war crimes of, 43–44, 45
Buchenwald concentration camp, 69
Burundi, 38, 98
Bush, George, 26, 150–51

Calley, William, 44, 113
Cambodia, 43, 98, 136, 138, 153–54
   justice unavailable in, 37–38
   U.S. response to, 26
Chicago *Daily News*, 79–80, 87
Chile, 98, 154
China, 14, 34
Chiu, Lisa, 112
C.I.A. (Central Intelligence Agency), 81
civilians
   in Bosnia, 124, 125
   as defendants in war trials, 22–23
   have improved human rights, 24
   as human shields, 37
   in Iraq, 36–37, 151
   kidnapping of, 70
   need semblance of justice, 91, 99
   Nuremberg tribunal on, 20
   rules of war for, 14, 37, 48, 50

   early history of, 14, 15–16, 17, 18
   in Rwanda, 40
   terrorized by rapists, 32–34
   "undesirable" group status of, 25
   in Vietnam, 76–77, 81–88
   as war protesters, 87
   see also Jews
Civil Rights Congress, 30
Civil War, 16, 49, 137
Clark, Ramsey, 144
Clarke, Sharon, 42
Clinton, Bill, 26
   on Bosnia, 28, 130
   on peacekeeping missions, 101
   supports International Criminal Court, 39
Coffey, Raymond R., 79–80
Cold War, 27, 93, 94, 145
concentration camps, 20
   in Austria, 61
   in Bosnia, 102–109, 122–28
   in Croatia, 124, 125, 132
   in Germany, 65, 69, 71, 157
   in Poland, 62, 63
Congressional Record, 87
Cook, Haruko Tayo and Theodore F., 115
Crimean War, 16, 50
Croatia, 94, 125, 156
   Bosnian refugees in, 108–109
   concentration camps in, 124, 132
   ethnic cleansing of, 34, 101, 122
   Serb cases in, 133
Czechoslovakia, 69

Dachau concentration camp, 69, 71
Dayton Peace Agreement, 94, 96–97, 127
death camps. *See* concentration camps
Dew v. Johnson, 18
Dodik, Milorad, 37–38, 131

Einsatzgruppen, 61–62, 71
El Salvador, 98
Ethiopia, 95, 96
ethnic cleansing
   in Bosnia, 101–11, 132, 156
   in Croatia, 101
   forced pregnancy as tool of, 33
   international response to, 139
   of Muslims, 132
   reveals evil, 155–57
   as sadistic pleasure, 109–10, 111
European Court, 148
evil studies, 156–57

Falkland Islands, 45
Four Hours in My Lai (Bilton/Sim), 114
France, 52–53, 55, 130
   helped to establish Nuremberg tribunal, 22

at Munich conference, 69
war crimes of, 30, 43
Franco-Austrian wars, 50
Franco-Prussian War, 16
Frank, Hans, 64, 68, 69
Fried, John H.E., 13
Fromkin, David, 152

General Treaty for the Renunciation of
War, 20
Geneva Conventions, 16–17, 92–93, 144
developed laws of war, 66, 152
on care of wounded, 50
on civilians, 37
on prisoners of war, 37, 80
did not address rape, 33
genocide, 24–31
committed by U.S., 29, 157
prevention of, 140
reveals evil, 155–57
see also concentration camps; ethnic
cleansing; massacres
Genocide Convention, 25, 29–31
German Labor Front, 68
German Supreme Court, 21
Germany, 52–53, 54, 55
attacked neutral country, 52
exterminated its own citizens, 20, 24
invades Russia, 70
Nuremberg Laws in, 56–62
reacts to Nuremberg trials, 130
war crimes punishment in, 16, 21
war crimes trials in, 18–19
after Nuremberg, 23
after World War I, 21, 66, 130
was warned of punishment for
atrocities, 21
see also Nuremberg trials
Goldhagen, Daniel Jonah, 26, 127, 131
Göring, Hermann, 22, 60–61, 67, 69, 88,
122, 130
charged with conspiracy, 74
on Jewish property, 70
suicide of, 74
during the trial, 64, 65, 68, 69, 72, 145
Greece, 14, 98
Grenada, 149
Gross, Leonard, 58, 59
Grotius, Hugo, 19, 146–47
guerrilla warfare, 17
Gulf War, 28, 36–37, 150
Gypsies, 20, 62

Hague Conventions, 50, 66, 152
on assassinations, 151
on naval rules, 51
Regulations of 1907, 17
Hague Tribunal, 16–17, 134, 144
Serbs on trial at, 93, 122–23, 133
Hale, Nathan, 48–49
Henle, Hans, 80–81
Hess, Rudolf, 68, 122
Heydrich, Reinhard, 60–61
Himmler, Heinrich, 63, 64, 67, 131–32
Hindenburg, Paul von, 21, 130

Hitler, Adolf, 67, 74, 98, 130, 155
conquers Poland, 71
scorched-earth policy of, 73
war plans of, 60, 69–70
Hitler's Willing Executioners (Goldhagen),
127
Holland, 53, 58
Holocaust, 61–63, 131, 157
renewed interest in, 26, 156
human rights movement, 24, 33, 148
Hussein, Saddam, 27, 136, 151
crimes of, 36–37
demonization of, 28, 155
U.S. opinion on, 28, 39
Hutus, 40, 92, 97, 131, 132, 140

Image, The (Boorstin), 127
INDICT campaign, 39
Inter-American Court for Human Rights,
148
International Court of Justice, 29, 39
could mediate disputes, 140
exemptions for U.S. under, 29–30
limited power of, 148, 149
International Criminal Court, 29–30, 34,
39–40, 142
based on faulty assumptions, 137–38
creation of, 94
enthusiasm for, 135–36
must exempt U.S. military, 46
must have financial support, 143
shares jurisdiction with national courts,
96
should be used as last resort, 39
will impinge on sovereign states, 136
will not be effective, 136–38
international law, 36, 145–49
on amnesty, 96
does not create change, 137
is instrument of peace, 53, 146–47
rights of defendants under, 93
rules of war as, 13, 17–18
suggests symbolic number of
prosecutions, 96
Universal Declaration of Human Rights
as, 31
U.S. policy on, 29, 30
International Law Commission, 94, 142
International Military Tribunals, 22, 67
Charter of, 67, 88
see also Nuremberg trials; Tokyo
tribunal
Iran-Iraq War, 36, 149
Iraq, 26, 28, 149, 150–51
American atrocities in, 43, 151
justice unavailable in, 37–38

Jackson, Robert H., 67, 145
during the Nuremberg trials, 64, 65,
68–69, 71, 72, 73
as U.S. Supreme Court justice, 65, 67
Japan, 14, 18–19, 157
medical training atrocities in, 115–19
reacts to tribunal, 130
Jasenovac concentration camp, 124, 125

Jews, 20, 30, 56–63, 64
  in Croatia, 124
  in Hungary, 73
  medical experiments on, 70
  in Poland, 71
  in Russia, 61
Johansen, Robert C., 139
Johnson, Lyndon, 76, 89
Johnson, Paul, 61, 62

Kaltenbrunner, Ernst, 64, 68
Karadzic, Radovan, 37, 38, 102, 129, 130,
  131, 132
Karsten, Thomas, 9–10
Kayabugoyi, Fidele, 90, 99
Kellogg-Briand Pact, 20, 55, 137
Ken, Yuasa, 115–20
Khmer Rouge leaders, 98, 153–54
Koljevic, Nikola, 126–27, 128
Kristallnacht (Night of Broken Glass), 59, 69
Kritz, Neil J., 90
Kurds, 10, 36, 37
Kuwait, 32–33, 36, 150

Lang, Daniel, 57–58
Langguth, Jack, 79, 87
Lansing, Robert, 53–54
Last Jews in Berlin, The (Gross), 58
Law for the Protection of German Blood
  and German Honor, 58–60
Law of War and Peace, The (Grotius),
  146–47
laws of war, 13–18, 66, 88, 141
  became military law, 50–51, 66
  on civilians, 14, 37, 48, 50
  did not limit the right to make war, 51
  formal recognition of, 13, 16–20, 48, 152
  ignored by powerful governments,
    144–45, 151
  Lieber Code as, 49–50
  motivated by commercial/military
    interests, 47–48
  on the navy, 51
  on prisoners of war, 14, 17, 48, 50, 80
  on soldiers, 13, 14, 16, 18, 48, 50, 92
  on spies, 48–49
League of Nations, 55
Libya, 148–49
Lieber, Francis, 49–50
Lloyd George, David, 53, 54
Lusitania, 52

Maass, Peter, 101
Making of a Quagmire, The (Halberstam), 79
massacres
  Amritsar, 44
  Armenian, 52, 98, 131, 132, 133
  Mameluke, 48
  My Lai, 44, 112–14, 157
  Rwanda, 40, 131, 132
Mathias, James, 9–10
Mauthausen camp (Austria), 61
media, 28–29, 147, 155
Mengistu regime, 95
Mischlinge, 59, 60

Mladic, Ratko, 37, 38, 129, 132, 137
  avoided justice, 74–75
Mohr, Charles, 85, 86–87
Mudende refugee camp, 40
Munich conference, 69
Muslim-Croat Federation, 133
Muslims, 90, 124, 125, 126, 128
  in Bosnian prison camps, 108–109, 122,
    123, 126, 132
  as rape victims, 34
My Lai massacre, 44, 112–14, 157

napalm, 76, 85–87
Native Americans, 29, 76
NATO (North Atlantic Treaty
  Organization), 37, 129
naval rules, 51
Nazis, 56–63, 67
  non-Jewish deaths caused by, 62, 64
  SS as, 61–62, 66, 71, 74
  suicides of, 65, 67, 68, 74
  were obsessed with racial purity, 58–59,
    62, 70
  see also Nuremberg trials
Neier, Aryeh, 135–36, 138
Newman, Amy, 56
New Republic, 9–10
New York Herald Tribune, 77, 78, 81, 82–83
New York Journal-American, 84
New York Post, 83
New York Times, 44, 77, 79, 80–81, 82, 85,
  86–87
Night of Broken Glass, 59, 69
Norden, Eric, 76
North Vietnam, 76, 80
Nuremberg, Germany, 22, 64
Nuremberg and Vietnam: An American
  Tragedy (Taylor), 9
Nuremberg Charter, 145
Nuremberg Laws, 56–62
Nuremberg trials, 18–19, 20, 64–75, 144
  accused only the defeated, 145
  defendants in, 22
    assigned blame to others, 65, 72
    deaths of, 22, 65, 74
    defense lawyers for, 72
    not guilty pleas of, 65, 68
  did not include rape, 34
  did not provide model, 153
  established legal precedents, 92, 142
  involvement of Soviet leaders in, 153
  judges for, 18–19, 22, 67, 68, 73, 74, 75
  length of, 65, 95, 130
  staffing for, 95

Omarska concentration camp, 104–109,
  122–28
Oosterveld, Valerie, 32
Ottoman Empire, 52, 130–31

Pan American Conference, 20
Paris Peace Conference, 53–54
Pasha, Said Halim, 131, 133
Pasha, Talaat, 131, 133
Pax Romana, 146

peacekeeping missions, 101, 102, 141, 143
Persian Gulf War, 28, 36–37, 150
Philosophy of Civilization, The (Schweitzer), 88–89
poison gas, 36, 52, 76
Poland, 62, 63, 71
Pol Pot, 30, 136
Power, Samantha, 24
prison camps. *See* concentration camps
prisoners of war
  from the Gulf War, 36
  interrogation methods for, 78, 86
  Red Cross access to, 80–81
  rules of war for, 14, 17, 48, 50, 80
    early history of, 15, 16
  as slave laborers, 15, 70
  as sources of information, 49
  used to train doctors, 115–19
  in Vietnam, 76–80
Program on International Policy Attitudes poll, 28
prosecutors, 25
  Arbour, Louise, 37
  Jackson, Robert H., 64, 65, 68–69, 71–73
  Karsten, Thomas, 9–10
  Mathias, James, 9–10
  Menthon, François de, 70
  Ribes, Champetier de, 25
  Taylor, Telford, 9, 47, 94, 131
Prussia, 16, 48

Quangngai province, 85–86
Quy, Ha Thi, 113–14

rape, 32–34, 36
  of daughters, 110
  following My Lai massacre, 114
  of Jewish women, 59
Reagan, Ronald, 26, 149
Red Cross, 50, 80–81
Reich Citizenship Law, 57–58
Republika Srpska, 37, 131, 133
Revolutionary War, 18
Ribbentrop, Joachim von, 68, 74
Rieff, David, 135
Rome treaty, 135, 136, 137
Roosevelt, Franklin D., 66, 67
Rosenberg, Alfred, 64, 68–69
rules of war. *See* laws of war
Russia, 61, 70
Rwanda, 90, 91–92, 136, 137
  criminal justice system in, 97
  massacres in, 40, 131, 132
  media coverage of, 29
  rape victims in, 33
  UN response to, 141
  U.S. response to, 26
  war crime penalties in, 97
Rwandan National Population Office, 33
Rwandan tribunal, 37, 38
  indictments in, 131
  lacks resources, 98–99
  organizational delays in, 94
  prosecutors in, 93, 95
  on rapists, 34

shares jurisdiction with national courts, 96
Schacht, Hjalmar, 70, 74
Scheffer, David J., 11, 35
Schindler's List, 26
Schweitzer, Albert, 88–89
Serbs, 94, 98, 101, 126
  amnesty for, 133
  claimed Islamic conspiracy, 125–26
  ethnic cleansing campaign of, 101–11, 132, 156
  exhumed victims of concentration camps, 127
  killed in Croatia, 124
  prison camps of, 102–11, 122–28
  as rapists, 34
  reburied their World War II dead, 127
  surrender to tribunal, 129
  on trial in Bosnia, 133
  as victims, 127
sexual violence. *See* rape
Sheehan, Neil, 85–86
Shnayerson, Robert, 64
Shore, Paul, 155
soldiers, 48
  adapt to inhumane orders, 71, 81, 84, 115–20
  are licensed to kill, 152
  kill or may be killed, 154
  loyalty requirements of, 19
  as rapists, 32–34
  rules of war for, 13, 14, 16, 18, 48, 50, 92
  see also United States, soldiers
Soldier's Medal, 112
Son My, Vietnam, 112–14
Speer, Albert, 72–73
spies, 48–49
Stakic, Milomir, 125–26
Stalin, Joseph, 132, 153
Star of David badge, 59, 60
Supreme Court, 18, 150

Tadic, Dusko, 109, 122–23, 124
Taylor, Telford, 9, 47, 94, 131
Thirty Years' War, 14, 48
Thomas, Ruth, 58, 60
Thuan, Pham Thi, 113–14
Tojo, Hideki, 22, 155
Tokyo tribunal, 18–19, 20, 22, 130
  established legal precedents, 142
  on rape charges, 34
Treaty of Commerce and Friendship, 16
Treaty of Paris, 55
Trnopolje, Bosnia, 102–104
Truce of God, 15–16
Truman, Harry, 25, 29, 30, 67
Turkey, 130–31, 132–33
Tutsis, 40, 90, 97, 140

U-boats, 52, 53, 72
United Nations, 21, 27, 109
  General Assembly, 94
    approved rules of war, 20
    funds tribunals, 38

passed Genocide Convention, 25
has created disillusion, 138
needs to be strengthened, 140–43
needs to generate revenue, 143
Nuremberg Principles of, 75
plans International Criminal Court, 39
Secretary-General, 98, 142
Security Council, 27, 42, 93
    briefed on Bosnian prison camps,
        108–109
    condemns rape, 33
    gatekeeper role of, 94
    on Iraq, 36, 150
    needs equal representation, 141
    role in International Criminal Court,
        39–40
    should be able to enforce
        international warrants, 143
    should require military training on
        rules of war, 142
U.S. debt to, 38
United States, 53
bombing of Libya, 148–49
committed to preventing genocide,
    25–26
Congress
    on Bosnia, 129
    can ignore international law, 147
    prior to Gulf War, 150
    stripped power of Genocide
        Convention, 29–30
Constitution, 146, 147, 148, 150
founded on domestic law, 145–46
has agreed to rules of war, 16
helped to establish Nuremberg tribunal,
    22
on International Criminal Court, 142
on international law, 29, 30
international lawsuits against, 148–49
military intervention of
    during the Cold War, 27
    has resembled Germany, 72
    has violated international law, 80
    supported with reports of mass
        killings, 28
    in Vietnam, 76–89
    see also United States, soldiers
opposes international laws, 146, 147–49
during Persian Gulf War, 150–51
and the Sandinista government, 148
should pay UN debts, 38
soldiers
    in Bosnia, 101–102
    in Iraq, 36, 151
    and laws of war, 49–51
    in My Lai massacre, 44, 112–14
    responsible for international security,
        40
    in Vietnam, 76–88
    see also soldiers
Supreme Court, 18, 150
unwilling to stop genocide, 26, 27, 28
war crimes of, 88, 145, 149, 150–51
    on African Americans, 30
    inquiry into, 43–44

in Iraq, 43, 151
in Japan, 157
on Native Americans, 157
in Vietnam, 30, 44, 112–14
and war reparations, 149
Universal Declaration of Human Rights, 31
U.S.S. Stark, 149

Versailles treaty, 19, 21, 54, 73
Vietnam War, 30, 43, 44, 76–89
Vulliamy, Ed, 122

war crimes, 18–21, 37
are defined by Western powers, 42–45
can be prevented through stronger UN,
    140–43
can be stopped by force, 136, 137
domestic prosecution of, 94–96
international prosecution of, 92
of powerful governments, 144, 145,
    149, 150–51
reveal evil, 156–57
as sadistic pleasure, 109–10, 111
see also genocide; laws of war; rape
War Crimes (Neier), 138
war crimes tribunals, 90–91
alternative approaches to, 98
are better than vengeance, 91, 132–33
backlash against, 130–31
defendant classifications in, 96–97
demand too much time, 130
do not deter criminals, 131–32
in England, 16
have destabilizing effect, 130, 154
offer symbolic justice, 131
record brutal facts, 132
temporary nature of, 142
U.S. assistance to, 129, 134
will enhance the virtues of capitalism,
    44–45
will not prosecute Western nations,
    43–45, 152, 153–54
will target individuals, 43, 45, 91, 93, 95
after World War I, 21, 53–54, 66
and World War II, 21–23
see also names of specific tribunals
War of the Flea, The (Taber), 87
Washington Post, 84–85
white phosphorus, 76, 85
Wilhelm II (kaiser of Germany), 19, 52, 53,
    54
Wilson, Woodrow, 53, 54
women. See rape
World Peace Through Law, 147
World War I, 52–54

Yugoslav tribunal, 37, 129
determining guilt in, 153
indictments in, 131
judges in, 42–43, 93
organizational delays in, 94
prosecutors in, 93, 95
on rapists, 33, 34
shares jurisdiction with national courts,
    96